SOCIAL SERVICES
for the ELDERLY

Elizabeth D. Huttman

THE FREE PRESS
A Division of Macmillan, Inc.
NEW YORK

Collier Macmillan Publishers
LONDON

To Mary Elizabeth Cashel and Nancy Sutter,
who encouraged and assisted me through the several
years of writing this book

The Free Press
A Division of Macmillan, Inc.
866 Third Avenue, New York, N.Y. 10022

Collier Macmillan Canada, Inc.

Printed in the United States of America

printing number

1 2 3 4 5 6 7 8 9 10

Library of Congress Cataloging in Publication Data

Huttman, Elizabeth D.
    Social services for the elderly.

    Includes bibliographical references and index.
    1. Aged—Services for—United States.   I. Title.
HV1461.H88   1985   362.6'0973   85-1593
ISBN 0-02-915600-9

Contents

Preface

The purpose of this book is to inform readers about the many types of services that can be of help to the elderly. Above all, it is to make readers aware of alternatives to the nursing home. This book should be of use to the practitioner, the student of gerontology, and the potential client or caretaker of a client.

Many persons have helped in the preparation of *Social Services for the Elderly*. Great appreciation goes to my Free Press editor, Laura Wolff, who provided useful suggestions and had enormous patience. I thank Edith Lewis of The Free Press for her work in producing the book. I thank Nancy Sutter for her help in typing the manuscript, as well as several typists in Zermatt who provided ready assistance in a time of need: Katja Bergman, Vreni Lembo, and Heidi Stadlman. I would like to thank the following people for useful advice: Kathleen Charmez, Anna Dickerson, Isabel Haigh, Elinore Lurie, Joan Nixon, Elizabeth Ratiu, and Phil and Lil Sturgeon. Ulrich Inderbinen, the Furrer family of Chez Beny, Brigadoi Myrta, and Cathy of François provided a pleasant atmosphere in which to write. Last, this book would not have been possible without the patience and help of my husband, Dr. John Huttman.

CHAPTER 1

Introduction: The Aged and Their Needs

Purpose of the Book

This book provides a detailed description of services that cover the basic needs of the aged. It highlights creative alternative programs and discusses current policy debates on appropriate types of service provision. Since these services or programs are often multidisciplinary, I draw on knowledge from many different fields. The information here should be valuable for health personnel, physical therapists, social workers, and students engaged in a wide range of jobs for agencies working with the elderly. Such agencies may call upon the services of sociologists, recreation workers, architects, lawyers, economists, and biologists, to name a few of the variety of disciplines involved.

The purpose of each chapter is to describe the service in question at some length. Equally important is the critical examination of both shortcomings and successes of these services. This will help students to develop new programs or reshape existing ones when they become practitioners. Likewise, students serving as caretakers for aged relatives can choose an appropriate support program to supplement the informal support provided by the family. Many research studies of services for the elderly have been used for my critical evaluation, including my own research on housing services for the aged in the United States, Canada, Great Britain, Holland, and Denmark.

1

Another goal of this book is to make students aware of the existing alternatives to institutionalization. Those unfamiliar with this field are often inclined to direct the frail elderly person with a health disability to a nursing home. The average person is unaware of the wide variety of community-based services that have been developed in the last decade—services which can prolong the aged person's stay in the community or can preclude use of the nursing home entirely.

We clearly need a continuum of care: different services directed to the aged in different degrees of health. The aged have a variety of needs; if they are to be met, services must be tailored to the individual's particular circumstances.

Outline of the Book

The first chapter examines the social and psychological characteristics of the American aged population. In this chapter I present a service model which serves as a conceptual tool for reading the rest of the book. In the second chapter the focus is initially on present issues at the national level concerning overall policymaking and planning for services to the aged, including the debate on Medicare reform. I then shift to a discussion of priority setting and coordination of activities planning at the local and state levels under the Older Americans Act (OAA). The next chapter deals with "linkage"—groups and programs set up to facilitate use of the service system, such as information and referral centers and case management services. The chapter concludes with an examination of the need to protect older people from abuse, and of the means available to achieve that goal. Chapter 5 provides a description of the natural support system for the aged, i.e., the family and the neighborhood network. Subsequent chapters are devoted to different programs and services within the formal support system. This entails detailed exploration, in chapters 6 and 7, of telephone contact services, friendly visiting, volunteer and paid work, senior citizen center programs, and meals and transportation services. Chapters 8 and 9 describe housing programs, first those in the aged's own home and then those in specially designed housing. Chapter 10 focuses on adult day care, while Chapter 11 treats long-term services for the chronically ill, from community home care to nursing homes. The last chapter covers income maintenance programs, with special attention to reform of the Social Security program.

Definition of Gerontology

It is important to define gerontology clearly at the outset. It is a fairly new field which started mainly as the scientific study of the aging process. When founded in 1945 the Gerontological Society of America centered its interests on such biological aspects of aging as physical changes in the organism which accompany advancing age: changes in cell structure, internal organs, and bone structure, as well as other changes in the body's general functioning. However, researchers trained in the social sciences became increasingly active in the field, developing theories on such matters as age stratification, role change, and disengagement. Writings inspired by the social gerontology viewpoint gradually gained recognition; in 1974 the Gerontological Society finally established a research project in social gerontology.

Social gerontology can be described as the scientific study of the social and psychological aspects of aging, i.e., adjustment to the later stage in the life cycle. It is concerned with group behavior and with the emotional–affectional aspects of development that occur as individuals advance through the last part of life.

For several decades gerontologists have been concerned with the implications of social gerontology for the manner in which we care for the oldest part of our population. Practitioners have used the social gerontologists' findings on adjustment to aging to help plan their programs for the elderly. From the first White House Conference on Aging in 1961 through the 1981 conference, both academics and practitioners have worked closely to make recommendations that would improve the well-being of the elderly.

Roles of the Gerontology Specialist

Human services experts work with individuals, groups, and the community. This work takes many forms. The worker may be directing a program for the elderly or using his special skills in such fields as social work, recreation, or medicine for a particular program in an agency. He works in a variety of settings: from a nonprofit social service organization to a community recreation program; from a special housing development for the aged to a community health clinic or hospital; from a mental health clinic to a federal agency such as the Social Security office; from a homemaker program or adult day care center to a nursing home or a company's retirement counseling office. The worker may provide direct service, such as counseling, to the elderly person. This counseling may be of an informational and referral nature or it may be individual, in-depth casework.

Another job of the human service worker is to inform older people of the services available. She may need to take the client to the service, help fill out forms, and otherwise act as guide through the bureaucracy. Since many of the aged have multiple needs, the worker may have to contact a number of agencies and counsel the family on different courses of action. She must be knowledgeable not only about the character of the programs, but also about their accessibility to the person involved and that person's ability to meet the programs' eligibility requirements.

The human service worker may try to encourage funding sources—private nonprofit organizations, local, state, or federal legislative bodies—to underwrite new programs. The worker may help plan the development of innovative programs such as adult day care centers. Groups like the Gray Panthers are also frequent advocates of new programs.

But the human service worker's main job may be to link services to each other; the worker acts as coordinator and broker in the field, trying to remedy gaps in services and overlapping.

Characteristics of the Elderly Population

A Diversified Group

Numbering over 26 million, the aged are as varied as the rest of the population in their life-styles, economic situations, religions, and their ethnic and social statuses. As for health, even those of the same chronological age are a diverse group: physiological changes are occurring, but deterioration does not affect all elderly at the same age in the same way.

In fact, the term "elderly" covers such a broad span of life, from age 65 to 90 or 100 or more, that one can hardly assume all elderly will experience the same physiological changes. We may classify persons 65 and over as aged, based on the social security pension definition. According to other definitions, age 60 (or even age 55) counts as "old." Clearly, we need to break this diverse grouping into subgroups. Some experts now divide the elderly into the young-old (65 to 75) and old-old (age 75 and over), or into the healthy aged and the frail aged. We can also divide them into single (usually female) households and husband–wife households. In spite of all these variations, however, we may generalize that for this entire aged population good health becomes less probable (especially after age 75), energy level decreases, and mobility declines. In addition, this group has lessened chances for employment and faces loss of income status.

At this point in the life cycle individuals also suffer increasingly from loss of kin and friends. The small urban family, often separated geographically from its aged members, and perhaps approaching retirement itself, is frequently unable to provide more than token support. The social service system must supplement what families of this sort can do. Before providing details on this family support system, however, let us examine some historical changes in the situation of the elderly.

The Historical Situation

The presence of a large population aged 65 and over is a relatively new phenomenon. It is only in the postwar period that this category of people has been widely singled out as a special group called "senior citizens" or "older Americans," although the demographic category of "65 and over" dates back to the Social Security Act of 1935. For most of our history the large majority of citizens died before 65 or, at the most, shortly after reaching that age. Average life expectancy in the seventeenth to nineteenth centuries was short; a retirement period as such was unlikely to occur. Life in the frontier farm communities, the mines, or the industrial towns was hard; working hours were long, and living conditions were primitive for many. Survival itself was difficult. Women often died in childbirth, infants at birth or shortly thereafter. The general population was exposed to killing epidemic diseases.

There were, of course, always some who reached 80, 90, or even 100 years, but their number was few. In 1900 the average life expectancy for children born in the United States was 47.3 years. The elderly—those 65 and over—represented only 4 percent of the population (Soldo, 1980).

The Present Demographic Picture

By the 1980s there had been startling changes. There were about 26 million Americans aged 65 and over in 1981; one out of nine Americans was classi- fied "elderly" (Brotman, 1982). Many "young elderly" under 75 had living parents and were members of four-generation families. The average life expectancy at birth in 1983 had reached 74.5 years, with it longer for women than men (U.S. Census, 1983). This meant that many of those reaching age 65 were likely to live on for another decade or more. For example, at age 65 the average man could expect to live for 14 or 15 more years, and the average woman for 18 or 19 more years. Modern medicine had eradicated many killing diseases; doctors had developed successful surgery and other treat- ments to keep vital organs functioning; pharmaceutical firms had developed "miracle drugs." Many people with serious illnesses were benefiting from these medical advances; they had high recovery rates and often lived on into their 70s or 80s, even after major surgery.

This latter group, those 75 and over—often referred to as the old-old— has thus become a larger part of the population than ever before. In 1950 less than 33 percent of all elderly were in the old-old group of 75 and over; by 1980, 38 percent were. Moreover this group increased more than the "young-old": from 1970 to 1980 it increased 48 percent, compared to a 27 percent increase on the part of the entire 65-and-over population (Soldo, 1980). The predictions for the next decade and a half (to the year 2000) are that the number of people who are 85 years old and over will increase 65 percent; those 75 and over are projected to gain in number by 53 percent. By the year 2000 almost half of the elderly will be 75 and over, and the elderly as a whole will constitute a sizeably larger proportion (one in eight) of our total population (Neugarten, 1977).

Since those 75 and over make up the population group most in need of medical or social services, its rapid growth means increased demand for these services. For example, if only 5 percent of the elderly need home care, this amounted to over 1.3 million people in 1983.

SEX

An additional reason that services will be needed is because such a large population of the old-old population consists of women living alone during widowhood. Because of the longer life expectancy of women, there is a significant gender imbalance in the older population: there are 67.6 males for every 100 females age 65 and over; by age 85 there are only about 43 men for every 100 women. Over 40 percent of women 65 and over live alone. This is because half of the women in this age group are widowed, another 4 percent are divorced, and 6 percent have never married. Males are far less likely to be widowed (about 13 percent) or to live alone (14 percent) (Soldo, 1980).

Of course, not all widowed women live alone; approximately one-fifth of them lives with relatives or someone else (Glick, 1979). Women in the age group 85 and over are the ones most likely to live with relatives because of health problems and because of reduced income. This *dependent* living arrangement is often not to their liking. Approximately 4 to 5 percent are residents of such institutions as nursing homes or mental hospitals.

LOCATION OF ELDERLY POPULATION

Geographically, the elderly are overrepresented in the inner cities because so many of them established homes there before the mass exodus to the suburbs occurred. However, some of the younger elderly were part of this out-migration which started in 1947; in the future, as suburbanites age, there will be a larger elderly population in this part of the landscape. This prospect is a troublesome one, for the low density of the suburban population makes it harder to develop programs for this group of the aged.

In rural areas, where—as in the cities—there is a sizeable aged population, the inadequacy of services has long been evident. People there must travel long distances to reach senior centers or health facilities. The new migration of retirees to rural areas may increase the call for, and eventual provision of, needed services, but distance will remain a problem: in such places the informal network of family and neighbors must play a larger role than elsewhere.

In general, the elderly who have living children tend to live near one or more of them (Shanas, 1980). They usually live near the place where they have resided most of their lives. While some middle-class elderly have moved to the Sunbelt, they represent only a small proportion of the total elderly; among the noninstitutionalized elderly, only 18 percent of those 65 to 74, and 16 percent of those 75 and over, have changed places of residence during the years 1975–79 (U.S. Census, 1983). When they do move, most of them remain within the same county. However, the small proportion that does move to Sunbelt areas substantially increases the elderly population there; for example, 18 percent of Florida's population in 1979 was elderly, while in St. Petersburg, it was nearly 30 percent (Soldo, 1980).

LABOR FORCE PARTICIPATION

Less than a fifth of all men 65 and over were employed in 1981. Half of those 60 to 64 were holding full-time, year-round jobs (U.S. Census, 1983). Some elderly do part-time work, but as a rule, retirement is total rather than gradual or partial. And it is starting earlier: In 1981, half of the male retirees had taken social security retirement before age 65; that is, they had retired with the reduced benefits provided for those in the age bracket 62–64. According to a Louis Harris poll (1975) most of these were voluntary retirements: the study found that only 14 percent were nonvoluntary. These were due mainly to ill health, disability or mandatory retirement policies. Some retirees are "discouraged workers" who, having been laid off during recession periods, discover that age discrimination, although illegal, works against their returning to the labor force.

INCOME

For many, early retirement is due to greater affluence, based on a substantial company or government service pension, social security benefits, assets acquired because of higher wages, and increased value of real estate (73 percent of the elderly own their own homes) (Soldo, 1980). It should be kept in mind that such assets are different from the income assets described below because they are nonliquid. The greatest financial asset for most, the house, is not a liquid asset. Since most elderly do not want to sell their homes, or even to mortgage or refinance them, this asset does not provide them with disposable income.

Income figures are the usual measure by which to judge the elderly population's financial situation. In 1981 the group's median income, while only slightly more than 50 percent that of younger American families, was high enough to keep most of its members above the poverty level. It was $12,965 for male-headed family households. Overall, 14 percent of the noninstitutionalized elderly were living below the poverty level. For elderly singles the situation was worse. For unrelated elderly individuals, the median income was $5746 for men and $4957 for women in 1981: this was very close to the poverty level. Twenty-five percent of unrelated males and almost 33 percent of unrelated females were defined as living in poverty, whereas only 8.2 percent of elderly family householders were in poverty (U.S. Census, 1983).

Since the poverty level of the aged is so low, especially for single elderly ($4,901 in 1982), many experts include the "near poor," that is, those with incomes 125 percent of the poverty level, in the general group of elderly poor. Adding this "near poor" group greatly enlarges the size of the elderly poor population. For example, in 1981 almost 30 percent of elderly couples' income was less than 125 percent of the poverty level, which was set at $6,875 for a couple (Rivlin, 1983). This meant that at least a quarter of the elderly were living in poverty or near-poverty. This does not count the "hidden poor" who live with adult children or other relatives.

The older elderly are more likely to be living in poverty because their assets and their pension benefits have been eroded by inflation or have decreased because of the number of years in retirement. The most hard-pressed group is that of older single women, 75 and over (Hess, 1980). These women try to maintain a house or apartment on less than $5,000 a year. Often they resort to stopping or curtailing their use of electricity and gas and to cutting down on food purchases. They sleep late in winter in order to conserve fuel; they eat less in order to cut food costs (Douglass, 1982).

Another economically deprived group is the black and other minority elderly. In 1981 there were 2 million black elderly, over one-third of whom lived below the poverty level (U.S. Census, 1983). The most needy group is that of the old-old black female group; approximately two-fifths of them live below the poverty level. The Hispanic and the Native American elderly population are also in a very bad economic position. Because these groups are underrepresented in the aged population because of lower life expectancy, and because they usually live in rural areas, on reservations, or with relatives, their plight has largely been ignored. Due to these factors and because of discrimination and language barriers, they make little use of the various services available, such as senior centers and nursing homes. But as their life expectancy and numbers increase, and the various services and workers become more accessible, they may partake of services more readily. Many groups, such as the Black Caucus, have advocacy organizations working to improve the situation (Jackson and Walls, 1978).

HEALTH STATUS

As life expectancy statistics indicate, the older population stays healthy longer today. The aged now suffer mainly from chronic, rather than acute, health problems: the leading examples are arthritis, hypertension, and heart disease (each affecting 20 percent or more of the aged), as well as diabetes. In fact, only 14 percent of the elderly surveyed in 1976 claimed that they did not have a chronic health problem (U.S. Department of Health and Human Services, 1980).

Not all of these chronic problems seriously limit the activities of the elderly. In a self-report study of noninstitutionalized elderly (65 and over), only about 18 percent said that they could not carry on major activities; 9 percent reported that by their definition they were in poor health. About 5 percent were housebound; only 1 percent reported being bedridden. As one would expect, members of the older age group (75 and over) in this study— some 23 percent—were more likely to be unable to pursue their usual major activities (Huttman, 1977).

The elderly are also more likely to be hospitalized—one out of six in 1979. In that year they occupied at least 30 percent of all U.S. hospital beds, and they endured longer stays than the average middle-aged patient. The aged in 1979 received a quarter of all drug prescriptions, although they comprised only 11 percent of the population. The noninstitutionalized elderly had an average of 6.3 visits to a physician each year (Soldo, 1980).

Biophysiological changes in the body cause these illnesses. Because the aging period takes up such a long time, it is hard to define the process of changes with the desirable precision. Biophysiological changes come at different ages for different people. Some develop degenerative problems in their 60s, others in their 80s. Even within the same person's body, changes occur at different times in different parts of the system (Rockstein and Sussman, 1979).

Decline in physical capacities is one aspect of biophysiological aging. Loss of energy is common, although preventitive measures, such as regular exercise, can minimize the loss. Physical energy may be reduced because of the system's lessened capacity to deliver oxygen and nutrients throughout the body and even to remove waste products. Most usually function less well as one ages. Changes in the bones and muscles generally cause a number of problems (Glass, 1977). Diminished bone and muscle mass, along with changes in the joints, cause an increased number of falls and fractures. Conditions such as arthritis (degenerative changes in the joints) cause stiffness that can effect psychomotor performance, limit mobility, and slow reaction time. Cardiovascular impairments may affect physical coordination and the ability to walk or to respond quickly.

Impaired hearing may be due to changes in structural and metabolic factors in the inner ear (Rockstein and Sussman, 1979). Communication becomes difficult; even if the speaker shouts to the hearing-impaired person, it may be heard as a booming of unintelligible sounds. Vision also changes as one grows older. The eye has trouble focusing on close objects, so that reading becomes difficult. The older person is more likely to develop cataracts.

Chronic conditions like heart disease, strokes, and cancer take a toll on many parts of the body. These illnesses also involve heavy emotional strain, and decrease the energy level. Chronic high blood pressure, along with the medication used to treat it, can cause dizziness (Finch and Hayflick, 1977).

In general, the nervous system, especially the brain, changes as part of the aging process. However, some problems that laymen often associate with the normal aging process, such as dulling of memory and/or learning disability, are not typical, but due to some prior incapacity or to debilitating change. The most common organic brain disorders fit this category, including senile dementia–Alzheimer's disease and arteriosclerotic psychosis; distinctions among these are hard to make (Kart, Metress, and Metress, 1978). The core manifestations are memory dysfunction, dislocation or disorientation, impairment of cognitive ability, such as comprehension and other intellectual functions, and emotional instability, such as depression and moodiness.

In concluding this section on physical impairments, let us remember that *most* elderly have more than one impairment, especially after the age of 75 or 80. On the other hand, these impairments, even if multiple, usually impose only mild limitations: most of the aged are able to cope with them. The burden can be eased, however, if services are available which make it easier for the person to function in an independent way.

Psychosocial Aspects of Aging

Aging takes on psychological dimensions for the elderly (Bengston, 1973). Individuals react differently to the changes that occur in later life; these reactions can, in turn, affect general functioning and social relations. Furthermore, physical health can be affected by the psychological and social problems associated with aging (Birren and Schaie, 1977).

Role Loss

A major social and psychological change that the elderly experience in this stage of life is role loss and role change. Here the term "role" means filling a certain recognized position, such as that of a mother or a lawyer. Most of the aged are given very limited roles in our society. With advancing age, they are forced to drop earlier roles; they gain few new ones. In their sixties, men and women usually move into job retirement and suffer role loss; in addition, women experience severe attenuation of the mothering role.

These losses are hard to take. In our society people are taught to carry on the roles of paid occupation (for men, and increasingly, for women), marriage, and parenthood. These institutionalized roles shape and direct identity and social status. Many people invest most of their time and energy in these roles. Women, for example, may devote their lives to caring for their children. Men—and increasingly women as well—invest themselves heavily in careers; either of the sexes may carry on the role of family "breadwinner." Yet employers usually want to retire older workers, largely because of society's belief that certain (debilitating) biological changes occur universally at specific chronological ages. Formerly, when life was usually shorter, one could assume continuation of one's work role until death. Now the 60-year-old employee may confront mandatory company retirement rules or an employer's desire to be rid of him in order to save money. At retirement, a man usually suffers from a loss of gratification heretofore provided by his job; the same thing may happen to the career woman (Hess, 1980). Retirement deprives one both of colleagues and of routine. Loneliness often replaces the social interaction typical of the work place. Retirement, especially if involuntary, also means loss of confidence in one's abilities; self-doubt can become the main theme of the retiree's existence (Kell and Patton, 1978).

The loss of an occupational position usually means loss of status and prestige associated with that job. The retiree may fear the loss of that part of his personality based on his occupational position; he is unlikely to see any prospect of a new, culturally significant role provided by society. He fears being displaced, unwanted, and even eventually a burden on others.

Working women also face these problems. In addition, most women also have to cope with the role loss resulting from an "empty nest" when their children leave home. To some, this opens a void in their lives; other women see this as a positive development, for they are glad to be finished with child rearing. They see this period as one which offers an opportunity to begin a new phase of life (Bernard, 1981). This type of woman is likely to relish the chance for a new career, for instance.

Other women fill this period with volunteer work or play the grand-parent role (Hill, 1977). However, the grandparent role is often artificial because adult children are geographically distant or too busy to integrate the elders into their lives. Just as the American workplace is unable to utilize the aged, the adult child in a basically nuclear, often two-worker, family is unable to absorb elderly parents into its normal, day-to-day activities.

The elderly, then, are often left without meaningful functions to perform; they find themselves excluded from many activities simply by virtue of their age. The elderly can easily become "roleless," as Burgess (1960) puts it in his "activity" theory. The fact is that our structuring of society, including provision of significant roles for the aged, has not caught up with demographic and technological changes. Among the most important of those changes are generally longer life spans, increased automation of the work-place, and splintered or geographically distant families. In any society, the concept of the life cycle is based on certain premises; in our own, the premises need to be changed. As Rose (1965) points out, we need to develop new roles, roles which give status to the aged so that they need not feel relegated to trivial pastimes while society waits for them to die.

The Gray Panthers and other groups are helping the elderly develop new roles or keep their former ones. The Gray Panthers are advocates of equal rights, equal opportunity, and dignity for the elderly. Unwilling retirees are no longer accepting inactivity and social or psychological stagnation. They are becoming "recycled, reconstituted" people, using their leisure to organize and to become active for social change. Estes (1979) argues strongly for the desirability of this process. She believes only a significant change in society's allocation of roles for older Americans will be effective in improving their lot; a shift in approaches to delivery of services and increased funding of services alone will not significantly improve their well-being.

Activity theorists prescribe a more general type of meaningful participation for the elderly, rather than a strictly advocacy role. They also mention more general benefits these activities give the elderly, speaking of lifelong satisfaction, for example. According to George Maddox (1963) the more activities one participates in, the more successful will one adapt to old age. He argues that virtually any avocation one develops will substitute for paid work; it is gratifying because it fits the American value of being productive and working hard. To the activity theorists the essence of a meaningful existence is social activity. Remaining active, they say, will improve physical and mental health, enhancing self-esteem, and give the elderly a sense that there is still an important place for them in the world.

Researchers who have tested this activity theory have, in general, supported the concept, but some indicate it must be modified. The present author's 1977 study indicated that the elderly do not put the same value on unpaid work as paid work, and are not eager to do it. Avocations are frequently viewed as nonproductive or not "real" work. Lemon, Bengston, and Peterson (1972), in their study of 411 southern California enrollees in a retirement home, found that it was largely social activity with friends, relatives, and neighbors that gave satisfaction, rather than social activity in formal groups. They also concluded that high morale was not related to the *number* of roles occupied, but to the degree of intimacy in relationships.

The Subculture Theory

One activity theorist, Arnold Rose (1965), sees the elderly establishing their own activities and their own meaningful social roles. Through transforming themselves into a group coexisting with other groups in American society, the elderly are able to pursue their own interests in competition with these other groups.

Rose sees group identification developing among some aged. They have found their own interests and goals and they express them through such organizations as senior citizen centers or advocacy groups such as the Gray Panthers. While Rose feels that such factors as relations with family members, some active employment, and television viewing will keep the aged integrated into the larger society, he also sees an increased willingness of the aged to identify mainly with their age-mates and participate in their activities. Activity is still the main component of this theory, but here it is not holding on to old roles and activities which counts, but replacing them with new ones and with greater identification with one's own age group.

Age Stratification Theory

According to this theory, as developed by Riley and Foner (1968), society is viewed as made up, among other things, of age classes or cohorts. Because a particular age cohort has gone through the same historical experience together, such as the Depression, that experience has a meaning for them that is different from the meaning it has for later generations. Those in a particular age cohort are likely to share certain general attitudes, outlooks, or political orientations. Each age cohort also has cohesion because its members are at the same period in their personal life cycle and are experiencing the same problems of adjusting to that particular stage in life. For example, most of its members face the problems of retirement and of failing health at about the same time.

Disengagement Theory

A different approach to what happens in old age and to which life-style is most compatible with life satisfaction and well-being is embodied in theories of disengagement. Cumming and Henry (1961) postulate that older persons, as they lose relatives and other important companions, and as they lose their traditional roles, gradually withdraw from extensive social contacts. Disengagement comes after the children leave, workers retire, and spouses die. These authors believe that the older person does not want to make new friends and engage in new activities; thus disengagement is often a mutually desired process; the social world moves away from the aged, while the aged have no great desire to stay in it.

Cumming and Henry see this as an inevitable process whereby roles are ended, relationships are severed, and those relationships that remain are altered. They see disengagement as having a positive function for the individual aged person who is ready for this change: withdrawal does not necessarily indicate lack of satisfaction with life, but rather a desire to be at peace with the world and prepare for death.

Some gerontologists argue that this theory applies only to a small proportion of the elderly, mainly in the old-old category (Hochschild, 1975). They use data to prove that many elderly do not withdraw. There is no question that the disengagement theory approves of reduced activity and withdrawal from society. Most social service practitioners do not approve of the theory's support for elderly remaining socially inactive and uninvolved. They agree with the activity theory's orientation to community involvement.

Application of This Information

As we work with the elderly as gerontology specialists, we must keep these theories and the supporting information in mind. We must understand why some elderly withdraw from society. Subscribing to the activity theory, we may want outreach programs—but we must also realize that an emphasis on participation can be overdone. Above all, we must understand the psychological and emotional problems that the elderly have because of role loss, and we must realize that it is our job to help develop new roles and new sources of status.

We should understand from Riley's theory of an age class and Rose's theory of an age subculture that many aged have a group consciousness and a desire to be with others with similar experiences. This can be a justification for age-segregated programs, such as specially designed housing or senior citizen programs. This world of common interests Rose talks about should be used as a basis for drawing the group together.

Riley's idea that an age cohort has similar historical experiences should be kept in mind in group counseling, where reminiscing can be a useful tool for establishing rapport; the aged generally enjoy recounting early experiences (Butler, 1968). Moreover, it should be realized that the aged's orientation to the past may cause them to have nostalgia for certain places, such as the home. They may want to remain in familiar places, such as the neighborhood they have always lived in. Specialists on housing programs involved in urban renewal or rehabilitation programs need to keep this in mind.

The information we have surveyed on physiological and psychological aspects of aging should alert us to many needs in running programs for the aged. In any program, the clients' health conditions must be taken into account. The designer of social housing for the aged or for a senior citizen center should realize that grab rails, ramps, and resting places should be included to accomodate those with lower energy levels or physical disabilities. The social worker must be aware of hearing and vision problems. Such workers need to know that many elderly take medication; they need to understand that some are confused and suffer from loss of memory. They need to know that many of their clients suffer physical limitations that necessitate transportation to and from the program. All of these factors should be integral to the worker's knowledge.

Social Services as a Functional Alternative to the Family

Besides understanding the aging process, the worker should understand the family's relations to its elderly members and the family's problems in caring for them.

Historically, the family was almost the sole institution which met the aged's needs, but demands for assistance were few in centuries past, partly because most people died early, partly because older people in larger families had useful economic, educational, and custodial tasks to accomplish. Most people grew old working the farm, surrounded by siblings, children, and other relatives. In cases where the aged person was ill, the family provided aid. Widows were cared for by their children.

In the late 1800s a number of changes began to occur in the family. With the development of an industrial urban society, many sons moved to cities. The son was usually no longer an apprentice to his father. The industrial system stressed individual success above family responsibility. The urban setting generally fostered smaller family units. The nuclear family became more important and obligations to this small unit grew more important than residual loyalties to the extended family.

By the 1970s the family had further weakened because of changes in its size and composition. Fewer children were born, and high divorce rates meant that there were more female-headed and single-male households. The heads of such units frequently had difficulties coping with the financial needs and the emotional problems of child rearing. Divorced adults became more likely to call on elderly parents for help than vice versa. As more middle-class married mothers entered the labor force, the traditional caretaker of the aged, the daughter, was less available to elderly parents. Often, too, because of longer life expectancy, the daughter was in her 60s herself, adjusting to her own retirement and therefore less available than had been the case in the past.

All of this does not mean that family support has disappeared entirely; indeed it remains a primary source of help for the aged. The family often retains its close emotional relations and provides mutual aid, although such aid may of necessity be inadequate and insufficient.

Social services supplement the family in meeting various needs of the elderly. However, only in the last twenty years have most services become a significant source of assistance. The big exception is the financial assistance provided by the Social Security programs that began in 1935. In 1965 many social services came in and payments for medical services were initiated under Medicare. In the 1970s these programs increased in numbers and funding. At the same time, Social Security (OASDI) payments increased considerably so that many of the elderly could be independent of their families in a way they could not have been in the past.

Today the point has been reached where experts rightly speak of the large role played by the government's social service system in meeting the needs of the older group of citizens. The government's social policies toward the elderly have moved toward selective assumption of societal responsibility; exclusive reliance on family responsibility is a thing of the past. Yet the family and the social service system have not been fully integrated to provide for needs; there are still important gaps in providing assistance, gaps which need to be filled.

This book is premised on the idea that more help should be given to the family: since it cannot meet all the needs of its frail, elderly members, it must receive supplementary help in its caretaking tasks. This supplemental help is more imperative today than ever before because of the family's lessened ability to carry on a variety of functions. The overburdened institution of the family, unable to fulfill some of its previous obligations to its aged members, needs a functional alternative to assume some of these tasks: it needs the social service system. The family and social service organizations are interrelated and interdependent. They can and should work together to meet the needs of the aged.

As I proceed to describe the various services available, it is wise to bear two facts in mind: we need to do more to create an interrelated system and fill the existing gaps, but we must remember that the family still plays a large role in meeting needs. A social worker must continually ask how the existing human resources, including the family, can be marshalled to facilitate a better functioning social system.

A Service Model

The service programs described in this work cover a wide range of needs. They are supplements to the provision of basic needs like income, shelter, and food; they cover such secondary needs as education and recreation/leisure. They also cover the services needed to alleviate the physical deterioration and psychological problems that the individual sustains in later years: this kind of aid is the underlying goal of recent federally funded programs such as the Older Americans Act (OAA).

Citing the needs to be met is only one way of classifying the social services available to or needed by the elderly. Before reading in detail about the specific characteristics of each service, it is useful to consider some of the general characteristics found for all service provision, that is, some of the other ways services can be classified. To begin with, one can classify provision of service according to income status. Some programs are provided to all income groups—are "universal" programs—while others are offered only to the poor, those found "income-eligible" by a means test or other methods. Provision of a service may be only to those of a particular health status. A useful health status topology is in terms of "well," "frail," or "chronically ill" elderly. Services can also be categorized by the locale or setting in which they are provided, with the major distinction being community versus institutional setting. Sometimes it is useful to classify service provision according to whether it is offered only to the elderly, that is, age-segregated, or to all age-groups. Service provision can also be characterized in terms of type of help given: financial assistance; intervention to give counseling and act as an advocate for the client; or many other kinds of help, here called nonfinancial services other than social intervention. Service provision can also be classified in terms of type of sponsor: public agencies, nonprofit agencies that depend heavily on government financing, or nonprofit agencies that depend mainly on nongovernment resources.

Health Status of Users

A detailed explanation of provision by health status is needed. Many services are devoted to a particular health group, such as the "frail"—that is, the partially health-impaired who are starting to have degenerating illnesses (the semiambulatory)—or to the severely handicapped, "chronically ill" aged. The concept of different services for those with different health conditions is integral to the modern idea of a "continuum of care": the elderly need different services at different stages in the aging process, each of which is likely to be attended by specific ailments and varying degrees of disability and immobility. Some aged, for example, need homemaker aid or services in a congregate setting because they are too incapacitated to do their own cooking or housework, other frail elderly need adult day care services, and some—the chronically ill—need permanent, 'round-the-clock, supervised nursing care.

Community-Based Versus Institutional Services

The locale of services can vary according to need. The emphasis today is on avoiding premature institutionalization. Society can decrease use of the expensive and debilitating nursing home in this way. This is not to say that institutional services should be eliminated entirely. The nursing home, or total institutional care, is still necessary. In cases of incontinence, immobility from a stroke, terminal illness, organic brain damage, and psychotic mental conditions, the elderly may need 24-hour nursing care. Those with Alzheimer's disease or the like, who cannot function alone, must be cared for in this sheltered setting or in a boarding home unless full-time caretakers and possibly a special day care facility are available.

The problem is that there has been overuse of institutional facilities. While the deinstitutionalization of mental hospital patients in the 1970s was beneficial for many, it also meant that some were simply transfered to a substitute institutional setting, that of the nursing home.

Age-Integrated Versus Age-Segregated

Age-integrated services cater to a variety of age groups; homemaker services or blood pressure tests programs may be age-integrated, for example. Programs that serve only the elderly are called age-segregated. Many policy makers, sociologists, and elderly are opposed to the age-segregated programs because they feel these programs isolate the elderly from the rest of the population and emphasize their condition as aging individuals. This group argues that the elderly enjoy being with younger people. Some experts, however, say that while most elderly enjoy seeing their children and grandchildren, they relate better to those in similar situations with similar aging problems (Anderson and Anderson, 1981).

One reason sociologists oppose programs that are solely for the elderly is their fear that younger Americans are beginning to resent older citizens' receiving such a high proportion of funds from the federal budget (a process sometimes called the "graying" of the budget). Some policymakers believe that one way to decrease this backlash is to have more age-integrated programs.

Type of Service

Some services give only financial assistance, some provide transportation, meals and other needs, and some are of the "intervention" type, as Lowy (1979) calls them. The latter do not require the person concerned to apply for a particular service. Instead the agency intervenes to counsel the elderly person who needs help with a problem. This may involve an outreach program for the isolated elderly, aimed at increasing their social contacts, or intervention on behalf of the mentally ill, homeless, alcoholic, or disabled elderly. Such service may provide information or counseling on use of services, or act as an advocate to see that other agencies respond properly to a person's needs.

Most programs are not of the intervention type. Usually, the person in need not only has to apply voluntarily for a service, but must be placed on a waiting list before qualifying for use of the service. In this introduction to the various categories of aid, these many varied services were differentiated from the others by the general title of "nonfinancial services other than social intervention." Section 8 housing is a good example. These services may also involve indirect income supplement (food stamps, for example), or programs providing for basic needs such as transportation or home health care.

Whereas the program types discussed at some length above have fallen into the categories of provision of nonfinancial services, other programs are purely financial assistance, such as federal social security. Of course, both financial and nonmonetary types of assistance have existed for a long time. In the United States, first local governments and then the states stepped in to give some meager income assistance to the elderly—e.g., state pensions. Voluntary associations did some visiting and provided nonfinancial services to the poor. During the Depression a large proportion of the elderly lived in poverty, arousing public concern. The Townsend movement, a group of elderly pressing for pensions in California, was joined by other newly founded organizations to push for a federal pension system. This pressure was a major factor in inspiring the 1935 Social Security Act with its OASDI payments to the elderly.

Thus, from 1935 onward the federal government provided substantial income assistance; however, it did not get involved in social services in a significant way until the late 1960s. Until then it was still considered appropriate for the private sector alone, such as churches and other philanthropic organizations to provide social services. Brown and O'Day (1981) report that 300 to 400 national organizations served the elderly in the late 1800s with as many as one-third of them devoting their efforts solely to this group. Interest in the aged's situation increased somewhat with the establishment of the U.S. Department on Aging and Geriatrics in 1951. Federal involvement increased in the 1960s. In 1961, the first White House Conference on Aging was held and the U.S. Senate Special Committee on Aging was established. From these groups came the recommendations that culminated in the Older Americans Act (1965) and in the Medicare legislation which provided national health insurance for the elderly (1965).

These developments shifted government subsidies from strictly income-maintenance programs, such as Social Security, to direct services and to indirect financial assistance. The best example of the latter was Medicare, a health insurance program covering a large portion of the elderly's hospital bills, and a sizeable part of other medical service costs under a provision entailing voluntary payment of the fee for enrollment. The Older Americans Act directed federal subsidies toward direct provision of social services. This legislation was premised on the idea that the elderly have a wide variety of needs, preventive as well as restorative; all elderly, middle-class as well as poor, can be viewed as potentially in need of the services required in the process of aging. The Older Americans Act aimed at meeting nutritional, transportation, and homemaker needs, in addition to a variety of others. The legislation set up a mechanism for coordination of existing programs as well (see Chapter 2). Title XX of the Social Security Act (now entitled Social Service Block Grants, or SSBG), was passed in 1975. It provided for community-based preventive and rehabilitative services, with approximately 10 percent of funding going to programs for the low-income elderly. All these variations in provision are included in the Service Model (see Table 1–1).

Types of Sponsors

Services for the elderly are provided by several types of sponsors. Today the federal government, under such legislation as the Older Americans Act and Title XX of the Social Security Act, provides funding to a variety of programs,

TABLE 1–1 Characteristics of Services Provision

NEEDS AND PROGRAM EXAMPLES	INCOME STATUS OF USERS		HEALTH STATUS OF USERS			LOCALE OF SERVICE		TYPE OF SERVICE					TYPE OF SPONSOR		
	All Citizens (Universal)	Poor Only (Income Eligible) (Means Tested)	Well Elderly	Frail Elderly	Ill Elderly	Community-Based	Institutional	Age-Segregated	Age-Integrated	1/Financial (Direct and Indirect)	2/Intervention, Counseling, Advocacy	3/Social Service Programs (except 2/)	Public-Govt.	Nonprofit Using Govt. Aid	Nonprofit w/o Govt. Aid
Economic Needs															
Social Security (OASDI)	x		x	x	x	x		x		x			x		
SSI		x	x	x	x	x		x		x			x		
Food and Nutrition															
OAA congregate meals	x		x	x		x		x				x		x	
OAA home-bound meals	x			x	x	x		x				x		x	
Voluntary agency Meals-on-Wheels	x			x	x	x		x	x^a			x			x
Food Stamps		x	x	x	x	x			x	x			x		
Brown Bag programs	x		x	x		x			x			x			x
Shelter—Housing															
Public housing for the Elderly		x	x	x		x		x				x	x		
Sec. 202 nonprofit housing complexes	x		x	x		x		x				x		x	

Tax postponement—Owners		x				x		x	
Property tax exemption	x	x				x		x	
Reverse annuity mortgage	x	x	x			x		x	
Community repair programs	xᵃ	x	x			x	x	x	ᵃ
House sharing—matching	x	x	x			x	x	x	xᵃ
Renovated hotels	xᵃ	x	x		xᵃ	x	x	x	xᵃ
Section 8 allowances	x	x	x			x		x	
Rehabilitation programs	x	x			x	x	x	x	
Mobility Needs—Transportation									
Specialized transportation	x	x	x			x	x	x	xᵃ
Dial-A-Ride	x	x	x			x	x	x	xᵃ
Mini-buses, taxis	x	x	x			x	x	x	xᵃ
Public-bus reduced fare	x	x	x		x	x	x		
Hydraulic lift public buses	x	x	x		x	x	x	x	
Health-Related Needs									
Medicare	x		x	x	x	x	x	x	
Medicaid	x	x	x	x	x	x		x	

(continued)

21

TABLE 1-1 (Continued)

Needs and Program Examples	Income Status of Users — All Citizens (Universal)	Income Status of Users — Poor Only (Income Eligible) (Means Tested)	Health Status of Users — Well Elderly	Health Status of Users — Frail Elderly	Health Status of Users — Ill Elderly	Locale of Service — Community-Based	Locale of Service — Institutional	Age-Segregated	Age-Integrated	Type of Service — 1/Financial (Direct and Indirect)	Type of Service — 2/Intervention, Counseling, Advocacy	Type of Service — 3/Social Service Programs (except 2/)	Type of Sponsor — Public-Govt.	Type of Sponsor — Nonprofit Using Govt. Aid	Type of Sponsor — Nonprofit w/o Govt. Aid
Nursing homes (Medicaid)		x			x		x		x	x			x	x	x
Visiting nurses	x			x	x	x			x			x	x	x^a	x
Home health–homemaker aides	x	x^a		x	x	x			x			x		x	
Hospice	x				x	x	x^a		x			x		x	x
Adult day care	x			x		x		x	x^a			x		x	x^a
Social Contact/Leisure Needs															
Multi-purpose senior centers	x		x	x		x		x				x	x	x	^{a}
Friendly visiting	x			x	x	x		x	x^a			x		x	x^a
Telephone reassurance	x			x	x	x		x	x^a			x		x	x^a
Recreation dept. programs	x		x	x	x	x	x	x	x^a			x	x		
Volunteer and part-time work (RSVP, Green Thumb, SCORE etc.)	x		x			x		x		x		x	x		x^a
Adult education programs	x		x	x	x	x	x	x	x^a			x	x		

^{a}Some programs for this service are one classification type and some are another classification type.

such as the homemaker service and meals service. Even the Department of Agriculture and the Department of Housing and Urban Development underwrite programs for the elderly. In some instances the government provides money to nonprofit agencies to run services rather than directly paying clients; in our model we call these "nonprofit, government aid." Both state and federal funds are used in such cases as Medicaid payments to nursing homes for patient care.

For still other programs, the local or county government is the primary funder, as with many recreation and adult education programs; these we list under "public" sponsors. A variety of nonprofit groups sponsor programs without government aid. Funds may come from the United Way or the Community Chest, some foundation, a service club, or the nonprofit group itself—or it may be a combination of all these. The funds may come from the group's national or local offices; in the case of churches, parish or diocese offices are *at least as likely* to be involved as the national organization.

Finally, the service may be one of many offered by the sponsoring body, as is true for Catholic Charities, or it may be the only service that the organization provides, which is the case with some adult day care centers.

Conclusion

The service model given in Table 1–1 provides the student some idea of the many dimensions of the services to be discussed. Classifications such as public versus nonprofit sponsorship may have emerged as a result of policy decisions on the best way to provide a service, or they may simply be historical accidents. Some classifications represent strategies for giving aid, such as universal- versus income-eligibility care, that are continually debated. In the next chapter we focus on a major controversy, that over the merits of community assistance as opposed to institutional care for the chronically ill. As the student reads about an individual service, he should keep all these classifications in mind.

CHAPTER 2

Planning and Policymaking for Services to the Elderly

The last chapter described the wide variety of services provided for specific groups of elderly under many different auspices. This is obviously a piecemeal system, each part of which has a different historical origin. Policymakers must reshape this system into a more comprehensive, coordinated entity.

Policymakers must also make some difficult decisions about federal spending on programs for the elderly. The central issue is how to cut back on expenditures. National policymakers are searching for cheaper alternatives to the present arrangements. The "graying of the federal budget" alarms many; they see costs going out of sight as the older population continues to live longer and thus increase in number, and they see medical expenses, a major contributor to cost increases, continuing to go up. In a period when an ideology of fiscal austerity for human services prevails, these policymakers are introducing a wide range of proposals to reshape and redirect services for the elderly in order to reduce costs while better meeting current needs. Such proposals come from Congress, the executive branch, the White House Conference on Aging, and from the many lobbying and research bodies concerned with the elderly. These policy-and-planning proposals are filtering down to state and local planning bodies. Gerontology students should be aware of this lively policy issue debate. Before reading chapters on individual services it is important to grasp this broad policy orientation and understand why different experts prefer one service or one type of provision over another.

Definition of Policymaking and Planning

Policymaking in the field we are concerned with amounts to defining a strategy or direction for provision of services. Policymaking starts with identification of goals as well as assessment of unmet needs. The goals reflect the policymaker's value orientations and practitioner's assumptions about the needs of a particular elderly population. For example, policymakers' values will clearly affect their decisions on whether the government should put more money into nursing home care or provide greater support for in-home services. Those who decide policy must also develop strategies to regulate programs, including eligibility requirements and utilization of staff. All decisions must be based on resource availability and cost/benefit analysis.

Planning, a term more descriptive of local and state decisionmaking, means coordination of different components of the formal support system. It includes detecting gaps in services, developing new resources to tailor services to meet the needs of different types of clients, and finding the best among existing alternatives.

Local and state planning, like national policymaking, must take the limited funds available into consideration in identifying priorities and making support decisions. The national debate on policy priorities, with its many political overtones, influences these state and local decisions; federal directives restrict local choices. However, federal funding resources allow states considerable leeway for alternatives, and this is increasing under "the New Federalism." States do their own planning and search for alternatives. Some of them, for example, have embarked on major in-home service programs backed by federal funding.

Local agencies develop their own priorities and do their own evaluation of gaps in services. Local nonprofit agencies may act as innovative components of the local care-giving system. Using special federal demonstration project monies or foundation funding, they explore new ways to fill gaps in meeting needs.

The National Policymaking Debate

Four issues dominate the current debate at the national level over the future direction of policy on elderly programs.

1. What proportion of the federal budget should be spent on the elderly? The "fiscal austerity" Reagan administration policymakers favor cuts in the programs. Others argue that cutting preventive services is not cost-effective.
2. What types of services should be provided? The main question is whether the institutional solution—the nursing home—isn't over-

used, and whether there should instead be more emphasis on community care and a "continuum of care." Proponents of the latter view regard it as more humane, more appropriate, and cheaper. Others argue that a shift to community services would mean very heavy utilization of existing resources and therefore a greater overall cost than is otherwise spent for nursing home reimbursements.
3. Are adequate services presently accessible to the poor? Who should be the main beneficiaries? Should there be eligibility criteria to concentrate on helping the poor, the frail, and certain other groups?
4. Where is the source of responsibility to be located? Should private and nonprofit providers replace public providers? Should the family be made to take more responsibility for its relatives?

Values and Priorities in Allocating Funds for Elderly Services

A major debate centers on how much of the federal budget should be spent on the elderly. The debate is conducted in an atmosphere favoring "fiscal austerity" in human services, at least on the federal level. This comes at a time when a continued "graying of the budget" is predicted, due to the high costs of the Medicare and Medicaid programs and to other increased costs resulting from the new growth of the elderly population.

FISCAL AUSTERITY

Cuts in social service spending by the federal government are part of an ideology whose advocacy comes easily in a period of economic uncertainty. Particularly under the Reagan administration, budget cuts have fallen unrelentingly on human services, especially those designed for the poor. The general public has largely accepted this ideology of austerity despite the protests of social service providers. Experts object that cuts in preventive programs can only mean higher costs later, for inattention to needs means deterioration of their clients' condition.

The Graying of the Federal Budget

Some younger workers consider themselves overtaxed to support benefits for this older population: many feel that the government devotes disproportionate resources to meeting the needs of the elderly. This sense that the older population is receiving more than its "fair share" is fueled by conservative experts' portrayal of today's elderly as well off. [This portrayal seems dubious in view of federal statistics which show 25 to 30 percent of the elderly are poor or near-poor, and that minority-group elderly are especially likely to live below the poverty level (Rivlin, 1983).] Negative attitudes

TABLE 2-1 Federal Outlays[a] Benefiting the Elderly

Program	FY 1981 (Actual)			FY 1982 (Estimate)			FY 1983 (Estimate)		
	Millions	% of Elderly Budget	% of Total Budget	Millions	% of Elderly Budget	% of Total Budget	Millions	% of Elderly Budget	% of Total Budget
Totals[b]	173,345	100.0	26.4	195,150	100.0	26.9	209,585	100.0	27.7
OASDI (Social Security)	$ 97,096	56.0	14.8	$109,708	56.2	15.1	$121,221	57.8	16.0
Medicare	35,752	20.6	5.4	41,833	21.4	5.8	46,916	22.4	6.2
Other retired disabled and[c] survivors' benefits	22,847	13.2	3.5	24,562	12.6	3.4	22,197	10.6	2.9
Medicaid	5,967	3.4	0.9	6,345	3.3	0.9	6,365	3.0	0.8
Housing	3,562	2.1	0.5	4,087	2.1	0.6	4,293	2.1	0.6
Supplemental Security Income	2,598	1.5	0.4	2,654	1.4	0.4	3,069	1.5	0.4
Other federal health care	2,229	1.3	0.3	2,516	1.3	0.4	2,741	1.3	0.4
Older Americans Act programs	993	0.6	0.2	905	0.5	0.1	758	0.4	0.1
Food stamps	906	0.5	0.1	899	0.5	0.1	660	0.3	0.1
Miscellaneous	701	0.4	0.1	829	0.4	0.1	751	0.3	0.1
Title XX Social Services[d]	595	0.3	0.1	647	0.3	0.1	445	0.2	0.1
ACTION	85	0.1	0.0	87	0.0	0.0	88	0.0	0.0
National Institute on Aging	70	0.0	0.0	76	0.0	0.0	81	0.0	0.0
White House Conference on Aging	4	0.0	0.0	2	0.0	0.0	0	0.0	0.0

[a]Reflects outlays, including effects of proposed legislation, for recipients aged 65 and over in most cases. These are estimates based on federal agency information, which may be administrative counts, samples, cr less accurate estimates from federal, state, and program staff. Other federal programs that assist the elderly (e.g., consumer activities, USDA extension services national park services) have been excluded due to date limitations.
[b]Totals may not add due to rounding.
[c]Includes veterans compensation and pensions.
[d]Includes energy assistance.

Source: U.S. Office of Management and Budget, Health and Income Maintenance Division. Reprinted in U.S. White House Conference on Aging, *Final Report: 1981*, Vol. 1. Washington, D.C.: WHCoA, 1982, p. 13.

toward high support payments for today's elderly increase as young workers in growing numbers come to believe that Social Security will not have sufficient funds in the 2020s to pay their own pension benefits. Thus, even though polls show that the public regards the elderly as a deserving group, support for programs designed for them is decreasing.

Without doubt, the proportion of the federal budget devoted to outlay for the elderly is high. The Office of Management and Budget estimated it at $195 billion in FY1982, or 26.9 percent of the federal budget; in FY1983 it was estimated to increase to 27.7 percent and to almost $210 billion (see Table 2–1). The major item, of course, consists of pension system (OASDI) payments. For FY1982 the portion of OASDI devoted to the elderly was estimated at almost $110 billion; some $121 billion, or 56 to 57 percent of total federal outlays benefiting the elderly, were estimated for FY1983 as falling under the OASDI category. Critics seldom point out that this part of the federal budget is a very special trust fund to which virtually all workers contribute. It is not part of U.S. general revenues, but a special contributory trust. Therefore, to say the cost of this contributory system is "graying the federal budget" is inaccurate. One must add, however, that at present there *are* problems making worker contributions cover recipient benefits. (See Chapter 11.)

Another major expense is the Medicare fund, again a special case. Like Social Security, Medicare expenses escalated from the late 1970s onward. Medicare benefits for elderly beneficiaries moved up from about $36 billion in FY1981 to about $47 billion in FY1983. By FY1983 Medicare was 22 percent of the total federal outlay for the elderly. A drastic increase in health costs themselves is the major reason for the "graying of the budget." As Rivlin stated in 1983, increased health costs, rather than an increase in Medicare beneficiaries, was responsible for the sad state of Medicare finances.

Runaway medical costs have affected another program, one which serves the elderly poor: Medicaid. The portion of Medicaid disbursed for elderly beneficiaries grew from about $6 billion in FY1981 to around $6.3 billion in FY1983 (Table 2–1). Increased nursing home costs, averaging over $1,400 per month in some states, contributed to this rise. Between 1973 and 1979 the increase in total nursing home expenditures was 148 percent, with public sources covering 57 percent of the total outlay (Crystal, 1982).

Payments for elderly beneficiaries (estimates) under these three programs added up to almost $175 billion in FY1983, or 83 percent of all federal expenditures for the elderly (Table 2–1). For both Medicare and Medicaid the increase in expense was largely due to soaring medical costs, a factor which afflicted all groups in the U.S. population.

Other federal programs for the elderly showed comparatively small increases. Social Service Block Grants (SSBG, formerly Title XX) accounted for an estimated $445 million in FY1983, or 0.2 percent of federal outlays for the elderly. Older Americans Act funding ($758 million in FY1983 or 0.4 percent of all outlays in this category) was very small in comparison. Even the Supplemental Security Income (SSI) to Social Security for elderly poor amounted to only $3 billion in 1983. The mixed category of income assistance programs that includes railroad pensions, veteran's compensation and pensions (that portion alloted to the elderly), and "other retired disabled and survivors" benefits, was larger: $22.20 billion (est.) in FY1983 (see Table 2–1).

Type of Service

At issue here is what type of care to provide: institutional care or community-based services, including in-home services. The question centers on services for those with chronic illnesses, a group whose numbers grow daily. The main concern is the fear of greater expenditures for the old–old population. Those 75 and over are, after all, the fastest-growing age group in our population. Although a major reason for increased spending for the elderly is the general rise in medical costs, future demand for services will be further exacerbated by the increase in the old–old population. Longer life expectancy, it is feared, will mean greater expenditures for long-term care. Medical "breakthroughs" mean that old people are less likely to die of heart attacks or cancer, but all the more likely to live on for years, suffering from debilitating chronic disorders such as Alzheimer's disease. The major question is how many will need the very expensive institutional care necessary to deal humanely with chronic illness, and how many can, or should, be diverted to less expensive alternatives.

The feasibility and cost-saving of various community long-term care alternatives is the topic of discussion and the focus of many research and demonstration projects today. Such discussion and research is based on the idea of a "continuum of care." The "continuum" refers to the provision of an appropriate level of service for elderly citizens in various stages of health and aging. The various levels range from the "well elderly," to the frail and often semiambulatory aged who do not need 24-hour nursing care, to the incapacitated elderly. This concept is utilized by states in planning their use of Medicaid, Older Americans Act, and SSBG funds.

NURSING HOME OVERUTILIZATION

The major alternative to the family as the last stage in the continuum of care is the nursing home for the chronically ill or frail elderly patient. The small proportion of our elderly population in institutional long-term care facilities costs the government a large amount of money. The problem in America is that we have always turned to institutions for long-term care for those without family caretakers. First we used almshouses and old-age homes. Later we used mental hospitals, and—finally—nursing homes. The latter gained prominence when government subsidies were provided to them from 1965 onward through Medicaid—and, to a limited degree, through Medicare. These nursing homes were privately operated for the most part. The owners, in order to meet their need for profit, cut costs and often fail—and continue to fail—in their obligation to provide quality care (see Chapter 10). Nursing homes, in most cases, have proved to be not only an unsatisfactory living environment, but an expensive way to care for the semiambulatory. They are in short supply, which makes matters worse.

Many patients do not need 24-hour nursing care. Instead, they require, for the most part, personal care. A Congressional Budget Office review of studies of nursing home care found that from 20 to 40 percent of intermediate-care patients and 10 to 20 percent of skilled nursing facility patients were inappropriately placed (Crystal, 1982). Understandably, therefore, there has been considerable controversy over the issue of whether the government, through Medicaid, should make nursing homes the main recipient of subsidies for long-term care cases.

In fact, the federal government has tried to stay away from provision of subsidies for long-term care in *any* setting; thus it has not funded alternatives to institutionalized care to any major degree. Its large payments to nursing homes are forced upon it by circumstances rather than policy. By deliberate policy, the government has supported only acute care, but not long-term care, in its universal Medicare program. Hardly any nursing home costs, except for short visits for acute illnesses, are covered by Medicare. The health coverage program for the poor, Medicaid, has been more lenient than Medicare; it pays the bills of elderly poor in nursing homes. Because Medicaid has been heavily utilized by long-term elderly in such facilities, nursing homes have become the main recipient of government long-term care funding. Ironically, this sole source of long-term care assistance is not readily available to the traditional poor, since most nursing homes are commercial enterprises which seldom admit the poor. Those covered are basically "conversion" cases—instances in which the patient has paid the nursing home bills for a number of months or years and then, after using up all assets, is poor enough to apply for Medicaid. This happens to at least a third of those in nursing homes; naturally, this entails a very high bill for the federal government—in fact, its highest expenditure for long-term care.

It might have been cheaper for the government to have supported community long-term care all along. But by giving aid only circuitously (i.e., after the recipient hits total poverty), and even then only to a service for the chronically ill—the kind of service that families are least likely to turn to—the government has hoped to limit use (Crystal, 1982). This strategy has not worked, however. As we have seen, inappropriate and overutilization is common by chronically ill patients who could best be served within their own communities. The government itself now sees the need to provide alternatives to the most expensive of long-term care services. In the current climate of opinion the nursing home is in bad repute; experts, more than ever, say it is both more humane and cheaper to use community facilities in most cases. Crystal (1982) predicts that the nursing home has had its day, and that the number of nursing home beds is unlikely to expand. The high cost of building new nursing homes in itself may limit expansion.

METHODS TO CUT INAPPROPRIATE USE OF NURSING HOMES

To control Medicaid costs, some states have limited nursing home bed approvals (Crystal, 1982), thus creating a shortage of supply. However, this tactic has made it harder for some in real need of a nursing home placement to get it, rather than stopping inappropriate use. Shortages of beds have meant waiting lists—which enable private sector nursing homes to exclude the severely ill, hard-to-care-for, expensive cases. Because the need is so great, nursing homes have little incentive to comply with stringent procedures for assessment of an applicant's need and with guidelines for appropriate placement.

All the same, some states are trying to enforce such control procedures. They are investigating nursing homes in regard to their Medicaid patients, encouraging the use of medical screening to determine whether the person in question really needs the nursing home, or could use other facilities more efficiently. In New York, for example, the appropriateness of nursing home care is judged by a diagnostic form that gives points for various impairments and special needs, based on an analysis of differences between samples from skilled nursing facilities and intermediate-care facilities (Crystal, 1982). Virginia has instituted a screening system based on face-to-face evaluations of nursing home applicants, both those covered by Medicaid and those self-paying admissions whose limited assets make conversion to Medicaid coverage within a few months likely. However, such screening is difficult when so many who will eventually require Medicaid coverage come in as private patients.

Screening of nursing home admissions can, nonetheless, be a positive entry in the ledger if those screened out of nursing homes are given help through community services. Some can stay in their own homes, possibly with adult day care, or can reside in a congregate housing facility, or utilize some other solution, such as a foster home. Screening may decrease a family's ability to "dump" an unwanted elderly relative in a nursing home when the aged person's health condition does not warrant such a measure. It is important to remember, however, that these community alternatives will work only if the individual family is willing to share responsibilities with the local facility.

IN-HOME SERVICES

Home care programs are the most appropriate alternative form of care for chronically and currently ill patients. New York and California are already modifying their Medicaid funding in this direction. In fact, Estes et al. (1983), in their survey of expenditures for, and utilization of, Medicaid in all fifty states, found that in many cases states were developing community-based alternatives to nursing homes. They found that new home-care programs, often small and limited in scope, were expanding—even though many similar programs were being cut back (see Chapter 11). These in-home services include homemaker services, home health care, and delivered meals; other services for the chronically ill include adult day care, respite services, delivery of library books, and volunteer visiting services.

Should the federal or other government increase its coverage of such programs, some fear that the many potential users would take unfair advantage of the services offered. This would again mean heavy expenditures for the government. Some experts think that by providing assistance to only a limited number of nursing home patients, the government avoids paying for many others who also need long-term care (Crystal, 1982). Families have usually been reluctant to put their aged parents in the dreaded nursing home, given its negative image. Home care does not suffer from the same negative image, although means tests and the like may discourage those who might otherwise participate. At a recent Senate Committee on Aging hearing (1983), experts reminded the senators that there is a very large eligible group of incapacitated elderly who need various home-care services. One senator commented that the total cost of home care for this large group of community in-home service users would likely be higher than the present cost for institutional care for a smaller group. This is even though studies show the per person cost would be lower for many in-home services (Crystal, 1982).

At the same hearing, some witnesses expressed concern that government assistance for those needing community care might further relieve the family of its responsibility for, and share in costs. Addressing this problem, Crystal (1982) concludes that once federal policymakers realize that it is probably impossible to reduce *total* long-term care costs by providing alternatives to institutionalization, they may be less eager to support such programs. However, one might argue that the cost of alternatives are so much more reasonable per user—especially if it is mainly a matter of home health–homemaker care for a few hours a day, or even a week—even with a greatly increased clientele (compared to nursing homes), the cost will not match the high nursing home costs. A number of states agree. They have taken advantage of the 1981 legislation allowing them to expand home care and related services, including respite care (temporary relief of the family caretaker from responsibility for the ill elderly person), case management, and transportation.

Eligibility Requirements and Accessibility

Some critics of current programs complain that funds are not targeted enough to the poor or that the existing programs are not easily available to the poor (Estes, 1979). Let us look at the present accessibility of programs, and then discuss the means which could increase "targeting" to certain groups, and the rationale for limiting programs to the poor or keeping them universal.

Certain programs are presently universal programs designed to serve all elderly, rich and poor. These include Medicare and the programs administered under the Older Americans Act. The latter include the nutrition meals program, information and referral services, and homemaking services. Other programs are designed for low income individuals. These services include Medicaid, SSI, and SSBG. Some are means-tested. Some programs, due to circumstances, are used more by the middle class than by the poor. Thus, even though Medicare is theoretically "universal," it has recently increased "deductibles," thereby limiting use by the elderly poor. Due to these and other factors, the elderly poor, compared to middle-class patients, have fewer hospital days, visit the doctor less often, and in general make less use of other medical services. Ironically, Medicaid—a means-tested program aimed at helping the poor with their medical bills—does not help the *traditional* poor in its major type of assistance to the elderly, i.e., nursing home payments. Most nursing homes are "private" and therefore unlikely to admit those already so poor they will have to use Medicaid to cover their expenses.

Minority groups find entry to nursing homes especially difficult. This may be due to the prospective patient's lack of money to pay for the required services for the initial period in the nursing home. Refusal may also be due to racial or ethnic prejudice. Many do not find a satisfactory nursing home available. Minority admittees are likely to be the very ill—transferred from other institutions by government officials (U.S. Census, 1976).

Because of the difficulty in finding nursing home placement, there is often a delay in hospital discharge for poor and minorities. This is expensive for the government, which pays the hospital bill. A New York study found that 15 to 30 percent of hospital patients in many hospitals were waiting for such placement (Crystal, 1982). These delays in hospital discharge costs the state of New York $100 million a year.

General budget cuts in social services by the Reagan administration have also affected accessibility to programs under Medicaid. Estes and Newcomer (1983b) found that many states had reduced the number eligible for Medicaid, or limited the amount, scope, and duration of services provided. Some states began to require copayments by Medicaid recipients for drugs and to place restrictions on the sums reimbursable for eyeglasses and dentures. The Reagan administration's major cutbacks in funding have limited the poor's access to Social Service Block Grants (SSBG) funds. Title XX, as the SSBG program was earlier known, has been the main social-service funding system in the United States, underwriting whole programs rather than individual income. It has paid for a wide variety of services to young and old. In 1981, a fifth of the total Title XX funds went to programs for the elderly. Because allowing the states considerable discretion in choice of services to fund, the program has supported innovative services by a variety of agencies. States are required to follow federal eligibility guidelines that require funded services to be mainly for the benefit of the poor, although these guidelines have been flexible enough to allow a wide variety of users. After Title XX became the SSBG in 1981, the program has been deregulated even in regard to federal eligibility guidelines. Some states, such as Missouri and Pennsylvania, have established "group" eligibility or "categorical" criteria (such as health condition) for certain programs. However, the main change resulting from federal cuts has been the introduction of copayments or sliding-scale fees for services. These are likely to deter many of the elderly poor from using the service in question. The states have also cut back on the number of those who can use the services, so that in all of the eight surveyed states there were waiting lists for many services for the elderly (Estes, 1983). The states also cut back on number of allowable hours for some services.

Problems of accessibility for the poor and minorities also exist under the Older Americans Act (OAA). The Older Americans Act programs were set up as "universal" services, thus one should expect a variety of users. While statistics show that many participants are at the lower end of the income scale, there is some "creaming"—that is, better-off individuals making high use of the programs. For a few programs, such as the homemaker service, OAA money is often used for those not eligible for the means-tested Medicaid program or the SSBG program designated for the poor. Accessibility for minorities is also limited in some OAA programs because the programs are run in English; as a consequence, many Spanish-speaking aged and others not fluent in English do not feel welcome. This is true for a large number of senior-center and congregate-meals programs.

The very nature of some OAA-sponsored programs, such as information and referral and senior centers, means they are not directed to the primary needs of the elderly poor. Estes (1983) complains that in general, social services for the aged (such as senior centers) are life-enhancing rather than life-supporting. She says what the traditional poor need are life-supporting services. Instead, the OAA-subsidized services in question are directed at the newly poor elderly, with the aim of helping them maintain their former way of life. Of course, one could argue that *all* elderly, with deteriorating health and social losses to deal with—have many unmet needs. Based on that premise, the initiators of the Older Americans Act decided on universal eligibility to its programs. At the same time, these planners suggested some targeting to the poor, and this is actually done. Second, some OAA programs such as those dealing with nutrition, are life-supporting.

The accusation that groups which lobby for the Older Americans Act provisions are oriented to middle-class elderly needs is probably true. Such powerful lobbying groups as American Association of Retired Persons (AARP) certainly represents a middle-class membership. Other organizations in the aging network, such as the Nation Council on Aging, are also largely middle-class in orientation.

Targeting in the Future

Some argue that more "targeting" of services is needed today to be sure the funds are used for those in greatest need. Estes et al. (1983), in their study of Area Agencies on Aging (AAA), found that in 1982 some AAAs distributed some of their service funding on a basis other than age; these criteria included income, race, and physical disability. Some state departments of aging are planning greater targeting of services in the future (Binstock, Grigsby, and Leavitt, 1983).

One type of targeting means concentrating on the "frail elderly," often identified as those 75 and over. In 1983 a number of states—Missouri and Pennsylvania among them—were beginning to concentrate on the at-risk frail elderly. Binstock, Grigsby, and Leavitt (1983), in a lengthy analysis of ways to reshape the OAA under 1984 reauthorization, consider this use of the 75 and over category as a possible way to focus funds and services on those most in need without using a means test. Certainly this frail older group is more likely to suffer from depleted assets, poor health, unemployment, widowhood, and isolated living.

Some experts discuss targeting in terms of applying a means test. Crystal (1982), for example, suggests use of a means test or sliding scale of payment for Medicare. The benefits of such testing include using funds only for those in greatest need and cutting administrative costs (but not per user costs) by reducing the total number of users. The main problem with means testing is that it threatens to return services to the Poor Law system, with its overtones of "charity" cases begging for assistance and the consequent stigmatization of users. If the government, as some recommend, applies this "lesser eligibility" criterion to our one universal health insurance program, Medicare for the elderly and disabled, it would move America further away from the type of universal health coverage all other modern industrial states have today. It would shift us even closer to a "residual system," in which eligibility is so limited that only the desperate will use it; the many elderly who do not want to be means-tested will no longer participate.

Source of Responsibility for Provision

Discussion of greater use of private suppliers is common today. Others favor greater use of the nonprofit sector or, as the Reagan administration says, a greater integration of nonprofit and public bodies. This administration also favors turning over more responsibility for frail elderly to the family.

The private sector is already involved in certain services. Unlike northern European countries the United States—through historical accident, philosophical orientation, and government cost-consciousness—let the private sector run some social and health services, most important among them the nursing home. As a private, commercial institution, the nursing home's emphasis is—and must be—on profit. It is therefore not surprising that studies show these private nursing homes are often of lower quality than the nonprofit ones (Kart, Metress, and Metress, 1978), nor that many try to keep out the severely ill patients who will require more care, or even evict Medicaid conversions now that this program's payments are so low.

Private firms are now expanding into the field of in-home care. Many observers such as Crystal (1982), are concerned that such firms may become the dominant providers. This might well limit provision of these services to poorer aged. The Reagan administration, favoring as it does the private supplier, has suggested that the poor could make use of vouchers in order to utilize such private services. It has even suggested that Medicare users should have such vouchers, so that they could be covered under private health insurance policies, if that were their choice.

The concern here is that such private suppliers will be selective as to whom they accept. Reliance on private insurance providers is especially dangerous for many of the frail elderly because there is no reasonably priced private insurance likely to cover all the expenses of this "at-risk" group. Private providers can not be trusted to cover long-term, expensive medical care. There are already indications that health maintenance organizations (HMOs)—the prepaid health plans—are reluctant to enroll elderly. With their cost-containment emphasis, HMOs prefer to serve younger, healthier clients. One result of this situation could be a dual-service system, such as we have had in the past for hospital use: one or two city hospitals serve the poor, while the rest are private hospitals for the non-poor.

Another locus of responsibility is nonprofit groups. They have long records of providing services for the aged and have often been reimbursed from OAA or SSBG funding. While present government policy is to encourage use of nonprofit groups, statistics show government purchase of nonprofit agency services is decreasing. Federal budget reductions have caused severe funding problems for these nonprofit agencies. It has meant cutbacks in their services to the elderly, especially in the areas of transportation, personal services, meals, and recreation.

The University of California Aging Health Policy Center reports that the public/private partnership heralded by the Reagan administration as an ideal delivery system does not seem to be developing according to plan in the states and communities studied. Foundations, in most cases, are not providing funds where government funding has been cut (Estes and Newcomer, 1983). Allocation of funds carries with it the power to make policy decisions. Under "the New Federalism," state discretionary powers on how to spend federal government monies are increasing. This has meant greater variations among states. Instead of uniform federal standards, one moves to more variable state regulations, where local prejudices and values come into play; groups that are regionally or locally considered less deserving are less likely to be targeted for funds than if the federal government had made the policy decisions.

The extent to which government takes responsibility for providing services necessarily reflects and affects the extent of the family's responsibility. The federal government continually fears that it will be in the position of taking over more of the family's care of its aged. It realizes the costs would be much higher if the family were not carrying so much of the caretaker job. Government experts realize that the American family, with its many burdens, is very willing to give up the role of caretaker for the aged (U.S. Senate, Special Committee on Aging, 1983); this is especially true for adult children who are retirees themselves. Adult children today have already moved away from making substantial payments for care of their parent by another provider, such as a nursing home. One University of Michigan study (1978) showed children contributed very little to their parent's nursing home bills. Recent efforts to revive the relatives' responsibility as it existed in state laws up to the 1950s are predicted by some experts to be unworkable. This applies especially to attempts to require adult children to pay part of their parent's nursing home bills, an option states now have under recent Medicaid directives. As of 1983, this option was being developed in Idaho, with Colorado and Wisconsin possibly to follow. Such actions reflect the Reagan administration's policy aimed at increasing family responsibility: this administration considers the family to be shirking its job. Such an approach to the family differs from that found in the recommendations of the 1981 White House Conference on Aging, which stressed provision of support systems *to help* the family, such as the hospice program.

Various states are adopting these White House Conference recommendations in different ways. Thus, some states are contracting with the family to share the burden of caring for the incapacitated elderly person, not only in terms of working with the home-care worker, but also in terms of using the family itself as the home-care worker. Michigan was a leader in this. According to one study, SSBG homemaker funding in Michigan often goes to family members to take care of relatives; 55 percent of the providers for the 11,000 or more clients in 1976 were family members (Emling, 1976).

Summary

These changes may not produce the "safety net" needed for the elderly. They may be changes mainly instituted to save money, although even this benefit may not always be realized. They may be minor additions to revisions of a system that needs a thorough reformulation and overhaul. The debate may focus on minor or peripheral issues—such as the "New Federalism," or on minor eligibility changes—rather than on the bigger picture. Our present splintered system with its various historical bases, multiplicity of goals, variety of regulatory arrangements, differing eligibility restrictions, and various administrative structures involving over fifty federal departments and agencies, needs to be integrated into one system providing a continuum of care for all Americans. In other words, there is an urgent need for planning on a grand scale.

Research, debate, and planning need to be followed by action. Present trends of scattered service provision, including demonstration projects, as with adult day care, need to be corrected; limited funding at token levels needs to be replaced by a real government commitment backed by conscientious planning and substantial funding. The federal government cannot logically herald certain community services, such as in-home services, as a new direction at the same time it introduces funding constraints requiring state and local government to cut back on allowable hours of homemaker assistance per week, or to skimp on nursing care. When the government provides only minimal assistance to a program such as adult day care, the service can not fill its role as an alternative to the nursing home or provide relief for the caretaker.

Restrictions placed by Medicare on use of community services such as home care need to be examined, as does the whole process whereby Medicare pays for acute care, while leaving families on their own to decide how to care for elderly relatives in need of expensive long-term care. Above all, the health care delivery system—with its escalating costs encouraged by an outdated fee-for-service system and provider determination of costs—needs to be thoroughly reformulated rather than just tinkered with. Medical costs are a major factor affecting reduced availability of service funding: we must therefore deal with the cost side of this delivery system. By necessity there will be "a quest for the holy grail" of cost containment (Crystal, 1982), especially in hospital and nursing home costs, but also in such alternatives as in-home services. Hospices, adult day care centers, and in-home care will all be evaluated from this cost-saving perspective. When hunting for cost savings, however, we should avoid an alarmist approach, which may well lead us to an inappropriate solution. We may be in danger of that with Medicare. Alarmist approaches to Medicare bankruptcy, or to fiscal austerity needs, or to the "graying of the budget" ignore America's general wealth, something Congress does not do when appropriating large defense budgets.

Perhaps the federal budget *can* support a high quality of life for all our elderly. Perhaps our government *can* produce the quality care for the chronically ill or generally frail elderly that northern European countries provide. Finally, and almost certainly, the government can decrease the inequitable treatment of the elderly poor, who cannot use medical services without paying deductibles (except under Medicaid), sharing costs, or suffering a means test. Indeed, even if they clear these hurdles they are likely to find few services available to them, as demonstrated by the case of nursing homes.

Some changes in this service system, then, are likely in the near future. We confront a highly volatile situation regarding the provision of services, for the whole service delivery system is in a state of flux. The Medicare debate is an outstanding example of this turmoil.

The Medicare Debate

Planning and policymaking for social and medical services do not, of course, occur in a political vacuum. Groups with different value orientations and different positions on such matters as accessibility, type of service, and source of responsibility take part in the controversy over legislation. The Medicare debate illustrates the interplay and conflicts among different interest groups and social values.

Medicare reform is today the most important issue in this field of services for the elderly—the crisis of the moment—because the Medicare program is near bankruptcy and reform measures are urgently needed. Decisions on strategies for this program will have ramifications throughout the whole service provision system.

The financial and philosophical orientation of the Congress and the Administration provide the basis for much policymaking. Without such government support, innovative programs and approaches are limited to serving a small population. For example, until recently, hospices were volunteer-supported, innovative alternatives to traditional hospital care for the terminally ill in a limited number of locales (see Chapter 11). Now hospice services for the terminally ill are covered under Medicare; it is expected that they will expand all over the country. A past example of a government change in funding that affected the whole service system was the dramatic decrease in support for mentally ill elderly in mental hospitals. Because Medicaid funding was available to cover these patients (if poor) in nursing homes, the number and size of nursing homes expanded greatly (though there still are not enough nursing homes available to accomodate all who apply).

The upcoming Congressional decisions on reshaping Medicare will strongly influence the nature of services for the elderly in the 1980s. A variety of measures will be used to cut costs in this system. As Alice Rivlin pointed out in the 1983 Senate Committee on Aging hearings, a long-term solution to the problem of rising medical costs will require changes throughout the entire medical care system.

Medicare Provisions

The Medicare program, a non-means-tested program, was introduced in 1965 to provide health insurance to those 65 and over. It is a special trust fund within the Social Security Administration; both employers and employees contribute to it. All Americans 65 or over are entitled to Medicare benefits, except for the few not covered under Social Security. In 1981 this program covered 29 million persons, 90 percent of whom were elderly; the rest were disabled of all ages.

Medicare is divided into Part A, hospital benefits that all receive, and Part B, medical benefits for those paying a voluntary premium (most do). Part A pays a proportion of medically necessary hospital costs. For the first 60 days of hospital care, most costs are covered under Part A, after an initial deductible is paid ($304 in 1983); for the next 30 days, a certain amount per day ($76 in 1983) is covered. If more than 90 days are needed in the "benefit period," a 60-day reserve for in-patient hospital care can be drawn on. Under Part A, Medicare pays for very restrictive specific use of skilled nursing facilities or home health services in cases involving acute care. Part B is a supplementary medical insurance program covering part of physicians' and surgeons' fees and some other services. Part B is financed from the premiums paid by enrollees and general revenue funds. Here again, there is a deductible. After that, Medicare pays 80 percent of covered services.

Medicare Deficits

Even though Medicare covers only about 40 percent of the elderly's medical costs (1982), the outlay of monies is so large the system is near bankruptcy: a Medicare deficit is expected as early as 1987. By 1995 the deficit will be $300 to $400 billion; after 1995 the annual cost may go down due to fewer new beneficiaries (U.S. Senate, Special Committee on Aging, 1983).

In 1982 Medicare spent almost $42 billion on those 65 and over (see Table 2–1). Almost three-fourths of the Medicare payments went for hospital care. In addition, Medicaid spent $6.3 billion for the elderly poor, mainly those in nursing homes. The Medicare budget is one of the largest and most rapidly expanding parts of the federal budget. In fiscal 1982 it represented 6 percent of the federal budget. Even though Medicare spending increased somewhat less in 1982 than it had in previous years due to cost constraints mentioned below, it grew at the annual rate of over 16 percent, a rate of increase somewhat more than 2.5 times the inflation rate and 3.5 percent more than the rate of increase in medical costs for all ages (Glenn, 1983).

Causes for the projected Medicare deficit include longer life expectancy of beneficiaries, increased services provided per patient, and higher rates of admission to hospitals (Rivlin, 1983). Deficits also loom due to the generally high inflation rate in the 1970s and the loss of revenues during the recession period of 1981 and 1982, when high unemployment meant lower employer and employee payments into the system. In addition, the Social Security fund has borrowed from the Medicare fund in recent years. Above all else, however, the culprit is high medical costs. In fact increased health costs far exceeded increase in number of beneficiaries as the main factor in this dramatic escalation of Medicare bills (Rivlin, 1983).

The increased cost of health care may mean Medicare's financial situation is harder to rectify than the Social Security deficit, which Congress tackled through amendments in 1983 (see Chapter 12). With Medicare the government must find means to constrain costs of a system it does not control. Health costs in the United States have risen dramatically in recent years. In 1965 only 6 percent of the GNP was devoted to the American public's medical expenses; by 1982 the figure was 10.4 percent. In 1982 over $320 billion was spent on medical services in the United States. Hospital bills have accounted for almost half the nation's total medical bills, and these hospital costs continue to rise. From 1981 to 1982 they increased three times as much as inflation. In the period of 1982 to 1995 hospital costs attributable to Medicare beneficiaries are projected to grow at the average annual rate of 13.2 per cent; growth in the number of beneficiaries and their increasing age explain only 2.2 per cent (Rivlin, 1983).

The hospital system is a hard one to reform. Across the United States it involves some 10,000 hospital providers; in addition it involves over 400,000 physicians (Davis, 1983). In setting about to change the system, one has to consider balances between primary care and high-technology fields, and between various medical specialites. To reform the system one would have to stop duplication of expensive equipment in the community and devise a remedy for the overspecialization of doctors in some geographic regions and their underavailability in others. Experiment would be necessary in order to find areas of work for those who could substitute for doctors, such as nurse-practitioners. To reform the system one would have to deal with a complex accounting system, with capital outlay costs, and third-party payment systems. And above all, one would have to come to grips with a system of *fees for service* in which, historically, the provider has had great freedom to determine the type of care given and the fee charged for that care. Finally, as a whole, the hospital system is oriented to research innovations and breakthroughs in treatment of acute-care patients, with little concern for cost.

Critics claim that our hospital system has too many surgeons and is too concerned with physicians' income. It is protected by the powerful lobby of the American Medical Association, which has thwarted many attempts to restrain costs. This system of private and nonprofit hospitals and other medical units is one in which the major funder, the U.S. government, has had little control over efficient operation of the components. This very limited role and lack of control by the government in decisionmaking regarding health care has been especially surprising because the heaviest users of medical facilities, the elderly, are the ones the government, through Medicare and Medicaid, is paying for. Today people over 65 use hospitals at 2.8 times the rate of those under 65, and their average length of stay is 1.75 times as long. Their hospital bills are accordingly higher than those of the younger population (U.S. Senate, Select Committee on Aging, 1983). The government is thus the major payee of the American health system. It is understandably trying to gain more control over the services it provides so much of the money for.

Reform of the Medicare System

In its reform attempts the government is heading in two directions: it seeks ways to control health costs, and ways to have the user pay more of the medical bill. In doing this, government agencies and legislators will have to deal with issues involving type of service; accessibility, eligibility, and locus of responsibility; public providers versus private suppliers; nonprofit agencies; and family hospital costs.

PROSPECTIVE HOSPITAL REIMBURSEMENT

This is an important area in the attempt to control hospital costs. In 1982 and 1983 Medicare changed the reimbursement method for hospitals. In the past hospitals were reimbursed by the federal government for whatever the individual hospital claimed as costs for a particular service for a Medicare beneficiary. This meant the government was paying different hospitals very different amounts for comparable services—for example from $2,100 to $8,200 for a hip replacement (Estes and Newcomer, 1983b). In the Tax Equity and Fiscal Responsibility Act of 1982 Congress changed the Medicare reimbursement system by setting limits on total hospital cost per inpatient, with adjustments to reflect each hospital's case mix (the composition and complexity of the hospital patient population in a given year). Thus, instead of payment being assumed retroactively, it is set prospectively, before treatment actually takes place. In 1983 the prospective hospital reimbursement system under Social Security amendments went further. A complex method of reimbursement based on categorizing patients into 467

"Diagnostic Related Groups" (DRGs) was introduced as a basis of payment. The payment is calculated in terms of the average cost of treatment for people with a particular ailment (Newcomer and Harrington, 1983). The new system controls increases in allowable payments over the years by limiting increases to "market basket" inflation plus another percent or so.

Prospective reimbursement is intended as a strong incentive to hospitals to cut costs. This new system is projected, by 1985, to decrease costs by 9 percent below the level they would have reached if government payments had continued to be based on actual costs. (U.S. Senate, Select Committee on Aging, 1983.) As this system goes into effect in the fall of 1983, critics predict a number of problems which may arise. It is possible that hospitals will try to recoup costs by upgrading the patient's DRG level in order to increase Medicare reimbursements (even though DRG coding is to be monitored). Even more serious, critics envision hospitals discharging patients earlier so as to save on costs. This will mean a need for more community services to assume the burden of care, whether this involves homemaker services, geriatric outpatient clinics, home-based hospices, or adult day care. In other words, this reimbursement scheme may change the types of services offered in hospitals. It may, for example, increase the use of ambulatory care so that patients do not stay overnight for operations. Again, more community services will be needed, such as home health care. Hospitals may be less willing to serve the severely ill who require more care than the set DRG payment allows, even though the DRG amount is supposedly based on a case mix formula that takes into account the severity of illnesses.

Teaching hospitals are most likely at present to serve the severely ill, so they may be especially affected. Another effect of DRG-based payments, already noted, is a likely drop in purchase of capital equipment; this may be beneficial in reducing duplication, but it could severely impede the process of updating technological aids to better treatment.

Experts before the 1983 Senate Committee on Aging hearings testified that this new system, besides leading hospitals to discharge patients early and then possibly readmit them so as to count their treatment more than once, may lead them to shift costs to the privately insured patient. This would, of course, increase insurance premiums and aggravate problems of accessibility by forcing even more of the low-income elderly to drop their supplemental private insurance (30 percent of all elderly lacked such insurance in 1982) (Davis, 1983). A two-class care system for the elderly may eventually develop and, if this reimbursement approach is kept long enough, hospitals may not want to accept elderly patients at all.

Another idea to cut costs is to freeze doctors' Medicare fee reimbursements for 15 months. In addition, to cut hospital costs, government policymakers may approve Medicare reimbursements for other types of services. For example, in 1983 they moved to allow reimbursement for hospice care for the terminally ill. Local and state groups that are experimenting with new approaches under demonstration projects are finding Medicare willing to issue waivers which allow reimbursements of other new types of programs.

HIGHER CLIENT PAYMENTS INTO THE SYSTEM

Constraints on hospital costs are supposed to cover about half the projected deficit. It is presently assumed that the rest will be made up by beneficiaries sharing the costs of medical care. An alternative approach would be for the government to provide more funds by using general revenues and increasing taxes in general. That scenario would be compatible with the welfare state philosophy that the state should cover basic needs of all citizens, including health care. Instead, the direction of present reform proposals for Medicare is that the users cover more costs. However, there is some concern for accessibility to the poor and attempts are made in *some* recommendations to see that user cost-sharing does not fall unduly hard on the low-income elderly.

The U.S. elderly are already paying a large proportion of their medical expenses, unlike their counterparts in northern European countries who are protected by elaborate health insurance programs. In 1982 our elderly paid about 56–58 percent of their medical expenses, either directly out of their own pockets or through private supplementary plans. For the many without private insurance, the burden imposed by these payments was considerable. The aged population devotes about a fifth of its income to medical costs. In 1983, their average per capita health expenses were estimated at $3,140, of which Medicare paid only 42.5 percent (U.S. Senate, Special Committee on Aging, 1983).

These medical costs fall hardest on the elderly poor and near-poor. In 1983, 68 percent of all Medicare beneficiaries had estimated family incomes of less than $20,000 per year. Almost a third had incomes of less than 125 percent of the poverty level, and thus qualified as poor or near-poor. A number of these did not qualify for Medicaid because they were not on SSI (Supplementary Security Income) and therefore had not taken its means test. A surprisingly small proportion, only 13 percent of Medicare beneficiaries, were also covered by Medicaid in 1981. Some were covered as "medically needy"—that is, those with enough income to take care of normal daily living expenses but not to meet their medical expenses. Even in the 34 states (1983) that covered the medically needy under Medicaid, in the general atmosphere charged with demands for budgetary cutbacks there was a move to stop support to this group as well. Only half of the poor or near-poor have private medical insurance (Rivlin, 1983). Studies show they underutilize hospitals, presumably due to inability to pay (Wilensky, 1983).

Because the reform proposals are based on a fiscal austerity orientation rather than on a welfare-state orientation, the reforms will mean that the elderly poor have to pay a larger share of their medical bills, especially in the first days of hospitalization; they may consequently use medical services even less. In fact this is already likely to be happening, for some increased cost sharing was introduced in 1982 and 1983 legislation.

In 1982 hospital and physician deductibles were raised. In 1983 the Part B premium was increased. The Reagan proposals would have hospital users pay not only the present first-day deductible, but also a small deductible for the second to fifteenth day, and a slightly smaller one for the sixteenth to sixtieth day, with the "catastrophic" insurance described below taking over after that. In other words, in the Reagan proposals, those who get sick would be heavily burdened with costs rather than all insured persons, both sick and well, equally covering the user costs. The Davis study group reported to the 1983 Senate Committee on Aging that raising the hospital deductible would mean that the fifth to a quarter of the elderly who are hospitalized each year would be the ones most heavily subsidizing Medicare's solvency. The Davis group estimates that if this Reagan proposal for hospital care sharing went through,

> Seven and one-half million sick disabled and elderly patients would face higher payments for hospital care. An elderly couple with a $7,000 income (and half of the hospital care received by the elderly in 1977 went to people with incomes below $7,000) could easily pay more than $3,000 for health care—including over $1,500 in hospital charges, and $1,500 in physician charges, prescription drug fees, and charges for other health care services not covered by Medicare.

Another Reagan provision, "catastrophic coverage," is aimed at helping those with long-term illnesses and high medical costs. The catastrophic coverage the Reagan administration proposed (1983) would pick up costs, without cost sharing, after 60 days of hospitalization. In other words, eligibility for complete coverage of medical bills would depend on how long one was ill.

Critics argue, however, that this provision would benefit only 150,000 Medicare beneficiaries, compared to the more than 7 million who would face higher charges due to increased cost-sharing deductibles. Less than 1 percent of beneficiaries ever use all 60 days of their hospital benefits.

The Reagan administration is suggesting that the eligible age for Medicare be moved from the present 65 to 67. It also proposes to make private enterprise and nonprofit groups a responsible part of the health provision system. Under such schemes, beneficiaries would have an option to use a Medicare voucher with a cash equivalent value to buy into a health insurance policy or to enroll in a HMO. The individual would have to pay any out-of-pocket costs for care not covered by this private insurer. This shifts the risk to the consumer and her health insurance policy. While the low cash equivalent of the Medicare voucher may motivate elderly to shop for low-priced insurance, the insurance finally chosen is not likely to cover all her needs. The aged will have trouble analyzing provisions of a plan and could easily fall victim to purchasing minimal coverage plans, as is already the case in Florida and elsewhere. The aged's option of using a medical insurance voucher would mean even more that there would be two levels of beneficiaries, those with additional private health insurance coverage, and those whose coverage is limited to what their insurer will cover under the Medicare voucher; the latter group would have to make out-of-pocket cash payments for any remaining costs. HMOs are likely to be promoted in these proposals; the government may give incentives to elderly to sign up for them. Administration experts, supported by research findings, estimate these prepaid plans to be cost efficient. The problem is that to date elderly have been slow to join HMOs and many HMOs have not been eager to give them membership.

Another proposal to increase revenue comes from the Congressional Budget Office. It is to couple a tax increase levied on well-off elderly with a mild version of some of the above recommendations. The idea is to have the elderly pay a tax surcharge which would replace the premium for Part B, which covers physician-related expenses. The Congressional Budget Office considers its proposal more equitable than other reform proposals because instead of making the elderly sick pay, it would draw more of the increased payment from the elderly with incomes over $20,000, who pay 85 percent of all taxes paid by the aged. This proposal would be less likely to decrease health care utilization by the poor. Another method, suggested in some quarters, would insure accessibility of the program to the poor by targeting the program mainly to them, making it a program for low-income individuals by using a means test for eligibility instead of retaining it as a program for *all* elderly. Others suggest payment according to a sliding scale, based on ability to pay. The rationale for either of these programs is the desire to save money. However, such steps would change Medicare in such major ways that relatively few would be eligible; because it would look like charity, few would want to use it (U.S. Senate, Special Committee on Aging, 1983).

The same would be likely to happen if another suggestion, to merge the Medicaid and Medicare programs by federalizing Medicaid, should occur. In addition there would be the problem of state payments. At present states pay about half the cost of Medicaid and have major discretionary powers. The states have different levels of payment; if Medicaid were federalized, with a federal payment only, in high-paying states Medicaid payments would be lower—a politically unfeasible move. With this proposal, financing would need to be restructured, since employers and employees cannot be asked to pay a special tax into a Medicaid system from which only the poor would benefit.

Better proposals are needed, especially those innovative enough to take into account the consumer contribution in relation to the pattern of Medicare use. The Medicare beneficiary population is not evenly distributed in terms of use patterns. A number of elderly—40 percent in 1978—did not use Medicare at all in that year. In 1978, 77 percent of the elderly received virtually no medical reimbursement, under $500 per person (this included those who got no funds back at all).

A small proportion of the elderly account for a large proportion of all expenses: in 1978, 9 percent of the elderly accounted for 70 percent of Medicare expenditures. This group's average bill was around $7,000 that year. Many in this group were near death, had long hospital stays, and were treated with expensive equipment. Davis reported in 1983 that in any given year, 6 percent of the Medicare beneficiaries die, and that this group accounts for 31 percent of Medicare expenditures. Thus, the very sick, those near death, are the ones who would pay more if cost sharing were increased. It could be that their estates after death might be required to pay some of the cost, but because inheritance is considered virtually sacred, such a proposal is unlikely to be enacted.

Conclusion

The basic philosophy behind most of these detailed reform proposals is that the consumer should pay more toward service costs; in one reform proposal the philosophy is that Medicare should be a selective service only for the poor. Both of these ideas lead our system further away from the welfare state philosophy that the state should provide for basic needs as a right, with medical need considered a primary one. Governments in Western European countries follow this philosophy and provide full medical coverage, even though in this recession period some adjustments have been made (a few services are now being cut back or provided free only to the poor). Many social service researchers, including the author, feel America should follow that approach and fully provide for this basic need. However, a realistic assessment of current American political trends including the vogue of fiscal austerity, suggests that full coverage of the elderly's medical expenses is unlikely; in the present climate I believe the emphasis should be on introducing "catastrophic coverage," whereby the government takes full responsibility for medical bills after a certain number of hospital days or a certain level of cost (a fairly low one) is reached. This should be universal for all elderly. Such a program would decrease the elderly's fear that huge medical bills will put them in debt. Support for such castrophic coverage does not mean the elderly should be made to pay a very high part of their initial bills; the elderly are already paying too much and, elderly poor are holding off in seeking needed care to avoid medical bills they cannot afford.

The most important need in reforming Medicare is to cut the high hospital, physician, and drug charges. The doctor's fee-for-service system needs to be changed. The DRG method of doing this needs to be refined or some other, better, method should be developed. Community aftercare for those discharged early from the hospital will need to be improved. Major efforts will need to be made to hold to a high level of care while cutting unnecessary costs. The sticky ethical question of how long we should keep the chronically ill or acute cases alive by life-saving machines will have to be addressed, since a large proportion of Medicare expenses are for those last days of life.

In ending this section let me remind the reader that the outcome of the Medicare debate can influence a whole range of community services utilized by discharged hospital cases—home health–homemaker services, for example. The results will have many ramifications for community planners of services. Local planning bodies will have to step in to meet needs created by changes in the medical system, coordinating and integrating all services into a unified, if diverse, support system.

CHAPTER 3

Priority Setting and Coordination of Services at the Local and State Level: The Older Americans Act

The national debate discussed in Chapter 2 on types of services to provide will be resolved not only through legislation, but through administrative decisions by and funding at the state and local levels. While general priorities evolve out of these national debates, it is at the local and state level that they must be carried out. State and local planning bodies must supplement the multiplicity of federal funding sources and federal provision of services with their own funding in the attempt to develop a coordinated, comprehensive system of social services for the elderly.

At these state and local levels, the crucial decisions involve how best to carry out federal mandates and priorities for use of funds where the nationwide programs allow some discretionary powers to states and communities. At the state level, for instance, each state has had to develop its own priorities for use of the decreased SSBG funds, while at the same time following federal directives. State units on aging (SUAs), usually designated as a department of aging, do the same for OAA programs. They develop priorities for local AAAs. In regard to these OAA and SSBG programs, as well as those in the health fields, the state bodies, including the state health planning agency, must assess regional needs, locate gaps in services, and develop priorities. They may use their own funding to cover needs unmet by federal programs, or may use federal demonstration projects or waivers of Medicare regulations to create their own approaches to delivery of services. Major sources for deciding on priorities and coordinating individual agency activities are the federal, state, national, and local divisions established under

the Older Americans Act; they are the national Administration on Aging
(AOA), the state units of aging (SUAs) and the local Area Agencies on Aging
(AAAs).

Planning personnel at the state and especially the local level must first
identify unmet needs by various methods—such as utilization-of-services
statistics, waiting-list data, information and referral office inquiry tabula-
tions, surveys of the local elderly, or initiatives sparked by meetings of local
residents and/or service providers. The next step is to analyze these data and
develop appropriate need priorities. At the local level, the personnel next
publicize findings, call groups together to explain the unmet needs, and take
part in campaigns to meet such needs, such as those to care for the homeless.
At this point available resources must be taken into account. Priorities cannot be developed autonomously but must take into account federal and state
funding guidelines. An active local planning group, however, can advocate
new programs and locate new funding. Such planning groups have some
leeway in their own use of funds and can direct them to unmet needs.

Assessing unmet needs and advocating programs to fill them are
important tasks, but coordination is the major task urgently required in all
local communities; this is true largely because of the prevailing high level of
fragmentation and duplication of services. Thus it is imperative to have a
local planning agency to concentrate on coordination.

OAA Priority-Setting Issues

Some of the issues these federal, state, and local levels of the OAA face are
the same as the national issues discussed in Chapter 2; others are specific to
the local government level.

A major OAA concern is the degree to which effort should be invested
in providing long-term care in the community. Other issues faced by the
OAA include:

1. Whether the OAA funds should focus on programs for the frail
   elderly or mainly for the well elderly (Binstock, 1983)
2. The degree the state and local units, rather than federal government should be the ones setting priorities (Newcomer, Benjamin,
   and Estes, 1983)
3. The degree of involvement of local citizens in AAA decision making
4. The ways in which the agency should be an advocate and how
   successful its advocacy activities are (Fritz, 1979)
5. The degree AAA funds should go for direct service provision versus
   nonservice expenditures (Branch and Branch, 1983)
6. The dimensions of the coordination role and to what degree does
   the AAA have power to stop duplication
7. How services can best be targeted to the poor (Binstock, 1983)

These issues arise out of the multitude of jobs prescribed in the Older Americans Act for its different levels of administration. This mandate needs to be described before the issues can be addressed in a knowledgable manner.

The Older Americans Act

The Older Americans Act originated in 1965 as the main focal point for needs of all the nation's elderly. It changed the federal government's focus from income maintenance to coordination and funding of a comprehensive service system for the elderly. Its orientation has been to the needs of all elderly and not to the poor alone, under the assumption that all the aging population is "at risk" when it comes to obtaining services. Thus, the OAA has used age 60 rather than income as the main criterion for participation, though it also encourages "targeting" of the poor and minorities.

The Structure of the Program

The Older Americans Act (OAA) set up a three-tiered administrative structure with a national Administration on Aging, various state units of aging (SUAs)—usually departments or commissions on aging, or a division of a human services department—and, within the states, local area agencies on aging (AAAs). In a few states there is only a single, statewide area agency on aging.

Local Area Agencies on Aging

The AAAs are the frontline forces in implementing the Older Americans Act. They carry out the theme of the program through their coordination, need assessment, and priority-setting efforts. In 1980 there were over 660 such agencies, following either county, city, health-planning, or other such boundaries, aside from the few statewide AAAs. The areas of operation are designated as planning and service areas (PSAs) by the state unit on aging (SUA). AAAs sometimes go under other names such as Council or Commission on Aging.

Funding of local services, that is contracting with other agencies to provide services on a non-means-tested basis, is part of the mandate of local AAAs. The "area planning and social services" provided for in Title III of the OAA received about a fourth of the act's total appropriations in 1983. More funding by far went to one specific program administered by the AAAs, namely the nutrition or meals program; it received well over a third of the

1983 OAA funds, while another program contracted out to other agencies at the national level, the Community Services Employment program (Title V of the act), got almost a third of the money (Estes, 1983).

Overall, funding for Older Americans Act activities is fairly low, considering that the programs serve a population of around 26 million elderly. In 1984, the total appropriation was only around $1 billion, slightly down from 1983. This, however, was still notably higher than 1973, when the appropriation had been only $253 million.

Besides the nutrition program, local AAAs are most involved with the multipurpose senior centers (funded under Title III) and with information and referral service. The information and referral service is the only one not usually contracted out but housed in the AAA office. About half of such services are operated by AAAs (Battle, 1977).

Priorities of Need

Other programs given significant OAA funding are determined by OAA priorities or objectives for a particular period. As already mentioned, a major purpose of the OAA is to set priorities and plan coordination of services for the elderly at the local, state, and federal levels. As one close observer of the program points out, the amount of money set aside for social services under this act is relatively small; its importance stems from its mandate to define need priorities and to create state and local planning and advocacy networks for the aged (Newcomer, Benjamin, and Estes, 1983).

Other services funded under the Older Americans Act—the flexible discretionary funding system of the Title III or Title IV demonstration projects and research activities—are primarily services relating to the national OAA objectives or to those given high priority by the various SUAs. With each amendment to the act new priorities are established, with decisionmaking as to priorities a major three-way process between local, state, and federal bodies. For example, the ten objectives stated in the original 1965 Older Americans Act were: adequate income; best possible physical and mental health; suitable housing; full restorative services; opportunity for employment without age discrimination; retirement in health, honor, and dignity; pursuit of meaningful activities; efficient community services when needed; immediate benefit from proven research knowledge; and freedom, independence, and unconstrained exercise of individual initiative. The priorities are today more specific. In the 1981 amendments these were established as: information and referral; transportation; in-home assistance (homemakers, health aides, visiting and telephone reassurance efforts); and legal services. A 1981 amendment also required that each state operate a nursing-home ombudsman system. In the OAA amendments the federal government

also told AAAs to provide counseling and information and referral to non–
English speaking elderly. They must, of course, also subcontract to provide
for the nutrition programs. These priorities come from the national level,·the
Administration on Aging (AOA).

Because the Administration on Aging organizes and funds the White
House Conference on Aging that takes place once per decade, it collects
information needed to perform its essential role of setting priorities in services for state and local offices. The federal office then mandates that the
AAAs use an adequate portion of their funds on one or more of these national
priorities.

The State Role

Under recent OAA amendments the position of the SUAs has been strengthened. States are encouraged to take the leadership in assessing need and
setting their own priorities. They often do this through recommendations of
assessed need based on statistics they get from the AAAs and their own
research on state needs. The states make up statewide plans and develop
new policy directives.

Some experts question whether the states will actually use the flexibil-
ity of "the new federalism" to become innovators in their region. Newcomer
and Harrington (1983) are skeptical whether most state agencies will step
forward to provide strong leadership to their own AAAs and develop their
own strategies. In the 1974–1979 period, most SUAs devoted their planned
service objectives mainly to federal priorities. However, there are some
indications that states are adding their own special needs to complement the
federal ones; for example, one state added such priorities as case management and crime security. And, as shown above, states are developing their
own complex targeting formulas.

At the AAA level the various service agencies help set priorities. These
AAAs organize a number of activities that bring together the whole network
of local agencies concerned with assistance to the aging. They organize
committees and bring together all the agencies from a wide number of
relevant fields, including long-term care, transportation, and housing. The
local AAA develops three-year plans in which, for each service, it must
identify needs from statistical material such as census reports, waiting lists,
and agency records; it then presents data on resources meeting the needs
and describes deficiencies and problems. After needs assessment, the AAA's
major job is to establish program priorities, keeping national and state guidelines in mind. It does this through hearings with social-services agencies and
the public. Once it gets its plan approved, the AAA's next step is decisionmaking about funding and about the units of service designated to deal with

these priorities. This process begins with the allocation of funding for information and referral, the ombudsman program, and the nutritional program (the latter has a separately authorized federal appropriation). It goes on to establish funding allocations for such items of prime concern as in-home services, health, transportation, and legal assistance.

The local AAA is now directed by SUAs to administer the various meals programs; while they have their own staffs, they report directly to the AAA. In accomplishing its priorities-setting job, the AAA also undertakes systems development to improve delivery in a broad area of services, such as long-term care—for which it may initiate a comprehensive, communitywide system—or it may improve the delivery model by utilizing a new type, such as the case-management model (see Chapter 4). The Area Agency on Aging is called upon to reach out to the isolated and those in economic and social need. It does this in a number of ways: through publicity, through meetings with target organizations serving these groups, by focusing its efforts on certain neighborhoods with high concentrations of minorities or low income, by providing bilingual staff and encouraging contracting agencies to hire such staff, by providing information and referral, and by encouraging telephone reassurance and friendly visiting to the isolated.

Coordination

One of the AAAs' main jobs, "coordination" includes resource development and community organization: working with non–Title III programs for the aging, establishing the local interagency committee on aging, and seeing to it that different community programs and groups work together to develop a comprehensive community-based service to older people in the area. This planning and coordination function operates on several levels, involving, for example, collaboration with major regional planning groups, including health planning units, with community service providers holding AAA contracts, and with other agencies receiving funding relevant to the elderly's welfare. The AAA staff also participates in the work of task forces made up of providers and consumers from both the private and public sectors. Examples of such working groups would be a transit coordinating council or a county affordable housing committee.

The burden of coordinating programs run by a variety of suppliers under federal funding or state directives, and by those who draw their monies from nonprofit sources, is not a light one. In larger communities, the continuum of care may include 100 to 300 or more agencies, all with services targeted upon different groups, all of them with different goals and limitations or gaps in provision. The AAA may also work with other bodies, such as a health planning unit and the local Community Chest or United Way, in its task of harmonizing the components of the social service providers for the elderly.

Coordination at the national level is of a different type. The Older Americans Act for the first time created a central administrative office concerned with the elderly within the federal government. This is the Administration on Aging (AOA). It is headed by a commissioner whose job includes coordination of programs for the aging which originate with such diverse government bodies as the Social Security Administration and the Department of Housing and Urban Development (HUD). In using its own funds, the AOA's primary purpose is to provide national leadership for state and local offices. In its role as the central spokesman and focal point for the concerns of the elderly, it tries to achieve interagency agreements whenever possible.

Targeting of Funds

Under the Older Americans Act, funds are devoted to persons 60 and over. However, additional targeting is done in many states to insure that the programs are utilized by disadvantaged groups. In such cases, each individual SUA disburses funds to AAAs according to a formula intended to meet this demand. While, as Cutler (1983) reports, this funding formula is often determined simply by proportion of population 60 plus in the locale served by AAAs, some states have recently developed additional criteria, such as the proportion of aged poor in the AAA region, the proportion of rural aged, the proportion of frail elderly (75 and over), or the proportion of minorities 60 and over (Binstock, 1983). Such targeting formulas meet the act's mandate to the states to assure preference is given to providing services to those in greatest economic or social need, including the rural elderly. SUAs are enjoined to serve as advocates at the state level for the poor elderly. In the future AAAs are more likely than ever to target their funds to benefit particular groups. While means tests are currently prohibited, AAAs are nonetheless encouraged to target their services to the economically and socially needy. Sliding-scale payments are being discussed, as are "donations" to the meals program; some adult day care programs already have such provisions (Newcomer, Benjamin, and Estes, 1983).

All AAA efforts, whether aimed at developing priorities, refining targeting formulas, or designing long-term care systems, are undertaken in collaboration with state departments of aging (SUAs), and with other statewide and regional planning groups, such as health departments. AAA reports and recommendations are passed on to the state office (SUA); these SUAs of course also have considerable power over the AAAs.

Current Issues in OAA Activities

In a year (1984) when the need for reauthorization has caused a reexamination of program goals and priorities, a number of issues have been debated. This periodic subjection of programs to congressional approval provides a time to reconsider the main issues, as Fritz (1979) points out.

One issue which concerns both the SUAs and the AAAs is the need to improve coordination and decrease duplication of effort. Since the OAA funds are very limited (and overwhelmingly for the nutrition program), the AOA's main mission must be to coordinate and provide priorities for the service network serving the aged. Coordination is necessary among the various information and referral services and also among the fragmented community long-term care services. The AOA, as a main supporter of homemaker–home health-care services, must deal with an area that is cluttered with a mélange of small and changing suppliers, both public and private. These sources not only need to be coordinated, but to be regulated as well. This is an area where it is hard, at the local level, to apply federal policy because of built-in restrictions in several federal programs, including those pertaining to homemaker– and home health-care services.

Another issue in question is the degree to which OAA funds should be focused on programs for the frail elderly. The considerable amount of money spent by the AAAs on homemaker services has certainly been used for the frail elderly. Many demonstration projects have been community programs to serve the frail elderly, as shown in Branch and Branch's (1983) analysis of OAA expenditures through the Massachusetts Department of Elder Affairs. Since community long-term care is so strongly advocated today there is considerable justification for devoting more funding to this purpose. At present several large programs under OAA are directed mainly at the well elderly; these include multipurpose senior centers and nutrition programs, although the latter also serve frail elderly in the homebound part of the program.

Besides increased targeting of the frail elderly there is continual discussion of doing the same for the poor and for minorities. The AOA has been seriously criticized for its support of programs serving the middle class more than the poor, the life-enhancing programs rather than the life-supporting ones, as Estes (1979) puts it. As stated earlier in this chapter, increased efforts are being made at the state level to target funds to communities serving the poor and minorities. At the local level more effort is being made to provide services to minority and low income areas, to employ minority staff, and, in general, to increase accessibility for these groups. Yet the criticisms of overemphasis on the middle class rightly continue in regard to the meals program, senior centers, and homemaker services (see chapters on these services).

Some of the above issues are linked to another serious concern: that is, who should be setting priorities? Under the "new federalism" more priority-setting power is given to the individual states, but some fear that they lack the imagination to support new programs (Newcomer, Benjamin, and Estes, 1983). Many experts feel the local area may be the best locale for setting priorities; each community situation is different, with different needs and different resources and degrees of local initiative available, as Schmandt, Bach, and Radin (1979) found for information- and referral centers. Another controversial issue related to setting priorities and other decisionmaking tasks is the degree to which users should have the power to determine policy. Collin (1979) complains that citizen representation on OAA advisory boards at different levels is largely a matter of rubber-stamping already decided policy.

The degree to which the units under OAA should play an advocacy role in pressing for new services and increased funding is also a matter of debate. Fritz (1979) believes this is a major mandate of the Older Americans Act and one that was poorly carried out at the national level in its early years. He says the first AOA commissioners did little to bring about a major shift of resources from other programs to those for the elderly; however, he believes that in the post-1973 period this changed, since many agreements were signed with other agencies to obtain more services for the elderly. He admits, however, that it is difficult to pursue an advocacy role when one is under severe restraints due to fixed resources and increasing competition for ever-fewer tax dollars.

Controversy rages as well over how specific or general the OAA mandate on service funding should be—what should be the breadth of services provided? The OAA has generally supported a broad variety of programs through its demonstration projects. Some policymakers say the mandate should be narrower, now that funding has been reduced. Others, including the author, would argue that a main advantage of the OAA funding structure is that it provides seed money for innovative programs. One could even argue further that it has too many of its funds tied up already in the nutrition program and the multipurpose centers.

A final issue under contention is the allegedly excessive expense of the nonservice (administrative) aspects of the OAA programs. Understanding the cost of nonservice expenditures is particularly important in a time of shrinking social service budgets—as Branch and Branch (1983) point out. They found that for the Massachusetts Department of Elder Affairs, expenditures—both for all the department's activities taken together and for the state's home-care program—were $.70 for services and $.30 for nonservice costs. For other services they found different service-to-nonservice costs. Amsden and Simowski (1982) found major differences in service-unit costs between different AAAs in Michigan, recommending that in this period of retrenchment such wide discrepancies as these be examined. They mention that a 1981 General Accounting Office (GAO) study cited numerous variances and inadequacies in cost standards for Title III-B of the OAA services.

Conclusion

This chapter on OAA policy and planning issues that effect all services provides a framework through which we can look at the individual services discussed in the rest of the chapters. This description of the Older American Act programs and the future issues involved in functioning of this important legislation gives details of the applied side of local and state policymaking and planning for the elderly, in terms of deciding on alternative policies and developing a coordinated planning effort for implementation of policy. The issue of targeting funds to frail and poor elderly was discussed; the issue of decisionmaking on alternative choices for dealing with long-term care needs was highlighted.

CHAPTER 4

Linkage and Protective Services

This chapter changes its focus to explore the planning of service delivery for individual clients. Several services are grouped together here: information and referral, case management, protective services, and programs related to abuse of the elderly.

Information and referral, and case management, are basic linkage services that assess clients' need and then connect them with the appropriate services. Linkage staff members act as brokers, negotiating between the person in need and the agencies able to help. A third service, protective services for the mentally impaired elderly, includes linkage functions. A different type of protective assistance, intended for the benefit of abused elderly, is included because here too, the program with primary responsibility refers the abused person to other services.

All these services have the common trait of acting as an intermediary, rather than mainly providing direct assistance themselves. However, each differs somewhat in its emphasis. Through information and referral the worker provides the general public with information on available services; the major job here is keeping files on available resources and, of course, informing others about them. In case management the emphasis is on the worker providing in-depth assistance to guide or channel the individual client with multiple problems to the right sources of aid. In protective services, before linkage to other programs is established, the social worker carries out the major jobs of intervening and assessing a mentally impaired person's competence to function and manage his own affairs. The aim is usually to determine whether the individual in question is such a danger to himself and others that legal action must be taken to force the unwilling client to cooperate and to utilize the services deemed necessary. After that, the client is referred to appropriate agencies. In services for abuse cases the purpose of assessment is first to verify reported abuse, and then refer the abused to needed services and work with the perpetrators to improve their relationship with those elderly whom they have mistreated.

In all these services assessment and diagnosis of need and of problems is, to varying degrees, part of the job. In all these services the worker performs some degree of outreach, rather than simply wait for clients to come to him. Information-and-referral workers locate those in need of services; this can also be true in case management. Protective service workers investigate cases of mentally incompetent elderly, and in abuse cases they investigate the home situation. These workers also act as advocates for their clients: they may pressure other agencies to assist their clients, or they may even advocate the introduction of new services. The social workers in this group also counsel clients to varying degrees from merely providing information and advice on minor problems, to providing in-depth casework services, to counseling caretakers who abuse the elderly in their charge.

Information and Referral Services

In most communities there is at least one, and often a number of information and referral services. Their basic job is to inform a potential client, often someone with an immediate and urgent need, of the service most appropriate to help him. Since it is estimated that less than 25 percent of the intended clientele for most programs—except for those who qualify for Social Security and Medicare—makes use of the program in question (Burkhardt, 1979), those concerned need to be made more aware of such programs. A good information and referral service does more: it negotiates the client's use of the program and assures his accessibility to it. While information and referral (I & R) is a service in its own right, it is really only a means to the utilization of other services. If a client uses *only* I & R, the end is not achieved, for the needed service is not used. In the broad sense, I & R's functions are information, transfer, linkage, outreach, and research and planning (Schmandt et al., 1979). The functions of a particular information and referral center are related to the size of its constituency (city- or statewide versus neighborhood) and the types of area and population it serves. One might also have different layers of I & R, with a state or regional service providing a detailed resource file (Georgia, for example, has such a statewide tie-line), as well as neighborhood I & R programs that center on personal assistance and outreach to those in need (Schmandt et al., 1979). I & R centers in urban areas may differ in function from those in rural areas; in urban areas the center needs to help the client negotiate the complex array of available services to find and utilize the most appropriate one, while in rural areas the agency may need to give personal assistance and provide transportation to the few existing services.

The following discussion covers the types of jobs an information and referral center might handle and then goes on to analyze the problems and issues likely to arise in the course of I & R work.

Functions

Information and referral is basically an access service intended to inform the elderly and their families of the great variety of services available to them in the community; those with unmet needs are likely to call upon it for advice. I & R is often the first contact that the elderly and their families have with an agency able to help them. It can answer questions for those who have a specific problem or want information on a specific service. It can also negotiate the delivery system for these clients, and educate them as to which, in the maze of services, is the most appropriate for them.

Many elderly or their relatives suddenly have a specific need—perhaps related to a hospital discharge, or to a change in their family situation. They often do not know where to turn. They may think they—or their aged relatives—are ineligible for services because they do not understand the complex regulations set up by the various bureaucracies concerned. I & R can inform them of the continuum of care, provide them with alternatives, and save them from turning unnecessarily to the nursing home. In order to do this job, the I & R office must first survey the pertinent resources in the community and develop a file system to make the information gained from the survey readily accessible. The resources covered are not limited to social service agencies but include health services, community organizations, and business resources as well. This file should include a variety of information, such as type of assistance given, eligibility requirements, and personnel involved. The information and referral staff needs to be thoroughly familiar with these different agencies and their limitations in order to judge whether the potential beneficiary can actually obtain the service needed from a given agency. The staff has to understand the occasionally subtle aspects of eligibility requirements, so that the aged person is not sent where she will not be served. As a part of this job, the I & R worker must continually update herself on changes in the various agencies' provisions; she must watch for the death of small agencies—and for the birth of new ones. Another I & R task is to train volunteers to use the reference file; volunteers must also be trained in communication and counseling skills. The entire staff must learn to what degree the drop-in or telephone client should be assisted before being sent on to another agency.

A basic aspect of this work involves contacting agencies to arrange appointments for the clients referred to them; this is especially true when clients do not speak English. The I & R worker may have to go further by personally taking elderly clients to the appropriate agencies. Thus, the I & R staff may have to pave the way for minority clients who fear that the recommended agency will not welcome them.

An information and referral office should keep records about instances when it cannot locate a service to meet various requests, since one of I & R's main roles is to take note of gaps in service, making these known to policymakers in the agencies responsible for the area concerned.

Furthermore, the I & R office must publicize its own existence—the most basic of all "outreach" functions. Typically, the office may advertise its availability, and the services it provides, by way of radio and television "public service announcements" (PSAs), as well as publicizing itself at senior centers. It may also distribute information at stores or in special target areas, such as minority communities.

Information and referral centers also do social work counseling. Often a staff social worker counsels a client who has first been screened by a volunteer or receptionist. This staff worker and others have to follow up on their clients. By doing this, either by phone or in face-to-face interviews, they find out if clients actually used the agency to which they were referred—and why they did not, if such is the case. This is important, for it serves to improve the office's referral system as well as to give further help to the client. If language problems contributed to the client's failure to use the service he was referred to, a bilingual escort might be recommended. If the client failed to benefit due to changes in agency regulations, the referral service needs to know this, too. The I & R service also needs to know about long waiting lists at the agency concerned—knowledge gained most directly through feedback from the clients themselves.

If the information and referral office is in an AAA, its job might include the kinds of coordination activities mentioned above. Early information and referral services were part of Community Chest–United Way organizations, and a number of them still are. But today, some 85 percent are public agencies (Battle, 1977). Information and referral offices are found in senior centers and in public departments of social services. However, they have expanded greatly under Title III of the Older Americans Act. About half of the public I & R offices are operated by the local AAA or its state equivalent (Battle, 1977). Title III of the OAA stipulates that information and referral agencies be reasonably accessible to all older persons: they must be walk-in and telephone centers, and their services must be well publicized. Client confidentiality must be assured as well.

Problems of Information and Referral Services

Proper staffing is a major difficulty faced by I & R offices. The functions of counseling and of creating a resource file are so different that it is hard to find a single individual with both talents. When it comes to counseling, there may not be enough professional social work staff, and the available volunteers may not have been trained adequately. Volunteers may lack communication skills, counseling techniques, and adequate experience in work with older adults.

Is the individual I & R service reasonably accessible to those who need it most? The cost of telephoning the county I & R office, or of taking a bus to get there, may be too much of a financial burden for poor people to sustain. Lack of publicity may also be a problem. Bilingual services may not be available. The informal network of churches, local service organizations, and family may not be sufficiently informed and motivated to increase information to the elderly, even though, of all sources, they are the ones Schmandt et al. (1979) found to be the most frequently contacted. Schmandt and his collaborators found that the centers they had surveyed had almost no personal outreach to the unaffiliated elderly. Battle (1977) found that about a third of I & R centers had some degree of outreach, but he found almost no door-to-door canvassing. There is certainly a need for greater publicity, for Battle found that the isolated and unattached seldom used the service, while Burkhardt (1979) reported that less than 2 percent of the elderly had contact with the program and that only 25 percent knew of it at all.

Another area of concern has to do with finding out whether the client used the referral offered, and if he did, how he fared. Unfortunately, referrals are often not followed through (Schmandt et al., 1979). Yet use of a specific service is the end product in view; the information and referral agency needs to know if, when, and why referrals do not work, so that it can investigate the situation. An I & R office needs to know if a given client faced barriers to accessibility due to waiting lists, income, minority status, or other such obstacles. In such cases, the I & R office needs to know whether it should make a greater effort to enter its client into the service system. Unfortunately, information and referral offices frequently lack adequate staff for such following-up of their initial recommendations. It is expensive to do so: witness the Wisconsin information and referral demonstration project of the mid-1970s, in which some fourteen centers had extensive follow-up programs, escorts for clientele, and a staff-training program. The Wisconsin project was initially considered to be a model for the whole country, but when federal funding ended, state policymakers decided that the program was too expensive, and thereupon suspended it (Schmandt et al., 1977).

Should I & R be a 24-hour crisis center, referring people to emergency care in appropriate agencies (Battle, 1977)? I & R emergency services are likely to discover dangerous gaps. For example, Rhode Island's Department of Elderly Affairs I & R service received many calls pertaining to abuse of the elderly and could thus provide the data required for significant action (Hall and Tucker, 1984). The failure of coordination between I & R offices and the various other services within their purview to develop a community-based, centralized information and referral office linked to the county service is all too common. One must also decide whether some specialized information and referral services might better be consolidated, or whether at least part of their jobs might be given to a central agency.

Summary

Information and referral is a necessary, frontline service. However, one must make sure the client goes beyond initial contact and actually *uses* the resources to which he is referred. A layered system of information and referral may be a good idea if it is designed in such a way as to avoid duplication. Information and referral needs to center more on outreach and accessibility. I & R needs to take its job of informing the local community about gaps in service more seriously.

Case Management

Case management, or service management, is an intensive type of intake service to provide the individual elderly person with what is appropriate for him along the continuum of care. This approach goes considerably farther than information and referral. The central task is to coordinate the provision of services by different providers for an individual person. Case management assigns a worker to a particular client, charging him to make an intense effort to see that his client utilizes appropriate care. This type of management is especially applicable to the frail or mentally impaired person who needs several services and/or has complex problems (Steinberg and Carter, 1983).

The case manager working with the elderly is defined by Monk (1981) as a permanent consultant or facilitator in the life of an older person. The latter, as the Federal Council on Aging (1979) says, may be largely capable of handling his or her life but "needs some help in coping with life's bureaucracies because of the accumulation of vicissitudes of increasing aging, not because of a single physical or mental trauma or a personal loss or role change." Some elderly persons needing case management may be so mentally impaired that the case manager has to initiate legal guardianship, a situation Monk focuses on (see below, pp. 74–75). The case management worker, with the help of other professionals, assesses the needs of the elderly person, plans her services, helps her achieve access to them, and follows up to insure accountability of the agencies involved. The worker maintains regular contacts with both the client and the agencies.

Case management programs try to integrate and coordinate services. Ideally, access to the whole service system is through one intake source, a single agency that does the need assessment, facilitates access, and helps clients make the appropriate choices. The case manager draws up a written service plan. Case management involves advocacy by the social worker on the part of his client in order to obtain the service(s) he needs.

Different Models for Case Management

The above description gives a general idea of the role of case management. However, as Johnson and Rubin (1983) point out, there are different types of case management. As they say, despite the increasing popularity of case management in attending to clients' multiple needs, the concept lacks clarity, since it covers several approaches. This popularity is attested to by the National Institute of Mental Health's (NIMH) having made case management a funding priority for serving the chronically mentally disabled and by the fact that funding sources have set up a "Long-Term Care Channeling Demonstration Project." But such developments mean that many different approaches, sponsored by a variety of agencies, are evolving. For example, there are statewide, impersonal case management programs in several states, set up to integrate services for particular clients; these include the Virginia Service Integration for Deinstitutionalization Project and the Florida Integrated Health and Rehabilitative Services (Johnson and Rubin, 1983).

A major difference among programs centers around the case manager's role. That role can range from the case manager who never makes contact with the client, simply reviewing records, assessing needs, and planning coordination of services, to the more usual kind of case management with the case manager in direct contact with the client, or to the type of case management that includes therapeutic counseling. In the Florida and Virginia programs mentioned above, according to Johnson and Rubin (1983) the case managers are not usually seen as service providers themselves, but as coordinators of cases and brokers of services whose task it is to expedite clients' contact with the many kinds of assistance available.

In the more usual sort of program, the case manager's role includes a major diagnosis and assessment effort. After initial screening there is a home visit, then the initiation of planning for the care program; if the client accepts the plan, then delivery of service begins, followed later by post service evaluation. (Guthrie and Brodbar [1983] give these as stages in the national "Long-Term Care Channeling Demonstration Project".) The case management worker tries to contact relatives or other supportive sources in order to integrate them into the helping system. In other words, the major job in case management is one of linkage, that is, negotiating the bureaucratic hurdles and arranging services for the client to use. The elderly client may be unable, by herself, to apply for the services she needs, or to understand the requirements for participation. The case manager, as Johnson and Rubin (1983) say, helps the client move across institutional, community, and agency boundaries.

Another job typical of the case manager is to monitor the client's use of the services and see why he has problems with use, if such is the case. Finally, the manager acts as an advocate, obtaining a needed service when it is not readily available, or interceding on behalf of his client if help is refused. In all this the case manager centers on an individual case and helps to integrate the services for his client's benefit, especially since the latter usually has multiple problems.

The case manager—especially when helping the mentally impaired—may go further and provide therapeutic counseling to the client. Johnson and Rubin (1983) report that in a mental health setting, practitioners are predisposed to including the traditional diagnostic and therapeutic function in case management, and that this is facilitated by the absence of a fully and clearly explicated definition of case management. They also say that case managers do this because unless they provide therapy they feel vulnerable to being called paraprofessionals; their agency may also want them to provide direct counseling service because this is mandated by the agency's funding.

Lamb (1980) justifies case managers taking on this therapeutic function rather than acting simply as service brokers; he maintains that the therapeutic service is a form of supportive counseling which focuses on day-to-day realities and survival in the community: this distinguishes it from in-depth counseling. As Johnson and Rubin (1983) point out, some argue that the case manager needs to provide both support and encouragement, and that these two functions cannot easily be separated, especially in meeting the unique needs of mentally impaired elderly. Such therapeutic counseling, it is said, helps the case manager recognize early signs of unmanageable stress and general deterioration. It helps the case manager establish a stable, close relationship with her client, one which makes it easier for her to secure the client's compliance with, and utilization of, her service plan.

Each of these models of case management puts its emphasis on different aspects of the job. One interesting case-management experiment for high-risk elderly patients in a hospital focuses mainly on the assessment process—its Model for Evaluation and Referral of Geriatrics (MERGE). The goal is to assist the physician in identifying, treating, referring and monitoring complex multiple problems of elderly patients (Sims and Packard, 1983). Here the physician himself might be called the case manager, although the nurse practitioners, using an assessment tool, evaluate the patients and present their cases to a project team made up of a geriatric psychiatrist, internists, a rehabilitation technician, a nutritionist, and the primary physician. This is only one of the many unique models we see developing.

Issues

One issue, already mentioned above, is what the case manager's functions ought to be. Should they include therapeutic counseling? The answer given to this question will influence one's approach to another issue: Who should do counseling? Some have suggested the use of paraprofessionals or individuals specially trained in case management instead of those with training in psychiatric social work. Ozarin (1978) argues that the case management function may be carried out by any one of a variety of disciplines and agencies. However, she would require the prospective case manager to possess special skills, training, and in-service experience. Those who see the therapeutic function as an integral part of the job usually argue that psychiatric social workers are best qualified. The latter, however, do not always want the job, or at least they often do not give it high priority. They prefer casework activity; many see the brokerage and advocacy jobs as artificial (Johnson and Rubin, 1983). One problem that bothers these social workers is the requirement that case managers be able to coordinate different sources of assistance.

The problem is to have community agencies accept a single agency as an intake source and accept its assessment of need. While case management is systematic and cost efficient, it diminishes the autonomy of the various agencies it deals with. There usually has to be an official mandate to authorize the creation of such a system. Pennsylvania adopted the service management approach under the auspices of its Older Americans Act SUA. It experimentally used it in some of the local AAAs; AAA personnel took on this case management as an extension of their coordinated delivery of multiple services to individual clients (Gottesman, Ishizaki, and MacBride, 1979). It was found that besides an official mandate, other needed ingredients included: (1) the existence of several services in the continuum of care, (2) one agency that could take on the role of being the primary manager and be accountable to the whole system, (3) acceptance, by all the other agencies in the system, that service management be performed by the designated agency, and (4) recognition on all sides of the special interests of cooperating agencies.

Gottesman, Ishizaki, and MacBride (1979) find that the type of client most likely to benefit from such a system is someone who needs personal advocacy support. It is often difficult, however, to locate enough services of the sort needed. The national "Long-Term Care Channeling Demonstration Project," which provides community care for functionally impaired elderly

at risk of institutionalization, uses two program models for case management, one with existing community services, and the other with access to an
expanded array of community services under a Medicaid and Medicare
waiver agreement (as reported by staffers of the Philadelphia Channeling
program and the Texas Project for the Elders in Gaitz et al., 1983).

Another problem has been the client attrition rate. The attrition rate
Guthrie and Brodbar (1983) report for the national "Long-Term Care Channeling Demonstration Project" seems to be high, although the case management approach adopted by this demonstration project is supposed to insure
that clients receive the services most appropriate to meet their needs. Case
management statistics reported by Guthrie and Brodbar show that of 426
clients accepted for case management, only 230 ended up as part of the
active case load. The attrition rate was especially high during the assessment
and home-visit stages.

Summary

Case management can help prevent clients from using the wrong services,
and it can even stop unnecessary institutionalization. The system can provide an impetus for coordination and consolidation of services. The best
example is Connecticut's Triage experiment which served 2,500 clients in
1974–81. The goal was to obtain the mix of services the clients needed from
local agencies (Gelfand, 1984). These clients were monitored for 54 months
as to utilization of 9 services. Interestingly, case management did not mean
indefinite use. Quinn et al. (1983) state that "effective Triage monitoring of
client status assured that in the majority of cases the provision of services was
reduced or terminated as appropriate."

Case management can humanize the whole social service system. I
believe that the service should be provided by psychiatric social workers. It
could be made even more viable by increasing the number of resources
available. However, at this writing (1984), this is unlikely, given the Reagan
administration's fiscal austerity orientation.

Protective Services

Case management plays a part in another type of service: protective services
for the mentally impaired elderly, people who can no longer manage their
own affairs. A broad definition of the human service worker's responsibility
toward the mentally impaired includes assessing or diagnosing their condition and then linking these clients with appropriate community services or
institutional arrangements that will ameliorate the at-risk situation. For the
client unable or unwilling to care for herself and unwilling to voluntarily

cooperate with the help offered her, the worker does more than link the client with social services. She initiates legal action that compels the client to make use of the recommended services.

The worker in protective services is dealing with a delicate matter, one that requires special skills. The worker, rather than the client, does the initiating in protective services. The worker, acting as a case manager for the person without a family, may come close to slipping into a paternal attitude toward his elderly client. In these protective cases the line between performing a voluntary function of coordination and linking services and providing court-ordered protective services can be a fine one, as Monk (1981) emphasizes.

The services the worker links the mentally impaired client to include home care, home health aid, visiting-nurse assistance, medical and paramedical care, counseling, and even friendly visiting and home repair services. Working in protective services also involves the coordination of the professionals involved, such as lawyers, psychiatrists, and medical personnel, in the legal action. As Wasser (1971) says in describing her classic model of casework services in this field, the caseworker acts as a central regulator, bringing in the ancillary services that play an indispensable collaborative part in meeting the needs of the mentally impaired. The human service worker's job is to act as a kind of case manager, or balance wheel, in the intermeshing of these highly varied areas of expertise (Wasser, 1971; Follett, 1977).

Types of People Served

The usual clients are elderly persons of varying degrees of incompetency— those who have difficulty in managing their daily living, financial matters, and personal decisionmaking. Their mental and physical functioning is so poor that it may result in harmful, even dangerous behavior; these are people who lack the ability to act efficiently on their own behalf.

The people who need protective services are most likely to be widow(er)s over 80 who suffer from an organic brain syndrome and who lack close relatives willing and able to deal with this incapacity. They are confused and forgetful enough to need someone else to handle their finances and their personal affairs. They may need protection from fraudulent schemes and exploitation, even by their own families. They may not maintain their personal appearance very well, or that of their dwelling; they may sleep on the street and roam the alleys.

Ruth Weber (1966) defines four circumstances in which the elderly need protective services: (1) the person is incapable of performing those functions necessary to meet his basic physical and health requirements; (2) the person is incapable of managing his finances; (3) the person's behavior is dangerous to himself and others, either directly or indirectly; (4) the person's behavior or circumstances bring him into serious conflict with the community. In general, the types of mentally impaired elderly that comes to the attention of social work agencies are those that show signs of some mental disturbance through unusual, bizarre, offensive, or self-neglectful behavior. Such behavior is often itself harmless in nature—but sometimes it is of a dangerous kind (Wasser, 1971). Some examples are:

> Mary N. is a wanderer. She leaves her home in the morning and wanders downtown. She looks in garbage pails and trash cans. She is oblivious to the many strangers who come up to her. She talks to herself. Mary N. has a large old house and other financial assets. She does not keep the house up and seldom eats regular meals. Her daughter is continually trying to correct the situation but Mary N. is adamant in continuing her ways. The daughter has now turned to a social service agency to see if there is any legal action that can be taken.
>
> Mrs. K. lives in an inner-city boarding house. She has very little money and eats irregularly. She wears old, ragged garments. Her landlord feels she needs someone to look after her interests. She has no relatives.
>
> Another case is Mary M. Her husband left her a large estate. She is now 89 and somewhat confused. She insists on living alone and handling her financial affairs. She is fairly religious and in the last year has been contacted a number of times by a religious group that has run into trouble with the law over its dubious fundraising activities. She has no children.

Some definitions have centered on the person without relatives, such as that used for the classic Blenkner study (1974). There it is said that the candidate for protective services is "the person 60 years and over whose behavior indicates that he is mentally incapable of caring for himself or his interests without serious consequences to himself or others and who has no relatives or other private individuals able and willing to assume the kind and degree of support and supervision required to control the situation" (Blenkner, 1974; see also Dunkle, 1983). Others do not limit the group needing protection to those without relatives; in fact guardianship by a relative is the most common kind. In such cases a social worker's advice may also be needed. However, the social worker is more likely to initiate the legal procedures when there are no relatives.

The definition of who is covered by protective services has broadened in the recent years. While in the 1950s it included mainly the extremely mentally incompetent, under Title XX of the Social Security Act it was broadened in the 1970s to cover cases of marginal incapacity. Under Title XX, now SSBG—one of the major funding sources for protective services— the definition includes not only the mentally incompetent of varying degrees, but those incapacitated due to ill health, or even ignorance; this program also broadens the array of supportive services eligible for funds, including household maintenance and financial management.

Role of the Social Worker

This broadening of the group included under the umbrella of protective services means that today, even more than in the past, the social service worker's job involves a great deal more than initiating legal action. In fact the emphasis is now on measures to avoid such drastic measures. Many cases are of the sort in which the client retains some degree of competency. This means that the degree and type of legal authority that the social worker exercises in the typical case has changed compared to the 1960s, when commitment of clients to a mental hospital was a major function of social workers, as Lehman (1961) points out in her classic article on protective services. In the early 1970s it was still widely assumed that clients should be committed to nursing homes, but by the 1980s more emphasis had come to be placed on community services. In recent years the complaint has been that there are insufficient funds for community services even though decreased use of mental hospitals and discharge of former patients has shifted a large part of the burden to the community; furthermore, the limited community mental health resources are sometimes not used for the seriously mentally ill (Johnson and Rubin, 1983). This often leaves mentally impaired elderly out on the streets.

The first step to take in relation to reported cases is, of course, investigation. Assessment of the problem can be hard, for, as Wishard and Wishard (1981) state, the line between foolishness or eccentricity and legal incompetency is a difficult one to draw. Each case must be decided on its own merits. Supportive services may make it unnecessary to resort to formal legal restrictions and loss of control by the client over her own affairs through legal guardianship; furthermore, halfway measures, such as limited power of attorney activated by the elderly person herself, may avoid court hearings on competency and full loss of control of decisionmaking powers. Today SSBG and AOA guidelines place more emphasis on prevention. The problem is what to do if the elderly person and her relatives, if any, are incapable of seeking these milder solutions—or refuse to do so. Legal action is definitely the last resort (Atchley, 1983). However, protective services do differ from other types in that the client contact may well be involuntary on the client's part, and that some form of legal intervention remains an option if cooperation is not forthcoming.

After preliminary investigation the social worker attempts to make an in-depth assessment of the problem. This is not always easy. The referring person, such as a neighbor, may provide an exaggerated description of the elderly person's degree of neglect and mental impairment. The worker may have a difficult time eliciting the facts of the situation because the client does not remember past events, admit to present deviant behavior, or show willingness to cooperate. He is often hostile toward the unwanted official entering his home. He may be unreceptive due to his fear that the worker will take away his freedom and independence of action, may intervene only on a superficial basis, or demand changes in his environment. The client may enjoy his isolation, consider his way of life acceptable, and feel no desire to change matters. The client may, in fact, be incapable of accepting help (Wasser, 1971). Resistance—for these reasons and others—makes the worker's job harder. (Of course some clients will not resist and will respond positively to help, even though they had not been capable of requesting it.)

In diagnosing the client's ability to function in an independent manner, the worker may need to call in a psychiatrist or utilize geriatric services to conduct assessment sessions such as those based on an Activities of Daily Living (ADL) scale (Lawton, 1972). The worker and other professionals need to differentiate carefully among different areas of functioning, for some people are impaired in one area but not in others. Some aspects of the aged person's mental processes may be relatively intact, rendering her still capable of some degree of decisionmaking and normal, everyday functioning if these aspects are supported.

After diagnosis is complete the worker needs to refer his client to the appropriate services. If the client resists help, a major decision on intervention needs to be made: whether to initiate legal action or leave him alone. The diagnosis must be reviewed to decide whether the behavior is simply bizarre and not harmful to the person or to others, or whether it is sufficiently serious to justify intervention against the client's will in order to insure that he receives proper care. The risks of keeping the client in his own home must be weighed carefully. As Wasser (1971) asks, Do the risks of remaining at home overbalance the client's gratification in doing so, and how much risk should be tolerated for the sake of the client if that involves violating the opposing interests of others? The worker, of course, may himself be able to decrease some risks by changing conditions in the home: diverting the aged person from collecting wood and old newspapers, or from filling the house with rubbish or stray animals, and similar measures. Furthermore, Wasser advises, the social worker may get outside authorities, such as fire and health departments, to present realistic standards to his client. The worker can then help his charge to meet these standards. On the other hand, if the worker, or the worker and the client's family, decide that legal action must be initiated, his role may change, so that he is called upon to demonstrate to the court that this elderly person is incapable of exercising rational judgement and making decisions in his own best interest.

Types of Legal Action

The legal component of protective services has several forms. A number are of a limited nature that apply mainly to management of financial affairs rather than to overall management of the client's affairs. The elderly person herself may initiate some such measure or, in cases where family members are involved, they may take such steps themselves. But if there is no help to be expected from the family, a social worker working with a public (or occasionally private) agency will initiate the process. Many states have public guardianship programs for such cases (Schmidt et al., 1981).

POWER OF ATTORNEY

Power of Attorney can be conferred upon another person by a legally competent elderly individual who does not want to be bothered by, or is forgetful about, routine financial affairs, such as bill payment. Legally competent elderly may do this because of severe illness or because managing their financial affairs has become too difficult for them. Power of attorney often involves another person, often a relative, in handling savings, checking, and other accounts. This is a limited power; the client retains ultimate control over his affairs. Sometimes a social service agency, including a welfare department, will have the power of attorney. In some states power of attorney expires automatically at the end of a year and must be renewed.

THE SUBSTITUTE PAYEE ACTION

Allowed by some federal agencies under certain conditions, substitute payee action is another form of limited financial management on behalf of an incompetent or incapacitated person. The agency providing a benefit check to an aged person appoints a substitute who will receive and use the funds for that person's maintenance. The substitute payee then accounts for expenses to the agency on a periodic basis. The substitute payee is usually a relative, but can also be another person or even an agency.

CONSERVATORSHIP

In this legal arrangement, a "conservator" is appointed by a court to supervise the client's financial and personal matters, but the elderly person keeps a number of legal rights, such as that of making certain contracts on his own. The older person retains the legal right to consult with the conservator about the management of his affairs, and it is assumed that the conservator will take into consideration the desires and preferences of the elderly person.

In many cases a conservatorship is set up for widows who inherit a large estate. The conservator mainly handles the dividends, interest, or other income from the estate. He is not supposed to dispose of the estate's assets unless he can demonstrate need and justification to the court (Wishard and Wishard, 1981). Banks and trust companies may act as limited conservators for estates of incompetent aged or even for competent elderly. They may handle investments and pass on the interest and dividends to the elderly person; they may also pay bills. State law usually requires that these financial institutions make a regular accounting of their stewardship as limited conservators.

GUARDIANSHIP

Guardianship is the most extreme legal procedure for handling the incompetent elderly's financial and personal matters. Unlike the case of conservatorship, there must be a court finding of incompetency. If this is obtained at the hearing, control of financial, as well as personal, affairs passes into the hands of the guardian, while the elderly person now becomes a ward. There is also such a thing as partial guardianship; for example, a bank can handle property, but not personal concerns.

Public welfare departments and other social agencies are often called on to be guardians of incompetent elderly who lack relatives able to assume the task. A judge may appoint as guardian either a relative or a county public guardian. This legal process is often used when the person who is judged incompetent refuses to voluntarily turn over responsibilities to the adult child or some other relative deemed appropriate by the court. For example:

> Mrs. Heley (85) is confused and often talks to herself; she also is a wanderer. Her husband left her several apartment houses. She seldom remembers to collect rents and is far behind in paying bills. She has refused help from her children and is argumentative over any of their suggestions for use of a real estate management firm. The family finally took legal measures, including a court hearing to establish the need for guardianship by the family.

The social worker's role here may be to give the judge evidence from the social investigation and from psychiatric and other evaluative studies. (Many states now use Geriatric Evaluation Services [GES].)

The grounds for judicial consent to the drastic step of guardianship have been tightened in some states in the last few years. The terms "incapacity" and "incompetency" have been more sharply defined, and the evidence required to prove that these conditions exist is more detailed and rigorous. Many states require a medical examination; some require a psychological examination (Schmidt et al., 1981; Regan and Springer, 1977).

The next step for the worker is the actual case management of the services by a public guardianship program or other social service agency to the person made a guardian. Or the court may decide to commit a ward to an institution, such as a nursing home or a mental hospital. There are some safeguards on commitment established by law in regard to mental hospital commitment. However, this is not true for nursing home commitments, and Monk (1981) maintains that some agencies are still overprotective and resort more than necessary to institutionalization. However, in general social workers are turning more and more to community resources. Blenkner's (1974) finding that those mentally impaired elderly in need of services who came under the supervision of a caseworker were more likely to be institutionalized than those who did not, may have had some effect on the profession's reorientation in this matter.

Within the community itself the social worker may utilize a hospital for some cases; the worker may bring in a visiting public health nurse or a homemaker, and may turn to such volunteer services as friendly visiting. Because of the client's helplessness, the worker may bear a heavy responsibility in arranging services (Heyman and Polansky, 1977). Even after guardianship (or lesser legal actions) has been established, the worker may have trouble getting her client to services because of her charge's hostility. It is not easy to move or otherwise help a person who, while in urgent need of assistance such as hospital care, is hostile, fearful, and helpless. It is difficult to move such a client from a dirty, unhealthy place that she nevertheless considers to be home to a large, alienating city hospital, for example. And the worker must ask herself: Will the client be destroyed in the process of moving her (Wasser, 1971; Zarit, 1980)?

Issues

Social service agencies have been reluctant to take on responsibility for protective services. As Blenkner's (1974) pioneer study shows, this is a complex field involving a variety of hard moral decisions. It has a legal dimension, too, which can even lead to lawsuits (Dunkle, 1983). It commits the worker to coordinate a number of services for the client, services that in reality may not be available in the community (Monk, 1981). Sometimes, as Zarit (1980) points out, the client is simply sent on a referral circuit with little resulting help. Or the services may be available only sporadically (Lowy, 1979). The worker must often become an organizer and advocate of services.

Provision of these services—or even case management—can be a costly activity. Schmidt et al. (1981) found that few states provided adequate funding for services under public guardianship programs. In addition, a major problem may arise from the fact that the decisionmaking responsibilities involved in protective services go against the social worker's basic philosophy of self-determination for the client. Even if every effort is made to involve the client, the situation is often such that, due to the client's confusion and incompetency, the worker has to assert his own authority and make decisions. He thus is intervening in the client's life without being asked, and forces measures on a client who may adamantly oppose them, as when hospital care may be deemed unavoidable. Intervention may even lead to commitment to a nursing home or—especially in the past—to a mental hospital.

QUESTIONS ABOUT THE USE OF LEGAL ACTION

Researchers seem less unanimous than ever before as to whether protecting the incompetent elderly through legal guardianship or conservatorship is the proper strategy. Writing in 1981, Monk reports that even when protective service is fully justified becase the elderly person is a danger to herself or a nuisance and danger to others, social workers often still experience moral trepidation and concern about the legality of intervention. He adds that they have a fear of improperly getting involved in others' business and of taking over others' lives. Agencies are afraid of legal suits being brought against them for recommending judicial action.

Blenkner's early research (1974) startled the social work world into realizing that its actions do not always improve clients' situations. She reported greater institutionalization and a higher mortality rate for those in her experimental group (those receiving counseling) than for her control group (those not receiving it). While methodological problems have been found with this research (Dunkle et al., 1983), the question of whether social work intervention is likely to improve a client's situation is still unresolved.

First, there is the issue of diagnosing incompetence. Some question whether the social worker does not often overreact to the client's situation, labeling it as intolerable and dangerous to the elderly person and possibly to the community as well, when in fact matters are not that serious (Wasser, 1971). As Zarit (1980) says, professionals often find themselves treating practical idiosyncracies or eccentricities that have no negative consequences for anyone. He suggests that they assess the consequences of behavior more rigorously. How much risk arises from this behavior? Any such risk should be weighed against the potential losses resultant from taking away an individual's independence. Is the bizarre behavior really hurting the community or the person? Does a dirty house and an unwashed physiognomy call for legal intervention?

Then too, there is the issue of whether the social worker's alternative is actually better for the client himself. In 1983 the Benjamin Rose Institute staff, the major researchers on this service, were especially concerned over the degree and type of intervention from which the protective-service client could truly benefit (Dunkle et al., 1983). After all, a move out of familiar surroundings may in itself be so traumatic that it increases the inability to function. As Zarit (1980) states, the risk of intervention may often be worse than that caused by the status quo. Relocation of the client to a retirement hotel may remove her personal control over important choices. If the move is to an institution, it may so deprive the person of her independence—possibly because of the use of tranquilizers and restraining wheel chair apparatus—that the benefits of receiving regular meals and sleeping in a clean room are likely to be of little importance to her well-being. As Wasser (1971) asks, Is the worker interested in survival per se, or in the quality of survival? And Cormican (1980), reviewing Wasser's evidence of chances of "transplant shock" from a move to a nursing home, suggests that practitioners ask what purpose is served by such a move.

Zarit, Wasser, and Dunkle et al., what is more, question the worker's aims as perhaps class-bound: even such a "self-evidently" worthwhile goal as a "safe" home is open to criticism. Is a middle-class standard being used for "safe" or "clean"? Are the goals realistic and specific? Are they individualized and obtainable for that particular client and acceptable to the client (Dunkle et al., 1983)?

These writers all advocate taking greater risks in keeping a person in his own home. Yet there are several problems in regard to this proposal. One is the social worker's own worry that if he does not intervene, a fire or some equally dangerous development may occur. Even if he feels the risk of keeping the client at home is worth taking, or the eccentricity involved is harmless, he must face the neighbors' complaints. Their appeal to a social service agency is often inspired not just by concern, but by revulsion as to what is going on. They may want the older person out of his home because they fear that a fire, or rodent infestation, might spread to their own homes; they are likely to be dismayed at the house's appearance and feel it affects negatively the appearance of the whole neighborhood. They can put considerable pressure on the worker to "do something about it."

The social worker faces other constraints. Actions may have to be taken quickly due to an emergency health need, an outcry from neighbors, or depletion of the client's funds. The worker may well lack sufficient time to establish rapport with her client, or to diagnose her needs carefully. It may prove difficult to link the client with proper services because they are absent or inadequate in the local community. In despair, the worker may respond to community pressure by using the nursing home: This will spell the end of her client's independence. Some observers of practices in this area (e.g., Cormican) were still saying in 1980 that the usual response by the practitioner to the elderly's need for protective services was institutionalization.

CLIENT RIGHTS

This situation has made client rights a major issue. Schmidt et al. (1981) report that by the late 1970s a number of state laws on the subject had written in a mandating review of guardianship policy. Monk (1981) reports that agencies are increasingly concerned about the client's civil rights. Horstman (1977) demands a "bill of rights" for all elderly that would limit the conditions under which they could be confined. There are increased efforts to see that the individual under consideration for guardianship be kept informed, take full part in the hearings, and have the right to counsel. This is clearly an area with great potential for extremely serious abuse, an area where the abuser, whether family or even public guardians, may be swayed by the potential for great financial gain. While, as Regan and Springer (1977) say, an incompetent includes one unable to manage the daily business of life and liable to dissipate an estate or become the victim of designing persons, the irony is that the guardian in more than one case has been known to do these very things. And at the same time the elderly person has lost his basic rights.

All these negative dimensions of protective services should not deter agencies from accepting responsibility. It is inhumane to ignore people who roam the streets or isolate themselves in a house, unable to care for themselves. As Wasser (1971) points out, if the agency fails to assume responsibility for these major problems, just at the critical point when the client has become unable to care for herself properly, this means the agency is denying, intentionally or not, a painful and difficult aspect of need in our society.

Programs and Services for the Abused Elderly

Social workers may have another role in protective services: they have a role in special projects for the abused elderly. In such programs they act as advocates for the rights of the aged when they are abused by others. In this endeavor they may work with legal aid societies or various social service organizations for the aged.

Abuse takes many forms. Abuse by unnecessary institutionalization of the elderly is one of them; there are many cases when aged people, often against their own wishes, are prematurely put in an institution. A serious problem in the past has been abuse of slightly confused elderly persons whose families have committed them to a mental hospital. Fortunately, in many states today involuntary commitment is limited by such legal safeguards as hearings and psychological reassessments at specific intervals. Some court decisions have further limited indiscriminate placement of the elderly in mental institutions. In *Donaldson* v. *O'Connor* (1975) the Supreme Court made clear the illegality of involuntary placement; it held that it is unconstitutional for a state to confine an individual in an institution when that person is not dangerous and is capable of surviving alone or with the help of family and friends.

Abuse of the confused elderly by wrongful and unnecessary placement in a nursing home is not protected by hearings and other safeguards. Yet through the use of drugs this institution can keep a confused aged person prisoner almost as effectively as a mental hospital. The newly formed ombudsman system described in Chapter 11 may rectify this situation to some small degree. The elderly sometimes, as alluded to above, need protection from their own families. Adult children have been known to put their aged parents in institutions so that they can obtain their house and other financial assets, often after they have been declared their parents' legal guardians.

An equally serious cause for concern is abuse by adult children when the elderly are living with the children or are otherwise dependent on them. This abuse of seniors—usually of frail mothers by their grown children—is not limited to the incompetent elderly, as Hall and Tucker (1984) point out. Abused elderly do not necessarily need a guardian, and certainly not the loss of their rights or other types of protective services. Instead, they need a champion, an "advocate" who will stop the family's abusive treatment. Consider the following example.

> Mrs. J. P. Smith . . . lived with her daughter. The son-in-law wanted Mrs. S. to turn over the whole social security check to him and to also give him half of the stock she had acquired when her husband died. She continually refused, and on several occasions he slapped her. He often threatened her, saying he would put her in a nursing home. The daughter just felt helpless to do anything.

In this case abuse took a physical form; however, mere verbal abuse may be involved. Abuse is also clearly present when the confused elderly person is left to wander about, is fed irregularly, or when the bedridden incontinent person does not have his sheets changed for 10–12 hours, or is otherwise left unattended for long periods. Steinmetz (1981) found that 40 percent of the adult children in her study admitted controlling their elderly parents by yelling and screaming at them. In this study 6 percent admitted to using physical restraint, forced feeding or medication, or threats to send their elderly parents to a nursing home. A still smaller percentage said they also threatened elderly parents with physical force or actually hit or slapped them. These are quite likely underestimates, as the perpetrators are obviously reluctant to admit such acts.

A number of researchers believe that a considerable proportion of the incompetent or dependent elderly is at risk of abuse; the number of cases reported to the authorities are numerous enough to be a concern, even though the elderly are extremely reluctant even to mention such mistreatment to others.

Steinmetz (1981) states that surveys of social service professionals and police statistics show that the most frequent abusers of the elderly are family members. She estimates that almost 10 percent of the dependent elderly are at risk. Seventeen percent of those responding to a mail survey of professionals (Hickey and Douglas, 1981) reported physical abuse of an elderly person and 44 percent reported verbal or emotional abuse by the family. O'Malley et al. (1979), in a carefully conducted mail survey of professionals and paraprofessionals, noted that 55 percent of the 332 respondents reported an incident of elder abuse during an 18-month period. Steinmetz (1981) finds that the Baltimore City Police Department reported 149 domestic assaults against persons 60 years or older in 1978. She says that about two-thirds of these assaults were committed by relatives other than a spouse.

Services

The evidence shows that abuse of the elderly is so serious that in each state some sort of adult protectives service has usually been established in state departments of social services with SSBG funds and/or that reporting services have been established in state departments of elderly affairs (these often have projects for the abused elderly, as in Massachusetts and New York). An example is the state of Rhode Island; in 1981 its Department of Elderly Affairs sponsored a Mandatory Reporting Bill on Elderly Abuse, which was passed by the legislature. The bill mandated the reporting of such abuse by professionals, levying a fine against those who did not comply. The state set up councils throughout the state to monitor elderly abuse; in Providence alone 52 public, private, and local agencies took part (Hall and Tucker, 1984).

A good deal of evidence on elderly abuse comes from these reporting systems. For example, the Connecticut reporting system enacted in 1978 required health care professionals, social services, and law enforcement agencies to report suspected cases of abuse, neglect, exploitation, and abandonment of the elderly. Walker and Potter (1983) report that private physicians and hospital staff were unlikely to provide abuse information to the authorities (only 2.9 percent of the verified complaints for noninstitutionalized abuse cases received in one year came from these groups, even though two-thirds of the cases involved physical abuse, mainly injuries to the head, neck, and face). The Connecticut statistics showed the majority of the perpetrators to be spouses, sons, or daughters. In the Rhode Island abuse statistics the son was by far the most likely perpetrator, followed by the daughter (Hall and Tucker, 1984).

Referrals in Rhode Island were made mainly to social service agencies. Some of these Rhode Island cases (15 percent, or 81 cases) involved institutionalizing the elderly, showing that giving help can lead to other problems for the abused elderly person. However, since almost 40 percent of the cases involved physical abuse, the workers concerned had little choice but try to intervene (Hall and Tucker, 1984).

Issues

As I have shown the dilemma for abused elderly is that because they are dependent on the abuser for basic services, they dare not report mistreatment. If they do, they not only risk further harm but also risk losing needed help, perhaps being placed in a nursing home or, if such is not available, being thrown out on their own. Agencies who intervene to stop such abuse are also faced with the problem of what happens to the dependent elderly person if they take this person out of the adult child's home.

A second dilemma is that the elderly may, in fact, be as abusive to the adult child as the adult child is to them. The very elderly person with physical and mental problems such as Alzheimer's disease, may be very abrasive, as detailed in Chapter 10. Their self-centeredness may mean they require full-time attention from the caretaker, usually a daughter. The burden of continual demands by the aged parent may put her under such stress that there is a strong potential for neglect or physical or verbal abuse (Rathbone-McCuan, 1982).

Counseling is indeed needed in abuse and neglect cases. The family must be confronted with such charges when they arise and then must be encouraged to improve conditions. In many cases the adult child needs respite services—that is, programs that provide free days or hours for the elderly person's caretaker. This respite service is becoming popular. It can be provided in a number of settings. For example, the respite service can be a planned, intermittent hospitalization to relieve the caretaker of his burden. Frenzel and Scharlach (1983) report that one VA hospital respite program improved the caretaker's health, sleep, and perception of the marital relationship—and definitely eased the burden of continued care; thus we could say it likely cut down on abuse. However, these researchers report that in this case the respite program increased the likelihood of institutionalization in one-third of the cases. The researchers therefore felt the role of a respite service in some cases might be to act as a transition to institutional life. Again we see the complexities involved in trying to work with elderly abuse (Wolf, 1984).

There are many other services mentioned in this book that can lighten the caretaker's load and therefore decrease the chances of abuse. They include adult day care. These services have to be made available to the family without straining its finances; at present the financial burden of care is one underlying cause of parent–child tension.

Conclusion

This chapter has centered on linkage services. To the social worker my advice is to put more effort into reaching out to those people in greatest need, and to make more than a superficial effort to connect them with the appropriate service. In doing this the worker needs to make a greater effort to accurately diagnose the case and to be realistic about truly useful services and benefits for the client. The worker needs to look at the bottom line—will his client be better off after this referral? He needs to follow up to prevent the development of a referral "circuit." He must realize that his help is useful only if the elderly person in need actually utilizes the services to which he is referred.

In doing her job the worker must deal with the informal caretaker, if one exists, and help her do her part without abusing the elderly person. The worker needs to bring in services to supplement those the caretaker can provide.

All these efforts at linkage can be successful only if adequate service resources exist in the community. If they are missing, limited in nature, or of poor quality, then linkage cannot be expected to work well, if at all.

CHAPTER 5

The Informal Support System: Kin and Community

The problem of providing for old people in modern society involves much more than the provision of public services. The elderly most often live in family and neighborhood systems, and society must therefore find ways to strengthen such networks and integrate the support they provide with more formal community services (Cantor, 1980).

Social service personnel too often characterize the elderly as isolated, poor, and without relatives, ignoring the fact that most of the aged have families—or neighbors—from whom they receive at least some support. In the United States the elderly usually turn first to children for help, even when there are outside agencies which could provide similar support. Social service professionals must understand how this "informal" support system works, so that they can integrate their own services more effectively into existing family-and-neighbor support systems.

An example may be useful here, one which shows how such integration or linkage of the informal, "natural" system with formal care might function:

> Mrs. K., 87, was discharged from the hospital after surgery for a hip fracture. Due to her limited mobility she did not go back to her own apartment, but moved in with her unmarried daughter, who taught school. The daughter was out of the house from 7:30 AM to 3:30 PM. Thus there was a question as to whether adequate care was possible for the mother, semi-bedridden, weak, and immobile. The mother needed someone to come in to provide some home health care. She also needed someone to prepare her lunch. The discharge department of

the hospital arranged for a homemaker—home health-care agency to send a woman in for a few hours a day.

The home health worker bathed Mrs. K, checked her temperature and blood pressure, and gave her her medication. She also prepared soup and a sandwich for Mrs. K's lunch.

The problem was that this service was provided only three times a week. On the other days the daughter was concerned about her mother's being alone. She sometimes rushed home at lunchtime; other days she called. The daughter was also worried that her mother's health was not improving and that she was also becoming somewhat confused. The strain of this situation was getting the daughter down. The home-health agency contacted a social worker to counsel the daughter.

There is an increased interest today in such integration of support systems—i.e., in bringing the informal and formal systems together and aiding the informal support system to do its tasks. Most gerontologists agree on the importance of fostering the family's willingness and ability to care for its aged relatives (Rathbone-McCuan, 1982). The programs recommended to accomplish this goal include counseling and education of caretakers, respite services for caretakers, homemaker and home health assistance, government subsidies to caretakers, and laws enforcing filial responsibility—such as mandatory contributions by grown children to the nursing home expenses of their parents.

Pressures to give families more support come from several sources. Local AAAs encourage agencies to work with families (Motenko, 1982). The national AOA sponsors a number of demonstration projects for innovative approaches (direct and indirect services) to the elderly, including self-help by families. The U.S. House of Representatives Select Committee on Aging (1982) recommends greater use of the aged's informal support system (relatives, friends and neighbors). The Gerontological Society's task force on the "Continuum of Support Required for Elderly Living at Home" addresses itself to coordinating support systems by AAAs: facilitating family helping systems, the "role of skilled family counseling," and collaboration between professionals and family members. The call is thus for greater coordination between social and health service intervention and the "natural support system," with a division of labor in which the family does what it is most capable of doing, and community agencies take on supportive tasks (Litwak, 1983).

Interest in the informal system of help is increasing, partially because during the current period of fiscal austerity this system is seen as reducing costs and providing assistance to ensure that the caretaker continues support when budgets are cut. There is also new pressure on those responsible to rely on community care for the frail aged in order to keep them out of institutional long-term care facilities, which are widely considered both more expensive and less humane than family and community services. In addition, helping informal caretakers makes good sense according to research findings that demonstrate less hospitalization (Goodman, 1984) or a better recovery in the posthospitalization period (Johnson and Catalano, 1982) if there is a strong family support system (a system that might, of course, need to be shored up by agency assistance). As Clayton (1982) states, the more successful continued residence of frail elderly in the home, and the longer the nursing home alternative is held off, the more successful is health care and resource utilization. In general the family support system is found to enhance the well-being of the aged, as Tsemberis and D'Ercole's (1982) study demonstrates.

In order to optimize use of the family, most policymakers realize they must provide considerable support, including counseling, respite services, and financial aid. Agency assistance is especially needed for caretakers of elderly with problems like alcholism, suicidal tendencies, terminal cancer, or Alzheimer's disease. For problems like these, self-help groups of caretakers—such as the growing number of Alzheimer's disease family-support groups, or local hospices for the terminally ill—are often initated by the social work agencies, which counsel and educate the groups concerned. Agencies also bring together neighbors to provide local support for the frail elderly (Fleisher and Kaplan, 1982) or to provide local crime-protection service. A number of agencies—because they relieve families of tasks or cooperate with them in various tasks—must work closely with the informal support network. This includes adult day care centers, which in many cases act as a respite service for caretakers (Huttman, 1979), more specific respite services to the elderly, or homemaker or home-health services (Groth-Junker and Zimmer, 1982). Included are hospices for terminal cancer patients (Koff, 1982), and hospital discharge planning services (Lurie, 1982).

These agencies take part in what we should recognize as a complex system of care, which includes a variety of parties. These informal and formal support systems divide a number of care-giving tasks among them. In this division of labor, as Daatland (1983) points out, "who" gives the care is linked to "what" type of care is involved. Daatland maintains that care should be a collective action, one which depends upon direct and indirect contributions from a number of different sources; the proper care system is based on a *complementary* type of cooperation. However, sometimes it goes astray, involving *substitution*—such as substitution of public services for family involvement, or even competition between the two. At times substitute help inhibits the ideal of complementation. This happens, for example, when nursing home services are organized in such a way as to inhibit cooperation from the family or to counteract the patient's ability or will to make use of self-help (Daatland, 1983).

Today's emphasis on trying returning to the complementary system is the focus of this chapter, with special attention to the family's contribution. "Complementation" in care giving does not simply mean that two or more parties—such as the family and the health agency—provide care for an elderly person; it also involves their negotiations with each other over the proper division of tasks. A social relationship between them, enabling these care-giving sources to work harmoniously together, is essential. Both formal and informal networks must be alert to the fact that the role each plays may change over time according to the family situation or the contemporary governmental attitude toward program funding. While in this chapter I focus on family caregivers, at the end I discuss their relationships with various agencies.

Agencies actually play a number of different roles in the care-giving system. We can delineate them as care provision (complementation to the family or substitution), support to the family caregiver (counseling, education, respite, or financial assistance), or care management (coordinating, arranging, mediating the care-giving system) (Daatland, 1983). The evidence shows that counseling and care management roles can enhance the chances that the family becomes an effective and successful caretaker. Projects attesting to such success include that of Clayton (1982). He reports that in care for the chronically ill, the additional help provided to the family by various social service agencies—including individual and family counseling, group discussions with òther providers, educational programs, and strength-enhancement sessions—result in more successful health-care and resource utilization. Such efforts produced a team effort which combined the best that both professionals and families could provide. Fleisher and Kaplan (1982), report that organizing local programs to strengthen the informal neighborhood support system had a positive impact on the elderly; however, they also feel that a strengthened informal system requires the backup of more formal services. Mace and Rabins (1982) also testified to the benefits of agency support for informal care-giving units; they reported that the families of senile dementia patients surveyed in the original study were overwhelmed by patients' behavior, and by their own feelings towards the patients' illness. By the time of the follow-up study, however, these families had resolved many of the issues bothering them—in part, because they were now able to manage formerly painful patient behavior through use of and by means of the family education program and through psychoactive medication.

Before human service workers invoke such improvements in family caretaking, however, they must understand the various elements involved in the care system, including the interrelationships among them. This is necessary both to do their jobs and to make consistent and accurate policy recommendations.

The rest of this book is intended to give the reader insights into government programs meeting various needs of the elderly. In the rest of this chapter, however, data from studies of the family's role and of the neighbors' role as caretakers serve to provide the worker with insights as to the services the informal support system is best able to provide; it also enables the worker to understand who, within the family network, and who, within the rest of the informal system (neighbors, friends, voluntary associations), is likely to do what tasks, for how long, and for what reasons (Litwak, 1983). The reasons which inspire such behavior may include a sense of reciprocation/mutuality or, as Lozier and Althouse (1975) call it, "social credit"; filial responsibility; guilt; humanitarian instincts or altruism; or enjoyment of an older person's company, to name just a few examples.

It is also important to consider at what stage in the elderly person's illness different parties are likely to assume responsibility for different tasks—and to recognize at what stage they are likely to become frustrated at doing so. There are important gradations of the degree to which members of the informal system—especially neighbors—are willing to involve themselves in helping older people with problems such as Alzheimer's disease, alcoholism, suicidal tendencies, or those who simply suffer from poverty.

The Nuclear Family as an Informal Support System

Mutual aid was an important feature of the traditional extended family, which provided an extensive supportive network available to an individual from birth to death. Often, too, the elderly in rural areas could expect help from friends and neighbors as well as kin.

In American rural areas, kinship ties became strained as young people migrated to urban areas. Yet for those who still live in rural areas, relations remain close; many researchers report that, to a large degree, family mutual aid continues to exist today. These areas can be seen as locales where traditional values, including family responsibility and respect for the aged, remain prevalent (Coyle, 1982).

Even in some urban areas there is a dense, cohesive population, often of the same ethnic background. In these "urban villages," such as the old Italian area of Boston, close family relations and neighborhood mutual aid continue to be powerful (Gans, 1965). Generally, however, the nuclear family—husband, wife, and children—characterizes urban life. The nuclear family is more fragile than the extended family by virtue of its small size and liability to disruption by the loss of even a single member. Despite the weak structure of the nuclear family and its emphasis on individual success, many still want to help their aged parents and attempt to do so. Even in urban areas family and kinship ties can be amazingly resilient and economically and socially effective, as members exchange gifts, advice, and financial assistance. In spite of social and demographic changes in society then, the elderly—especially in times of illness, difficulty, crisis, or on ceremonial occasions—value their relatives and often turn to them for assistance.

Young family members still place a high value on filial responsibility and feel guilty if they do not care adequately for their elderly parents. This filial sense of duty is particularly strong in working-class families. Because of this, many grown-up children attempt to take care of their parents too long, trying to avoid institutionalization. I will discuss the cost of this care, in terms of stress on family members later in this chapter.

Types of Mutual Aid

Most elderly in America today receive some help from their children; the main types of mutual aid are repairs, gifts, and care during illness (Shanas, 1979a). Taking parents places, help with personal finances, help with household chores, running errands, and emotional support are also common forms of such help (Robinson and Thurnher, 1979). Young family members can also help with legal problems, such as the writing and signing of contracts. Money, however, is less often given (Robinson and Thurnher, 1979); when given, it is most often given in token amounts, rather than in substantial sums.

Several researchers find emotional support to be the main kind of help. When parents are still healthy, other exchanges are only token. For example, visiting between the elderly and their children is fairly common. Often adult children allocate a day—typically Sunday—to visit elderly parents, particularly if these parents live near them. Shanas (1980) reports that over half the elderly live close to their children, either in the same home, next door, or a few blocks away. Half of the old who live alone are within ten minutes of one or more of their children. Middle-class adults are likely to live further away from parents than do their lower class counterparts (Troll et al., 1979). Of course, when children do live too far away to visit frequently they often make up for it with longer visits (Litwak, 1983); besides, they often have brothers or sisters who live closer to their parents.

Family members may also take on another job for elderly parents— that of mediating with agencies and coping with bureaucracy: they act as negotiators with the hospital or the welfare office, for example. Often the whole family goes as a group to the hospital or other agency. Sometimes they do this because the older person cannot drive, but more often in order to provide emotional support or to help the older person negotiate the complexities of applying for and using a health or social service agency program. Any professional working with the elderly should be sensitive to the reasons for the family's involvement, recognize its value, and work with the family to the maximum extent possible. This family role of negotiating with and even modifying bureaucratic structure so that it functions in a more satisfactory way for old people and their kin may be even more important in the future (Munnichs, 1977).

Decline in Family Support for the Elderly

The traditional family extended considerable help to elderly parents. Urban city dwellers often attempt to give this care to family members but are likely to be less successful in doing so. For many reasons, aid to the ill elderly—and even to the well elderly—may be diminishing in our society. An individualistic philosophy which places high value on independence and reciprocal relationships, changes in family structure due to geographic and social mobility, and increased longevity make it increasingly difficult for family members to sustain support for elderly parents in the time-honored fashion. The upshot of all this is that adult children often resort to only token concern. Visiting, for example, may consist only of a pro forma call on ceremonial occasions such as birthdays and holidays (Barrows and Smith, 1979). The elderly may find these token visits unsatisfactory and even emotionally disturbing (Johnson and Bursk, 1977). The relationship between children and elderly is seldom one which entirely prevents loneliness and demoralization among the latter (Blau, 1973). Over time, the pleasure of visiting relatives can turn to negative feelings; such visits can become burdensome for the children and their elderly parents are likely to notice this (Robinson and Thurnher, 1979).

Close relationships are more apt to be maintained if children and elderly parents continue sharing the same values as to such things as manners, religion, child rearing, and drinking. Financial security of the elderly parents, not income alone, can contribute to better relations, mutual trust, and respect. Positive attitudes to aging by the elderly help bring about better child–parent feelings. Working-class people seem to have more rapport, as well as more contact, with their parents, which suggests that family and kin relations enjoy a high priority within this group (Lang and Brody, 1983).

Impact of Values on Support for the Elderly

Emphasis on individualism and success can undermine family relations, particularly if parents become dependent and unable to support themselves. The American family values reciprocal aid in child–parent relationships, a balance of giving and receiving. But in spite of the value of reciprocity implicit in such relationships, parent–child relations are seldom reciprocal in the true sense: parents tend to give more, even after their children have grown up (Frankfather et al., 1981). For example, elderly parents baby-sit, give financial help or loans, buy the children houses, or do carpentry for them (Shanas, 1980). Parents value their children's success, and even well into their elderly years they often strive to help their children achieve it.

At the same time they contribute to their children's success, elderly parents work hard to maintain "intimacy at a distance" (Rosenmayr and Kockeis, 1963; Rosenmayr, 1977). They want to avoid infringing upon their adult children's lives or representing a burden to them. A delicate balance in the relationship between the elderly and their adult children requires, in our society, a "respectful detachment" from each other's family affairs. Each party should, ideally, remain independent while maintaining a warm and continuous interaction (Rosenmayr and Kockeis, 1963; Rosenmayr, 1977). Emotional ties are important: gifts of symbolic value are given, indicating parental willingness to help if necessary. But sensitivity about being a burden means that parents usually try to maintain a certain distance. Those working with the elderly need to understand the delicacy and nuances of this complex relationship if they are to avoid overstepping the unmarked—but nonetheless very real—boundaries in such relationships.

Some elderly do not themselves understand this reciprocal, delicate balance; they demand more from their children than they can reasonably expect to get. If they yearn for the kind of relationship provided by the extended family, expecting to live near their children for mutual aid and affection, they are often disappointed. They are less apt to be disappointed if they understand and anticipate today's nuclear-type relationship, in which elders expect neither to live near their children nor to receive aid from them.

Extended illness or death of one of the older partners can disturb this delicate balance. The reciprocal relationship may then become one in which the remaining elderly parent needs, and therefore receives, more help. Roles are reversed when the adult child is expected to provide more—and may even need to make vital decisions on behalf of an elderly parent whose independence is limited by ill health. The former not uncommonly begins to play an almost authoritarian role vis-à-vis the dependent, aged parent.

New widows or widowers sometimes go to live with their children. For a short time after their spouse's death, they usually receive a flurry of support from family members, but this will not long endure (Lopata, 1979). Within a few weeks widowed persons usually find themselves pretty much on their own. The high value family members place on independence, reciprocal relationships, and the demands of their own private or professional lives make it difficult for family members to sustain support for an ill or bereaved older parent.

Changes in Family Structure

Geographic and socioeconomic mobility contribute to changes in family structure; this in turn leads to diminished support for elderly parents. Our society is increasingly mobile geographically—one in five Americans move each year. Grown-up children often move to urban areas, leaving their parents behind in rural areas; some move to the West Coast, leaving their parents in the East or Midwest; economically successful adult children leave their old neighborhoods for the suburbs. Geographic distance, of course, affects the type and frequency of support for elderly parents (Litwak, 1983).

Over the years, American families have become smaller; thus fewer children are able to give assistance. As women have moved in increasing numbers into the labor force, daughters—who traditionally provided support for aging and ill parents—are more limited in their ability to be caretakers for their parents. Clearly, insofar as more women work, there will be fewer full-time family caretakers available (Brody, 1981).

The increased divorce rate also contributes to changes in family structure and to diminished support for the elderly. About half of all marriages in the United States today are likely to end in divorce. This means that many adult children themselves are struggling to survive—and therefore have little energy available to help their aging parents. Divorced women must often care for their children with very limited incomes. In their financial need, some may return to their parents' homes and receive—rather than give—support. But such arrangements may also meet some needs of the elderly person for companionship and assistance in housekeeping chores. Here too, human service workers need to understand how divorce may affect help from children and possibly increased need for agency assistance.

Increased Longevity and Diminished Support

Another major reason for diminished familial support is the current longevity of the elderly and the stage of life their children are in when their parents become ill. Modern medical advances keep people alive longer, though their health gradually fails and they may suffer prolonged illnesses. Many elderly who live into their eighties need long-term care—just at the time their children are retiring from work and other family responsibilities. Middle-aged people, looking forward to freedom from family responsibility when their children are grown, often now find that they must assume care—and often financial support—of their own elderly parents. That they may resent the imposition of such responsibilities is human, all too human.

Stress Related to Family Care

The family can—and does—respond to short-term crises, as well as to day-to-day needs for emotional gratification. Today's family often lacks, however, the structural, organizational, and economic resources to care for the elderly ill over a long period of time (Schmidt, 1980). The stress of care increases along with the stages of the parent's illness. Over time, many adult children caring for their ill parents develop attitudes ranging from irritation to exasperation to desperation. They usually experience growing anxiety, tension, and a sense of confinement. Eventually the job of looking after the parent(s) becomes a burden, one borne only with resentment (Zarit, 1980). Prolonged illness increases tension for family members, especially when support from outside sources diminishes (Cantor, 1980). In the earlier stages of illness, when the elderly are frail but ambulatory, neighbors and friends may give support. Later, particularly when the older person is confined to bed, immediate family members are the main helpers.

The elderly person's attitude toward illness may also affect the parent–child relationship. When the elderly enter a stage of serious illness, they are likely to experience less satisfaction with life or self-esteem for themselves. They resent their increased dependence on their adult children. Consequently they express dissatisfaction, rather than gratitude, in spite of their children's best efforts to provide support. Families with strained relations prior to illness are particularly vulnerable to the stress entailed by long-term illness. As the health of the parent worsens, family relationships deteriorate.

Mental decline on the part of the parent may produce a new type of parent–child relationship (Robinson and Thurnher, 1979). When mental deterioration is involved, the parent herself is often confused and cannot be trusted to act as an independent, responsible individual. Some grown-up children despair that their parent is no longer able to communicate clearly with them. They find it hard to accept that the old relationship—with close communications between parent and child—has given way to confusion (Schmidt, 1980). In time, family members become desperate for relief. This need for help may lead them to use adult day care centers for their parent(s). Usually they try to avoid putting their aged parents in a convalescent or nursing home. This is an important time for human service workers to counsel the family and to find ways to lighten its task.

Support for the Elderly from Siblings and Grandchildren

Fortunately, adult children are usually not the only source of support for frail, elderly parents. Brothers and sisters of about the same age may be a major source of support. As the elderly continue to live longer, grand-children, and even great-grandchildren, may share in support.

Sibling Mutual Aid

Sibling relationships are often overlooked in the existing gerontological literature as far as sources of intimacy and companionship for the elderly are concerned. This is true even though many studies show that the bonds between siblings typically extend throughout life and are second only to mother–child ties in intensity and longevity (Lamb and Sutton-Smith, 1982). Sibling ties are the most common kinship roles among the elderly in general, and renewal of close relations with brothers and sisters in later years is quite common. As old age sets in, many elderly try to resume old bonds; siblings are very much a part of this, even if they live far away. The elderly usually mention a sibling as a source of aid in times of trouble or need. Next to adult children, sisters and brothers are the best source for providing older people with a home. Brothers and sisters are a major source of assistance to the elderly in part because there are more of them than there are adult children, especially in rural areas where children have moved away (Cicirelli, 1982). Elderly persons over 75 have usually come from a family of about five children, on the average, but they themselves have usually had only one or two children. In the nation at large, eight of ten elderly women have a sibling who is still alive—but only half of them still have husbands (Shanas, 1980). Youmans (1977) reports that in one rural area, 82 percent of all adults still had at least one sibling.

Elderly siblings apparently maintain frequent contacts with each other. At least a third of them see their brothers or sisters weekly or more often, while many talk to their siblings every week on the telephone. Never-married siblings tend to maintain even closer ties: three-fourths of them engage in weekly contact (Shanas, 1980). Many elderly find brothers and sisters, rather than their own children, best able to understand their problems. Sibling relationships, in addition, tend to have a more moderate emotional tone than adult children–parent relationships, in which feelings of guilt, filial or parental duty, and worry over infringement on time tend to intrude (Cicirelli, 1982). Many of the elderly, reluctant to lean heavily on their children for fear of disrupting their lives or of becoming an unwelcome burden upon them, prefer to turn to a sibling (Zarit, Reever, and Bach-Peterson, 1980). Then too, as some say, old prefer old: The elderly often find much comfort with siblings who have shared a lifetime of experiences with them (Lowy, 1977).

Death, of course, reduces the number of siblings; younger siblings are thus likely to have relatively few living brothers and sisters to whom they can turn for support. For those who have never married, sibling relations constitute a special category of mutual aid (Lamb and Sutton-Smith, 1982). Quite often two never-married sisters live together, or a widowed sister will move in with a never-married sister. Sibling relations will undoubtedly grow in importance as social and geographic mobility, along with increased divorce and remarriage rates, make it harder for the elderly to obtain the kind of support they need from their children alone.

Support from Grandchildren

Today many older people have grandchildren—or even great-grand-children—to whom they can turn. In some cases, a close relationship develops between elderly and grandchildren. If bitterness exists between aged parents and their adult children, the elderly may turn to the grandchildren for affection.

Usually the relationship is one in which the grandparent gives and the grandchildren receive. Hill (1977) reports that grandparents give more than grandchildren in economic terms, although in terms of emotional gratification, household management, and help during illness, the pattern is reversed. In few cases is the grandparent–grandchild relationship one of constant interaction, for only about 5 percent of grandchildren live with their grandparents.

The Neighborhood and Friends as a Source of Support

Neighbors in Rural and Urban Areas

Neighbors can be important in all communities, including cities and suburbs, but they tend to give mutual aid more frequently in rural areas, partly because of the smaller size of towns. Daily interaction is more likely in a small town, where social and economic interdependence are more pronounced and necessary (Windley and Scheidt, 1982). The longer one lives in the area, the more numerous one's friendships are likely to be (Taietz, 1982). Residence in a small town, high density of old people in an area, high socioeconomic status, and good health are all positively related to a large number of friendships for older people.

Neighbors in small towns often "adopt" single elderly (Shanas, 1980). However, such a sense of community does not include all elderly in a rural area; Cottrell (1975) reports that in his study of a rural community he found twenty isolated older people whose existence was not known to a single organization in the community.

Nor are urban areas always devoid of daily contacts and social interdependence. Some inner-city areas—"urban villages," with dense populations of the same ethnic background—have old-time residents with close contacts with other residents who exchange a considerable amount of mutual help (Gans, 1965).

Mutual aid can also exist in urban apartment houses with dense populations of elderly. In one study of a Cleveland apartment house's elderly tenant population, many of whom had little money and were in poor health, neighbors served as an important reference group (Rosow, 1967). Although they almost never asked each other for financial help, the residents often supplied other types of assistance, especially in times of illness. While less than 10 percent of the old people who lived with someone else received help from outside the family, for those who lived alone—particularly if they had no local family—neighbors provided significant assistance.

In "specially designed elderly housing," that is, special apartment or congregate living complexes, the elderly often find neighbors who are willing to help them in case of need (see Chapter 9). In some developments either the tenants or the management establishes a "buddy system," whereby residents are assigned a "buddy," i.e., another resident, to whom they provide assistance; in other cases, one resident on each floor or wing acts as a semiofficial friend to the rest of the residents in his area. Hochschild (1973) describes similarly close helping relationships in an urban commune of elderly, while Sheila Johnson (1971) reports the active functioning of mutual aid in a trailer park inhabited mainly by elderly. Finally, widows are especially likely to develop a circle of friends for mutual support (Lopata, 1979); Groups of them often get together for companionship and to go places with one another.

Social Credit

Thus neighbors and friends are important social supports for the elderly (Coyle, 1982). However, not all of the older population is willing to call upon them for help. Particularly in rural areas, the elderly seem more willing to ask for help if they have built up "social credit,"—that is, if they have already helped others enough to count on a reservoir of good will that they can draw upon when they themselves are frail and in need. Since help under such circumstances has been "earned" and is not a form of charity, the elderly can accept it without losing their sense of dignity. Those working with the elderly should keep such values in mind, making the most of them. They should learn from their clients to whom they have given earlier assistance; the wisest course is to call on these, rather than other friends, for the help their clients may now need. The dimensions of this reciprocal relation among the Appalachian rural aged are described by Lozier and Althouse (1975). Those under study spend a good deal of time sitting on their porches; this is the habitual spot from which they receive help from neighbors, take delivery of groceries or mail, or whence they depart on rides to stores or elsewhere. The authors show how use of the porch does not *create* a claim on others: rather, it *facilitates* the assertion of claims which have *already* been developed. The study illustrates other ways the elderly may use to keep their claims in evidence before the relevant public. For example, an elderly man may leave his new bathtub on the porch and talk about installing it until his neighbors finally assist him. Or he may let a neighbor use some of his land, receiving vegetables or fruit in return.

    Not all elderly in rural areas can claim social credit. One has to have "social standing" and cannot be a "no-account" person. Also, some elderly have developed their personal resources more narrowly within a society of kinsfolk, and thus depend less on the community at large. Lozier and Althouse (1975) mention other circumstances under which help is less likely to be given. Those who have worked and lived outside the community for a large part of their lives have correspondingly less opportunity to accumulate social credit; they may well find it necessary to pay cash or to negotiate for services.

There are rules of behavior in giving and receiving the kind of aid Lozier and Althouse are interested in, just as there are also informal rules as to when and to what degree an elderly person can start drawing on social credit. Some people make a claim on their social credit too early—when they are not seriously ill, for example. If a person does not seem to be in real need (typically, if he is still mobile), the community will find a way to return him to active participation (Lozier and Althouse, 1975). Old age is seen in terms of successive stages, each of which entails its own degree of ability to make claims on social credit. Full retirement to the porch comes when a man no longer participates in activities beyond the house and yard, perhaps because his health is failing, or because others can relieve him of obligations which would take him further afield. This is the time when a man begins to accept the idea of being dependent on others. He ceases to accumulate further social credit, and instead uses the porch as a springboard to occasional involvement in activities of others; he remains increasingly on the porch: others come to him. His relative immobility is socially acknowledged and he acquires the privilege of requesting services from local passersby. If an elderly person becomes too demanding in asking for help, the community may cut back on assistance. For example, its members may refuse to drive him to the grocery store every day.

The social credit tradition can also apply to the many retirees now moving to rural areas, some of whom were raised in that particular community. Some fit into the local rural social credit system because in their healthy years of retirement they help others and are active in senior citizens' clubs and churches and thus interact with the locals in such a way as to develop social credit. For example:

> Helen and Mary, sisters who were both city school teachers, bought a small house in this rural summer resort community. They have several local elderly and other older urban retirees as neighbors. When any of these are ill they provide cakes and casseroles and they get their mail. One neighbor's husband has cancer; the wife cannot drive. They share taking her to the store with other neighbors.

In summing up this section on mutual support from neighbors and friends, one can say that there is much evidence to show that it is an important type of support to many elderly, especially the rural elderly. The degree and type of help that is given varies with circumstances, including the degree to which an elderly person has accumulated social credit.

As Coyle (1982) says, a social service worker need not see this rural value system as a negative factor, one which necessarily engenders resistance to more formal means of assistance. It is more appropriate to view it as part of a positive emphasis on self-help. The worker should build on the social credit orientation by utilizing the help neighbors are willing to give. Instead of the homemaker, visiting nurse, or agency home visitor cutting neighbors off, these workers should call on them, explain what they, as workers, are able to do, and try to get these neighbors to continue to fill in at other times or in other ways. For example, a homemaker can explain to the helping neighbors (identified as such by the elderly client) that she will be coming in three mornings a week but that on other days someone will be needed to keep a watchful eye on the client, cook some meals, or whatever. If good rapport is established, this homemaker and the neighbors may become a doubly effective helping team.

Support from Voluntary Associations

Voluntary associations can provide social interaction for the aged, and their volunteers and staff can provide various forms of assistance. Some voluntary associations are occupation-related, however, and elderly drop out when they retire. Some elderly may continue to attend their church and service clubs, such as Rotary and Lions. Poor health, lack of transportation, or lack of money are serious detriments to participation. Lower-class elderly may feel out of place in these mainly middle-class voluntary associations; members of the lower-class, even when young, have a low rate of participation in voluntary associations in any case.

The church is the voluntary association elderly people are most likely to belong to. However, they can feel neglected by the church in a number of ways: many churches tend to emphasize programs for adolescents and young families, lack outreach programs for older people, and tend to push them out of positions of responsibility within the church (Moberg, 1977). Churches may provide few social services to the aged, perhaps because of a strong emphasis on individual responsibility. One study of Presbyterian churches revealed that, while they have age-segregated social groups, very few have homemaker, health, or employment services. Jewish organizations and the Catholic church have a useful variety of programs and a considerable array of health services open to older people. Both have convalescent homes; indeed, the Jewish homes for the aged are often the best in the community.

However, it is still surprising that many individual churches do so little for their elderly (Huttman, 1977). While they may provide transportation to church services or lend their facilities to senior citizen groups, their lack of outreach is particularly notable. Some help with housing, but the retirement housing complexes for the aged provided by these religious denominations, such as the Episcopalians, are quite expensive; often one has to buy one's own apartment in the development. Ministers, priests, or rabbis do visit the sick, at least in the hospital and occasionally at home. Ellor et al. (1983), however, found that even programs for the homebound were infrequent.

Some service clubs, such as the Masons, run homes for their elderly members. They may, like churches, also lend their facilities for subsidized meals programs and for other senior citizen programs. They sometimes have special fundraising efforts to raise money for the blind, for a minibus to a senior center, for a group living facility, or for other such charitable causes.

Social Services to Supplement Family and Neighbors' Aid

Family, neighbors, friends, and voluntary associations give considerable informal support to the aged, but care of an elderly ill person is a heavy burden. Informal help must be linked to the formal system in an effective way at the policy and practice levels, so that shared responsibility becomes a reality. Health and social services should *supplement* help given by family and neighbors; moreover, formal care must be provided in a way that will *bolster* the available informal assistance. While the family usually needs no public pressure to continue its responsibilities for older members, it cannot and should not be expected to perform beyond its means. A more satisfactory division of labor could alleviate obvious stresses which are harmful to both older people and the families caring for them (Litwak, 1983).

Linkage between the formal agencies and the informal support system should be done, then, in a way that integrates them into a single effective care system. Adult day care centers provide an example of effective integration of care. The services provided there allow the family to care for the frail aged, but relieve them of this task during part of the day. Unfortunately, such linkage has often been inadequate in the past. Too frequently, the various government-backed services have ignored the role the family plays, and failed to allocate resources to families caring for elderly. Still worse, agency services too often attempt to *replace* the family rather than *supplement* it (Sussman, 1979). An unequal distribution of social services favors those without families. This does not mean the state has not provided some programs to relieve the family of its load, for indeed it has, especially as far as financial support is concerned. There has been, in Lowy's (1979) terms, a selective assumption of societal responsibility.

The major problem today is that health care and personal care for the elderly are usually provided under government auspices either as full-time care—usually in an institutional setting—or not at all. In other words, the state pays the full bill for certain specific types of care, but pays no bills for other kinds. For example, the government gives help to aged in nursing homes; when the aged persons's financial resources are depleted, Medicaid takes over the monthly payments (also using his or her SSI check). But the state gives very little help, except SSI, to families that take on the onerous task of caring for their ill, aged parents.

S. Brody (1973) describes the narrow way government programs help—and the way they ignore—family needs in his study of Medicare and homemaking services. Medicare demands, for example, that the aged person be virtually housebound in order to get help; yet it implies that he should be able to provide for himself all sustaining services, such as cooking and housework, other than those related to nursing and personal care. Because Medicare reimburses only services which fit its strictly defined health criteria, most home health agencies have not provided homemakers, but have limited their help instead to the professional services of visiting nurses or physical therapists, for which Medicare reimbursement is assured. Calling it a Catch-22 situation, S. Brody (1973) states that the administration appears to have been reluctant to fund those services related to patient maintenance because they seemed too closely related to funding a housekeeper and seemed inappropriate to a health program. In other words, even though the homemaker service would allow the elderly to stay in their homes, often with some family care available, the service was not provided—thus forcing the elderly person, in many cases, to enter a nursing home.

In summary, in some cases, government assistance completely replaces the family if used; in other cases, aid is very narrowly defined such as provision of a home and health aide once a week—which still leaves the family overburdened; and in other cases, aid goes only to those who have exhausted their assets.

Integrating the Provision of Care to the Elderly

This situation must improve if the family is to be encouraged to keep its caretaking role and even expand it. Policymakers and gerontologists are calling for expansion of support to caretakers (although at the same time U. S. senators and others, concerned about costs, are predicting that such services, aimed at keeping the elderly ill in the community and with their families, will be more costly than nursing home care due to the many potential users).

In any case, meshing the assistance available from different providers will be necessary. As I mentioned at the beginning, there are several roles the formal agency can assume. These include, according to Daatland (1983), direct care provision, complementing the family's role; support to the family and other caregiving sources in the informal part of the care system; and care management, including organizing the cooperation between caregiving parties, as described below.

Now let us discuss these three roles separately, keeping in mind the characteristics of caregivers as described in the previous section. The first role, care provision to the elderly person to complement the family care, is certainly necessary. Johnson and Bursk (1977) and Robinson and Thurnher (1979), in their studies of aged parent/adult child relationships each point out the need to provide home care lest the family reach its breaking point. Johnson and Bursk suggest adult day care, while Robinson and Thurnher would expand the social support system in such areas as home meals, housekeeping help, and transportation assistance. These authors also recommend greater home health care, since it is likely to improve the health of adult children themselves by lessening the stress on them as caretakers. Furthermore, home help to the family allows hospitalized elderly to be discharged to the family earlier. Some experts suggest as well that government, should, in some instances, pay the adult child to care for her aged parent(s), thus cutting the costs of institutional care. Demonstration projects show that such financial help is often needed (Gray, 1983).

These direct services are covered in other chapters of this text. The focus of this chapter is support to the family to assist it in its own caring activities; such support to families include skilled counseling and information and referral services. Counseling should be directed at the family caretaker's own stresses and not just at the elderly person's problems. Counseling in regard to several types of stress may be necessary, including the actual care of parents, loss of a meaningful relationship due to the aged person's mental deterioration, parental resentment of role reversal, and feelings of guilt associated with the decision to place a parent in a nursing home. Counseling is also needed about special health problems. For example, it can improve family relations in cases of Alzheimer's disease (Coons, 1983). Or, as Richman (1982) reports, family therapy can revive the family's healing and cohesive influence to diminish the incidence of suicide by the elderly.

Before counseling the elderly, it is thus important to understand typical adult child/aged parent relations, because this knowledge will make it easier to develop intervention strategies which can improve intergenerational relations (Cantor, 1980; Oktay and Palley, 1981).

Education of the family about proper care and the special dimensions of the aged person's illness (such as terminal cancer) is another job for agency staff (Mellor, 1982). Included in this task is an analysis, undertaken in cooperation with the family concerned, of the agency's assessment of the elderly person's needs. In addition, information and referral sources often educate the family about sources of in-home care.

The other part of the agency role in the system is, according to Daatland (1983), *care management* itself: establishing and supervising the linkage among all the parties, resources, agencies, and informal caretakers aiding the elderly person, helping decide what tasks need to be done and by whom, and possibly even monitoring day-to-day contacts. This means sustaining the relationships among these various caregiving parties, mediating and negotiating their interaction. In pointing this out, Daatland (1983) adds that the expansion of public services for the aged has increased the importance of care management, making the role of mediator between the formal and informal care system more vital than ever. He holds that care management should also be involved in adjusting for the changes in the family and in compensating for the different providers' inability to supply full care.

The agency handling care management may be one which itself delivers some direct care; alternatively, it may be largely devoted to providing support to the family or its function may be restricted, for the most part, to care management itself. An AAA, for example, may establish a demonstration program to refer family caretakers to agencies such as in-home care sources (Motenko, 1982). An information and referral service may perform such linkage, as may a home health–homemaker service. By the same token, care management may be handled by a hospital discharge department which decides what kind of formal care is needed in the period after hospitalization in order to supplement the informal or natural system's care (Lurie, 1982); visits to the family home may be necessary to assess needs properly. In other cases care management is managed through senior centers, or through some special program, such as Cohen and Adler's project (1984) involving social workers in the identification and utilization of the natural network for elderly living in Manhattan Single Resident Occupancy (SRO) hotels.

In its advocacy role the agency—whatever its official nomenclature— may also help the family to negotiate more effectively with the bureaucracies it must deal with, as in the nursing home or the hospital (Mellor, 1982). Social service workers help the family use such institutions in ways that works for it and helps it to understand what is happening to the aged relative. The worker may also help the doctor or nursing home official understand the family's special circumstances, as well as mediating with Medicare and Medicaid when necessary.

In performing these support tasks and case management jobs, agency staff needs to understand how families go about seeking help and at what stage they usually look for it. Knowing this is important for one of the case management worker's duties, which is to assist in the optimum division of tasks between the formal and informal caretaking systems. In this area agencies can become more knowledgeable by studying findings such as those of Mindel and Wright (1982) who discovered that for their sample of 1,343 elderly the family was better at providing personal services (homemaker, nursing, personal care), while the formal system was more effective—and likely to be used—for maintenance and medical services; this was especially true for black elderly (See also Jackson, 1982). Many studies show the family's inability or unwillingness to take on heavy financial responsibility for their elderly (Lowy, 1977; Frankfather et al., 1981).

Distance is likely to affect the natural system's division of tasks. Litwak (1988) points out that the family, when distant from the elderly relative in need, is likely to provide mainly emotional support—typically over the phone—plus some financial support in some instances. Neighbors may be useful for day-to-day help (getting the mail, bringing in food, and the like). Ward et al. (1984), however, found that many neighbors did not even give this kind of help, functioning more as confidants than as helpers. The agency concerned must assess use of these sources in the division of labor; it should consider how friends and even a church's helping system can best contribute. At the same time the agency must be careful not to overburden these parties, keeping in mind the type of assistance each is most suited to provide.

Not only the limitations of neighbor and friends, but those of the family itself must be ascertained if there is to be an effective division of labor in helping the aged person. Soldo (1982) found that the size and availability of the family can determine the degree and type of help at hand; for example, the presence of one or more daughters, rather than sons alone, can have an important bearing on the family's role. In addition, employment, health, and financial status have important effects on the caregiver's ability, as do his living arrangements, location, life-style, other obligations, and even his attitude toward filial responsibility. And of course the age of the caretaker, as mentioned earlier, can have a major effect (Schmidt, 1980).

Day-to-Day Relationship

An overall case management plan for coordinating care from different sources is not enough; it is too static for a situation in constant flux. The agency providing family support or the case management agency (often the same entity) needs to watch for changes in the day-to-day division of labor between the formal and informal network if it is to do a good job. For example, the agency needs to watch for a worsening in the elderly person's condition that might mean more in-home care is needed. Rapport with the family is important in this regard. The agency needs to have more than a formal division of labor with the caretakers: it needs good day-to-day relations. Are its professional workers dictatorial toward the family, or do they respect the family as an equal partner in the caregiving system, a partner willing to tell them about important changes? Do they realize that the family may need to seek some kind of modification in their agency's bureaucratic requirements, such as the number of hours a person can be admitted to a day care center? As self-help family support groups develop (such as those designed for victims of terminal cancer or Alzheimer's disease), a respectful, day-to-day partnership becomes even more necessary. The hospice program (described in Chapter 11) is a good example of such a relationship. Professionals must beware of overburdening the family, of demanding too much, of not being aware of the day-to-day changes which occur in a particular family's ability to care for an aged relative. Otherwise they risk alienating the family, their most important ally. If the social workers are encouraging neighbors and friends to give assistance, do they realize these groups' own limitations and do they understand what type of aid they are most able to provide?

A major potential barrier to maximizing support is the professional's lack of comprehension of the changes occurring in the patient's health. Many do not understand the elderly person's mental problems. Doctors and other health care staff are often those most oblivious to the patient's mental state, whether it manifests itself in hostile behavior to the caretaker, in confusion, or in depression. Staff who treat the elderly person as alert when she is actually confused not only do not help the family handle its burden but are counterproductive in other ways as well. They may, for example, exclude the family from their consultation with the patient—who is so confused that she cannot understand the medical treatment prescribed.

The family, rather than the agency, may be the source of strain between the two. Its members may no longer want to give care because the elderly person has presumed too long upon their goodwill. The family may give priority to the needs of younger family members. As mentioned earlier, the family may believe that agencies or government should now take over care. When help from the state is available, the family may overutilize it, doing so at an even earlier stage than is actually necessary. (The author [1982] found this to be true with regard to homemaker care in Denmark and residential care in the Netherlands.) The complementary care relationship may become difficult to maintain because of changes in the family's situation, such as employment of a female caretaker, divorce, the retirement or death of a caretaker within the family, or geographic mobility. In rural areas the family may, instead of overutilizing services, present the opposing problem by refusing to use available services due to the value it places on independence and individualism (Coyle, 1982). Such families are likely instead to risk bankruptcy or breakup before turning to the total care provided by a nursing home; only after using up the old person's assets are they likely to enlist the assistance available from Medicaid. There is a special need in rural areas to be careful in coordinating and integrating the informal with the formal agency service system because of this delicate situation. As Harbert and Ginsberg (1979) point out:

> One of the biggest problems of the rural elderly is that programs established to meet their needs are often not designed to fit their way of life. Most rural older people have been very self-reliant all their lives. . . . When crises arose, neighbors quietly chipped in, often without being asked.

Yet help from the formal system is needed, for while kinship ties are strong and neighborly help is a valuable tradition, these elderly in many cases have lost the support of their adult children, who in many cases have gone off to the cities. Furthermore, these rural aged are poorer and, in general, a more disadvantaged group than the urban aged (Windley and Scheidt, 1982).

Conclusion

All these needs for more services and integration of the informal and formal system, whether in rural or urban areas, depend on finance. An agency typically suffers from the problem of being understaffed due to financial limitations. It thus finds it hard to monitor the elderly person's situation and the ability of the family to provide care on a day-to-day basis, bringing in agency reinforcements if necessary. An agency may be able to initiate aid to the family caretaker, but it may well have too limited a staff to keep up with periodic changes in the situation. Its own workers, such as home health aides, may not inform their supervisors of changes in the family situation or of new needs; even if they do, the supervisor may be too overworked to follow through. If services from other agencies are needed, he may not consider it his job to be a broker between agencies. Not only support and linkage between families and agencies need improvement, but also the linkage among agencies.

It is worth stressing again that there is a complex care-giving system for the elderly in the United States; it includes an informal part—family, neighbors, friends, voluntary associations—and a formal part, which in itself plays a variety of roles. The agencies are important to the system as a whole, even though policymakers are right in considering the family, with its traditionally strong sense of filial responsibility, to be the source to call on first for the care of its aged members. It is, after all, "a flexible and optional system which contains a storehouse of social resources that are potentially available." As these writers add, the family is so flexible that it can very quickly activate resources held in reserve (Johnson and Catalano, 1982).

However, family resources often need to be complemented, especially for long-term care, if they are to be effective and are to play a major role for a long period. The government cannot throw the whole burden on the familial caretakers; it can no longer say to the daughter, for example, this is your job alone: many American women today have career aspirations that exclude that option (Hess, 1983). We need more programs to give them partial relief or they may reject the caretaking role, even while feeling guilty about doing so. The government must give more financial support for home care, for respite services, for adult day care programs, and even for reimbursement of the poorer groups among family caretakers. In fact we must recognize that the family caretaker may need several types of services. As Gray (1983) points out in describing a demonstration family caretaker reimbursement program, "Although money was viewed as important the training and support was more significant to the caretaker."

CHAPTER 6

Social Contact Services

People need social contacts to keep them alert, active, and integrated into the community. These social contacts provide roles and status which are important to one's sense of identity. Old age disturbs many social relationships: friends and relatives die, children move away, companies impose retirement. Role exits such as widowhood and retirement can be devastating, especially if they occur earlier than for others in one's peer group.

The elderly may respond to such dimunition of social function or role by withdrawing, retreating into the past. This disengagement is an inevitable phase of growing old in our society, say some theorists (Cumming and Henry, 1961); they assume that the elderly will have less and less interaction with others, becoming more preoccupied with their own health condition instead. Other theorists argue that this disengagement is neither automatic nor total, but is a *differential* disengagement, as the elderly lose some roles, but assume others to take their place (Hochschild, 1975). Finding a new, optional role to replace a lost obligatory role requires a degree of initiative and discipline which many elderly lack. The elderly person who does manage to remain active socially and avoid shrinkage of his social world benefits both emotionally and physically. It is only fair, however, to remind the reader that research shows that some of those with low levels of participation do have high morale and life satisfaction (Reichard, 1979).

Agencies serving the aged must find ways to encourage sociability and reverse tendencies to social isolation. Helping elderly persons learn how to utilize their leisure time is one of the great challenges for staff and volunteers working in such agencies.

Use of Leisure Time

Today's older Americans have more leisure time than their parents ever had. Many do not use it well because they find leisure activities boring or unsatisfying—or because they lack the skills necessary to take part in them. Having oriented their lives previously to paid work, they find leisure "play" dull, perhaps even sinful. Poor health, lack of money, and inaccessibility of activities often further contribute to lack of participation. Finally, those elderly who have not cultivated an appreciation of cultural, educational, and arts activities earlier find it hard to acquire a taste for such activities in their senior years.

Research studies show, however, that many elderly would like to use their leisure time productively. Many would like to go back to school, to participate in exercise classes, simply be with others during their leisure time. What they do not want, however, is "fun" or "busy work" designed simply to fill out their time. They prefer productive activities which use skills and knowledge in which they can take some pride.

The rest of this chapter covers a variety of social contact activities for the elderly. The major focus is on the best known of these: senior centers and activities in churches, libraries, or other community settings. The last section discusses volunteer and paid employment under the Older Americans Act and other special government programs; these programs are the major channel through which many thousands of elderly find their way to interaction with the larger community.

Senior Centers

One major focal point for social contact services is the local senior center. This is likely to be the hub of activities for the elderly and the community's flagship, which shows its concern for the aged. Today most senior centers, with the support of AOA funding, have evolved into multipurpose centers offering wide variety of services. Thus the old stereotype of the center—as a sort of club where middle-class elderly come to play cards and gossip—does not describe the range of activities in a large number of them today (Fallcreek and Gilbert, 1981). Senior centers vary in programs. They also vary in facilities, from beautiful new buildings to rooms in older community buildings, recreation centers, churches, service clubs, or public housing projects for the elderly. Of today's centers, a third or more has its own buildings. Many, such as the senior center at Jacksonville, Florida, completed in 1981, provide an enviable range of facilities and services. They are designed with ramps and other features to promote accessibility. The *Senior Center Report* (1981) describes the Jacksonville center as an

> innovatively designed, $2.5 million, 34,000-square-foot (Architectural Design Award) facility occupying a four-acre block in the city's downtown section. In addition to a dining room and auditorium, each seating 150 persons, it contains class rooms, a crafts room, ceramics studio, game room, library, miniature golf, huge fireplace, ramps and walkways and "dating corners" for private conversations. It can comfortably accommodate 800 people, and provides ample parking.
>
> Among services and activities offered at the center are nutritious lunches, food coupon exchange, employment, information and referral, volunteer opportunities, macrame, clothing construction, choral music, exercise, drama and painting.

Then there are small rural centers such as those in Monongalia County, West Virginia, described in Harbert and Ginsberg (1979). Five centers existed in rural parts of the county in 1977. The largest, at Everettville, met daily, offering a hot lunch under the federal Senior Nutrition Center program, a crafts course, Bible study, organized shopping trips, and other activities. The second most active center was open once a week; it offered a warm lunch and such activities as ceramic classes. The other three rural centers had monthly meetings—but one, at Blacksville, was in the process of becoming a Senior Nutrition Center, which would be open daily. Of these rural centers, two were housed in old school buildings and three in churches (Harbert and Ginsberg, 1979).

Over 5,000 senior centers exist today; in addition there are around 4,000 senior clubs that meet less than once a week (*Senior Center Report*, 1981).

Clubs for the aged are not in themselves something new. But the multipurpose type of senior center, which provides an array of services under one roof, was first tried out in New York City under the sponsorship of the Welfare Department in 1942: its purpose was to serve the low-income elderly. A number of multipurpose centers were later developed to serve all income groups; they include the well-known Palo Alto center (supported by private funds), and the San Francisco and Philadelphia centers. Many other senior facilities in the early postwar period were mainly recreational clubs for the middle-class elderly rather than centers for delivery of social services. Nineteen seventy-three was a benchmark year, both as to changes in the centers' functions and as to their increase in number.

In 1973 Congress enacted the Older Americans Act Title V (now Title III) program to provide financial support for multipurpose centers. To qualify for funding, the AOA requires that such facilities actively foster the provision of a broad spectrum of health, social, and educational services. The act also mandates that the centers reach out to the low-income and minority

elderly in their area. In fact, Title III explicitly states, "Priority consideration will be given to facilities located in areas with high concentrations of
low-income minority older persons." As a consequence, about half of the
users have been from blue-collar backgrounds (Leanse and Wagner, 1975).

Types of Programs and Activities

The recreation–education programs—still the most visible and regularly
scheduled programs in almost any senior center—include arts and crafts
courses, dancing, concerts, singing, a wide range of games such as bingo,
bridge, billiards, and chess, exercise classes, and special birthday and holiday parties and dinners. Recreational activities vary according to the preferences and needs of area residents. In ethnically mixed areas, games popular
with specific ethnic groups, such as majong for Chinese–Americans or bocce
for those of Italian extraction, may be appropriate. Senior centers also sponsor a variety of outings to musicals, plays, zoos, city shopping areas, or to
holiday resorts and parks.

Some recreation activities, such as movies or sing-alongs, are directed
at the frail and the somewhat confused elderly who find games, dancing, or
other physical activities beyond their capacity. Even a lounge program that
simply provides a comfortable, pleasant place to have coffee is suitable for
these frail elderly; a staff worker may direct such a program, becoming
acquainted with the regular participants in the hope of serving them in other
ways. Some participants may need help with alcohol or drug abuse.

Educational activities, offered at most centers, include English as a
second language, health and nutritional care courses, oral history, and consumer education. Most centers have a library which features reading programs and makes books in Braille and in large print available.

Many centers today offer such services as friendly visiting or telephone
reassurance services, run by volunteers. Community health professionals
who come to the center at an appointed time offer a variety of health services. Community medical personnel, whether public health nurses, hospital outpatient staff, or community health clinic personnel, take blood pressure, give medications, do medical tests, and provide foot care and a host of
other kinds of assistance.

There may be religious services at the center; most likely there will be
a meals program. Many of these centers have been designated by their AAAs
to run the local branch of the AOA's Senior Nutrition Center program.
Others, such as the one in Hayward, California, develop their own meals
programs, which draw on a minimum of local funding and depend heavily on
elderly volunteers.

Outside staff are responsible for many of the activities; they come from
community agencies, including adult education and recreation departments.

Outside volunteer groups also run programs: in Hayward, for example, the center's large dance band is a volunteer group.

In fact volunteers are a mainstay of any senior center. The 1981 *Senior Center Report* describes a large midwest center in which about 30 volunteers work in a program involving between 300 and 500 participants per day. The center's director estimates that it would take six full-time staffers to replace the volunteers.

Although the center is often not the formal AOA information and referral office for the community, it does provide service information. Centers have bulletin boards with announcements of various services, and tables full of pamphlets on sundry programs. Staffs are knowledgeable about services besides their own, and can recommend the suitable ones to elderly who need them. Some community agency personnel, such as SSI officials, come to the centers in person to explain their programs.

To counter the charge that senior centers are serving a select, middle class constituency, the centers, encouraged by their AOA funders, have embarked on outreach programs for special groups. For example, a multi-purpose center in Springfield, Illinois has a lip-reading program for those with hearing problems (National Institute of Senior Centers, 1978). In their outreach efforts staffs attempt to locate isolated elderly who need services (by 1975, almost 60 percent of the users were those living alone), and also to bring ethnic minorities into their centers.

Despite outreach efforts, minority group elderly are infrequent users; only about 15 percent of the users have been minorities, according to a nationwide study of senior centers sponsored by the National Institute of Senior Centers (Leanse and Wagner, 1975). Some have added minority staff whose job includes contacting minority elderly. For example, at the Hayward center a young professional of Mexican–American background has been hired to contact Spanish-speaking elderly and encourage them to use the facility. She does this through local Catholic churches and Spanish-speaking organizations. In Hayward those contacted seem more interested in specific services than in social activities. This seems true in many centers; hard-to-reach elderly are reported to be mainly receptive to use of such special services as those relevant to their health. Of course, running some programs in Spanish or Chinese instead of English can increase that specific ethnic group's interest in attending regular recreational activities. Provision of games or recreational activities popular with local ethnic groups also helps, as does celebration of ethnic festivals. Some centers have even established satellite centers in ethnic neighborhoods.

Frail and handicapped elderly are also underrepresented in senior centers; one study reported that only 25 to 30 percent of the users were 75 and over (Leanse and Wagner, 1975). Outreach to the frail and handicapped elderly takes a variety of forms. It may mean providing transportation to the center and instituting less active programs for their benefit; it may mean introducing this group to useful services available to them at the center. It may also mean seeing to it that necessary services reach them in their own homes; this might well include visits from a public health nurse or more informal friendly visiting. For the handicapped elderly, outreach may include verbal assurances that the senior center has special bathrooms and grab rails. Outreach personnel need to make all such groups realize that the centers are for them—and that they should feel at home there.

In rural areas the elderly are easily isolated from services and are often not inclined to use any service that seems like government charity. Here the need for outreach is especially high, as the Advocacy for Rural Elderly Committee pointed out to the 1981 White House Conference on Aging. This committee recommended that the relevant federally funded agencies be required to provide outreach services to rural elderly, increase their funding to expand these services, and provide for effective training of outreach workers. It also suggested that federal sources develop the "traveling van" concept of outreach services: this involves transporting medical, mental health, and legal assistance experts to senior centers and private homes, where they provide information and counseling to rural elderly.

Satellite Centers

A senior center can best fulfill its functions if it is in a location convenient to the users. Senior centers have traditionally been situated downtown, but even as cities have grown, many elderly are located in outlying areas; other elderly live in ethnic enclaves within the city. To attract these kinds of elderly, the parent center often creates satellite branches. Satellite centers are better able to meet special neighborhood needs including those of ethnic groups. They can draw people into the program and then encourage them to use the more plentiful resources of the parent center.

Satellite centers, especially in rural areas, may provide a limited program a few days a week to communities unable to sustain a full program themselves. A satellite affiliated with a parent center is likely to be a low-budget operation, staffed by paraprofessionals backed up by the professional staff and resources of the parent center. In some cases these professionals circulate among the different satellite centers, or the mobile unit from the parent center goes to different satellite centers on specific days to offer services (such as health screening or an arts or music program) which require equipment too expensive for individual satellites to buy.

There are, of course, some disadvantages to developing satellite centers. One is that such programs may drain resources from the parent facility. Such satellite centers will also, by necessity, have limited resources and programs. It may often be better to develop a single strong program, with a variety of services, at the parent center. Such a program can be made more highly visible and thus attract more community attention and contributions. Seniors attending will not only have a wider range of recreational activities and services but will meet a greater variety of elderly.

Functions of the Senior Center

Through all these activities the senior center fills a number of functions for its elderly clientele. It provides a substitute for the workplace, whether the aged person involved is on the advisory board or simply a participant. Being a committee member or volunteer helps to develop an active decisionmaking role and leadership capability that can be useful to the whole community. Old skills can still be used and new skills can be developed, both through volunteer activities and through classes in various arts and crafts. Such work in turn gives the elderly person a greater feeling of productivity. Both classes and volunteer work help restore a sense of usefulness and dignity which may have diminished with retirement and the departure of children. Participation in the center's activities provides structure and routine to a person's day. As a social contact source the center often helps to overcome loneliness, especially after the loss of a spouse or friends (Krout, 1983).

> Mrs. Carter lost her husband last year. Her children all lived in other parts of the country. She had few close friends. She usually spent most of the day at home except for a walk to the local grocery store. She felt lonely and bored. One day a next-door neighbor she hardly knew persuaded her to go to the local senior center with her. They had a sing-along that morning and she enjoyed the singing. Then they stayed for the lunch and she met a number of people. Soon she became a regular participant and a volunteer for the meals program.

The center serves as a bridge to reconnect the elderly with the community, decreasing their isolation: it allows the participant to belong to a group again, while establishing a new group identity. The center provides a supportive setting in which the elderly person feels safe, comfortable, and able to get help for the problems of old age, whether they involve reduced income or physical limitations. It acts as a special community where the elderly can view problems of everyday living from their own point of view. For example, it provides a place to adjust to retirement or to adopt to new circumstances, new ideas, and new roles.

The senior center also serves as an accessible and acceptable vehicle through which the elderly can tap the resources of the community as needed. It is a setting that brings together initially all services relevant to them, one in which the staff can help them overcome bureaucratic barriers. The center can also help those it serves to save money—either by advising them of free or discount services or by listing shared housing opportunities. Its activities provide a forum to discuss how to survive on a reduced income with others. Some centers help low-income elderly earn more—either through volunteer programs which offer a small stipend or provide free meals, or through sale of handmade goods in the centers' own stores. Through employment listings such centers can also help find baby-sitting and other jobs. Low-cost midday meals and free or inexpensive recreation also help seniors save money.

Funding

The main impetus for the recent growth of senior centers has come from Title V (now part of Title III) of the Older Americans Act. Before this, subsidies came mostly from private groups such as Community Chest and local government. OAA funding is designed to expand the number of senior centers and to turn existing centers into multipurpose facilities which provide a wide range of services. Title III authorizes grants of up to 75 percent of the costs of acquiring, altering, or renovating existing facilities—since 1978 the construction of a center has been covered as well. Federal money is thus available both to buy initial equipment and to furnish other facilities intended to serve multipurpose senior centers. The AOA channels funds through the SUAs, which then disperse funds. Each such state agency is charged to make sure that an equitable portion is reserved for each planning and service area in the state, and that the AAAs and other local agencies participate in the selection of facilities. Any organization designated to develop or expand multipurpose senior centers must devise an overall plan which obtains written commitments from other public or private nonprofit agencies to use the facility in question in order to deliver services or contribute resources which will expand the existing program(s).

The Local Public Works Development and Investment Act of 1965 is another source of money for construction, renovation, and repair. Construction money for senior centers also comes from Community Block Grants of HUD; in the 1974 housing act, funds were made available for the expansion of community services, principally for persons of low-to-moderate income. Funding for services also comes from Title III of the Older Americans Act, as well as from SSBG, which is a general source of funding for specific social services in a variety of settings. These services include friendly visiting, recreational services, telephone reassurance, and other social group services for seniors. Since the SSBG program is supposed to focus on the low-income elderly, there is a problem of eligibility for use of SSBG-funded services.

This makes it hard to coordinate SSBG programs with the other, open-eligibility OAA initiatives in the general area of care for the elderly.

Volunteers can be funded under a variety of programs, especially the programs administered through ACTION, such as the RSVP or Senior Companion program described elsewhere. The meals at the center may be funded under the Senior Nutrition program of the OAA.

Problems of Senior Centers

A major problem is underutilization of some centers due to limited hours (Collin, 1979). Lack of use by minorities and by low-income groups is another problem. More effort must go into making them feel welcome; outreach programs and the move to create satellite centers in minority-group and low-income areas should alleviate this situation. Improved transportation to the centers may also help; a large proportion (39 percent) of the minority-group elderly surveyed in one study said they would like to take part in their program but found that transportation to them was problematic (Brown and O'Day, 1981).

Changing the image of the centers from that of social clubs to that of places to receive important social services is another problem; such a change would attract those who do not feel comfortable in social situations as well as the frail and old-old elderly who do not want to participate in vigorous activities. This reworking of the centers image is still far from complete. Users in 1978 (as compared with nonusers in one study) were more likely to be socially oriented, to belong to other groups as well, and to see themselves as healthier than most of their peers (Hanssen et al., 1978). Many centers, long in existence as "clubs" or recreational centers, resist a change in focus, as Brown and O'Day (1981) point out. The American centers also need more men. Unlike those in Holland which the author visited, our centers have a great predominance of women: only a fourth of the users are men, according to one nationwide report (Leanse and Wagner, 1975). The National Council on Aging was so concerned about this that it put out a book (Jacobs and Magann, 1974), describing the specific needs and interests of men and effective methods for involving them in the activities of senior centers.

In general, such centers are underutilized; as Tissue (1971) points out, only a small proportion of the total American population over 60 uses them. Because of this, some critics question the centers' utility as a focal point for provision of elderly services (Brown and O'Day, 1981); one could then argue that federal funding should not concentrate on them. Yet such funding is necessary if they are to survive (Fallcreek and Gilbert, 1981). Funding is in fact a continual problem. Year-to-year negotiations on funding challenge the viability of senior centers as the "hub of social service delivery" for the elderly. Senior centers have been seriously affected by a loss of local funds, by the drop in SSBG funding, and by the discontinuation of CETA programs. Lack of adequate funding has a negative effect on ability to retain professional staff. Many centers are run by part-time personnel who usually lack graduate degrees—or even proper undergraduate training.

Social Contact Activities in Churches, Libraries, and Other Settings

Churches

A very important source of socialization for the elderly is the church or synagogue. (In what follows, "church" should be understood to include all the major religious denominations and sects.) Most churches run a number of social activities that are, to a large degree, attended by their older members. These include suppers, weekly or monthly women's club meetings, Bible classes, and a variety of other activities and special events. Some churches also have special senior programs. In addition, the church, through its volunteers and minister, priest, or rabbi, often provides transportation to church and visits members who are homebound, hospitalized, or in nursing homes. Churches may allow their facilities to be used for such community projects as the AOA meals program or senior citizens clubs.

Service Clubs

A variety of other community groups provide social opportunities and a wide range of useful services for their elderly members. The typical service club may well have within its membership a retired group that holds its own special meetings. (Occupational organizations do likewise; for example, there are many retired military officers' clubs.) Some service clubs sponsor special events such as Christmas parties for certain groups—nursing home residents, for example.

Libraries

Libraries often have special programs for the aged; Boston's "Never Too Late" group is a good example. Such programs are oriented to retirement planning, rights of the elderly, and acquisition of new skills. Libraries service the elderly through book delivery to the housebound; provision of books, often in large print, to senior centers; circulation of mobile library vans in rural areas; and provision of "talking books," cassettes, records, and tape recordings to the elderly who do not see well. Libraries often also run volunteer programs as well. They use the aged as senior aides to help administer library branches (Vermont) or even to run the senior program, such as the "Over Sixty" service in Milwaukee (Irwin, 1978).

Educational Programs

The elderly are increasingly becoming an integral part of America's education system; there are curricula designed specifically for them, including adult education programs and emeritus colleges. In addition, standard college courses appeal to more and more elderly (Lebel, 1982). Participation in educational programs provides intellectual stimulation for the aged and keeps them mentally alert. It facilitates social contact with other old and young people. Education may also serve other purposes: for example, increasing self-reliance and a do-it-yourself ability (thus decreasing living expenses) through learning basic skills like auto maintenance, tax preparation, plumbing techniques, and accounting methods. Or education may serve the practical goal of learning the language and cultural history of a country where one plans to spend a vacation—or even retire.

Enrollment in college or special programs may help the relatively young newly retired start a new career. These early retirees may want to use the years ahead profitably through part- or full-time work in some other occupation. On the other hand, the elderly individual may simply wish to pursue "knowledge for knowledge's sake." This includes increasing one's understanding of art, music, science, or a variety of other fields. Or the elderly may want to take exercise classes, yoga, swimming, or the like in order to keep physically fit.

For others, further education fulfills lifetime dreams of getting a university degree or even a high-school diploma. At almost every college graduation ceremony today, gray-haired students walk across the platform to receive their diplomas:

> Mary Q. Hillman . . . had left college in 1932 to marry and then bear two children. Mary always felt handicapped because she had only one year of college, while most of her friends had a degree and her husband had a doctorate. Three years ago, after her two children had finished college, she returned to the university to finish her education. This year she graduated with honors. Her husband and her children came to the graduation ceremony to witness this great event.

TYPES OF EDUCATIONAL PROGRAMS

The elderly vary greatly in the kinds of programs they select due to these different aims and to their diverse educational backgrounds: some are barely able to read, write, or understand English, while others have college or postgraduate degrees (Suhart et al., 1982).

Junior colleges usually encourage the elderly to attend: they may audit courses or take them for credit. (They need not take a full course load; they are usually allowed to take just one or two courses.) These students need not meet all the normal educational requirements; they may or may not need to have completed high school or the GED exam.

Some junior colleges go still further; they have formed an emeritus college—a college for older students within the regular junior college. Here some special, short, noncredit courses especially applicable to the elderly are offered. Marin Junior College in northern California has such an emeritus college. Examples of its short courses are: "Feeling Fit at 55," "The Older American Years," "The Law and How to Use It," "Leisure: A New Lifestyle." Emeritus colleges usually involve their students in an emeritus center program. The center's staff runs reentry orientation sessions and offers individual and group counseling. These elderly students may, of course, take the regular college courses as well.

Four-year colleges also encourage older citizens to become students; some of them charge only a small fee instead of standard tuition. These elderly students enroll in regular courses on a noncredit or on a credit basis. These students must usually fill the same educational requirements applicable to others. However, at many four-year colleges they get the benefit of a special reentry program. Some colleges go farther. The City University of New York (CUNY) system in 1980 had a college designed specifically for older students. Here, at Lehman College, those 65 and over could enroll for a small fee in credit courses without pursuing a degree.

An informal education program available at a number of colleges in the summer is organized nationwide by Elderhostel Inc. In 1981 over 200 colleges offered a week or more of Elderhostel programs; approximately 37,000 elderly, many from out of state, participated (Gelfand, 1984). The main goal is intellectual stimulation: the program includes a number of lectures, field trips, etc. The elderly "students" live in dormitories and eat on campus at moderate prices. They can use any of the available facilities, such as libraries and tennis courts.

Friendly Visiting and Telephone Reassurance

Isolation and loneliness are serious problems for many elderly, especially for the 5 percent whose health limitations confine them to their homes. This loneliness, more prevalent among woman than men, causes depression and feelings of uselessness. A related problem is the fear that no one would help them if they should have a sudden accident or illness. The elderly have all heard stories of others who had accidents and could not reach the phone for help, lying on the floor in pain for hours—even for days—before someone found them. Two social contact services, telephone reassurance and friendly visiting, reach out to the homebound elderly to meet these needs.

The provision of a regular contact, either by phone or in person, is reassuring to the isolated elderly. This gives them the knowledge that someone cares about them; such contact also gives them something to look forward to every day. Elderly clients have reported, "It makes me feel like I'm still someone worth talking to," or, "It gives me a chance to speak of things in my heart." The contact people can communicate the needs of the elderly to appropriate agencies or, in many instances, they can themselves take care of some needs, such as grocery shopping or transportation to medical appointments.

Telephone reassurance provides for a volunteer to call a "regular" client or clients each day at a specified time. He inquires about the health and needs of the client and engages in general conversation, passing along requests for assistance or handling them himself. If the client does not answer the phone, a designated friend, neighbor, relative, fireman, or the like checks to see if there has been an accident. If there is an emergency, he or she contacts the appropriate resource, as determined by the program supervisors. Clients who plan to be away from home at the time of the volunteer's call inform him in advance. Clients are encouraged to call the volunteer on their own initiative if they need unforseen help—or are simply depressed and want to talk. The telephone reassurance program is popular with volunteers because it makes relatively few demands on them. The volunteer spends only 15 minutes or so a day calling the aged client(s) from her own phone. It is popular with the elderly as well, because it means an assured daily contact. As one homebound elderly woman of age 83 said, "I don't worry as much now about breaking a hip or something and lying on the floor for hours with no one to help. I've got Mrs. Young calling me every morning. She'll even go to the drugstore and get my prescription for me."

Variations of the telephone reassurance idea have developed in different areas. One is "Dial-A-Listener," in which the aged individual is given a telephone number to call if he feels lonely and needs someone to talk to, if he has a need that volunteers can take care of—or, of course, in case of an emergency. Davenport, Iowa, has such a service. The Red Cross in New York City has sponsored another type, a "Telephone Club" for homebound, isolated people. "Lifeline" is a another service: though the program differs in form from place to place, in its newest form, the elderly user wears an apparatus with a button that he presses in case of a medical emergency. This alerts a medical service, such as a hospital, which calls a designated neighbor, relative, or government staff—such as the police—to investigate, or directly sends staff (volunteer or paid) to render assistance (Dibner, 1982).

"Friendly visiting" is similar in some ways to the contact services just described. However, in this case, volunteers go to the client's home or visit clients in nursing homes. Visits do not usually take place daily, but once or twice a week. Volunteers may simply visit the aged, play cards, or write letters for them. They may do minor chores for the elderly, such as going to the grocery store or pharmacy, or even doing some minor cleaning. As with telephone contact services, the volunteers check on their clients' health and report any immediate needs to the proper resources.

The friendly visiting program sponsored by the International Ladies Garment Workers Union (ILGWU) in New York City serves as a model for many others (Irwin, 1978). In the late 1970s it had a staff of 90 visitors, more than 70 of whom were themselves elderly. The ILGWU hired its own retirees—former finishers, cutters, and so on—and even used some personnel from other unions, such as bakers, furriers, and postmen. They called on around 28,000 retirees a year. They not only visit but act as an information and referral source; they also help fill out forms for Medicaid, public housing, etc. Locating appropriate clients is an important part of the program. It is best suited for the frail elderly with health limitations who seldom leave their homes. They can be located most easily through churches, senior center outreach programs, information and referral sources, service clubs, and hospital discharge programs.

Volunteers for these programs must be carefully selected. For friendly visiting, because it involves face-to-face contact, it is better if the volunteers have certain interests in common with the clients—up to and including similar education levels, class backgrounds, and ethnic or racial origins. They should be trained as to how to deal with their clients and what resources to refer them to. Visitors should be taught to recognize the early symptoms of various illnesses. (Telephone reassurance volunteers should also be trained to detect early signs of illness over the phone—slurring of speech and odd tones of voice, for example.) Volunteers for friendly visiting should also be instructed about how to recognize nutrition problems. If they see that clients do not eat regular or balanced meals, they should try to help them improve this situation, even encouraging use of the Meals-on-Wheels program. The volunteers should have pleasant dispositions and be able to relate well to the elderly or, if aged themselves, to other elderly. They should not dwell on the depressing aspects of the client's illness, but create a cheerful atmosphere. As Heyman and Polansky (1977) point out, friendly visitors should gear themselves to their clients' needs rather than to their own; they should be interested in their clients as people; they must have enough tact to refrain from comments that may be upsetting or depressing; and they must be dependable. A good friendly visitor, as Lowy (1981) points out, can establish a visiting relationship similar to the casework services of the past that stressed the importance of having a friend in bolstering the morale and general health of clients.

The importance of the contact services described above has been recognized, and public support and funding are provided in many states through SSBGs and by private, nonprofit groups which provide services at a minimal cost. Such services are both easy to manage and inexpensive to run. Their volunteer staffs and few professional supervisors largely account for this. It is not surprising that they are considered essential social services for the homebound and isolated in virtually any community. They are inexpensive—but they make the difference between security and insecurity, perhaps even between life and death, for many homebound elderly.

Volunteers in Social Contact Services

In the two social contact programs described above, the volunteers are often elderly. Volunteer work by the elderly can in itself represent an opportunity for them to get out of the house and increase their contact with the larger community. Part-time employment in the same cause can do the same thing. The federal government has set up a group of programs under ACTION, the same organization that runs the Peace Corps; included are the Retired Senior Volunteer Program (RSVP), the Foster Grandparent Program (FGP), and the Senior Companions and Service Corps of Retired Executives (SCORE). Volunteers in these programs may receive reimbursement for their work, their transportation, or for other expenses. In addition, with OAA funding, the Senior Community Service Employment Program (SCSEP), through the Department of Labor. has made contracts with various organizations to use elderly employees in providing services. The organizations involved include the American Association of Retired Persons (AARP), the National Council on Aging (NCOA), the National Council of Senior Citizens (NCSC), the U.S. Forest Service, and the National Farmers Union. The programs include "Senior Aides" (NCSC) and "Green Thumb" (National Farmers Union).

Volunteer Programs Under ACTION

RSVP originated under the auspices of the OAA, but it is now channeled through the ACTION program. RSVP's focus is to enhance the older person's sense of being useful—namely by giving service; it seeks to employ his or her time in productive activity (Sugarman, 1982). RSVP does not pay these elderly volunteers. In 1981 about 300,000 of them, aged 60 and over, served in different health, nutrition, or other community programs under RSVP sponsorship; there were 800–900 projects in all. RSVP volunteers work in a very broad range of programs: in hospitals, nursing homes, and many of the other social services mentioned in this book. Local senior centers sponsor a variety of RSVP programs, such as friendly visiting, and use RSVP volunteers in their own centers. Besides serving other aged, RSVP volunteers work with children in schools, delinquents in institutions, and neglected children in foster homes. Funding depends upon government grants to nonprofit agencies, either to establish or to expand volunteer activities. The program, although providing no wage compensation, does pay for accident insurance and reimburses the volunteer for out-of-pocket expenses. With such financial aid the government hopes to increase the incentives and opportunities for volunteering to work with other elderly and children. RSVP organizations often have fund raisings and social activities. There is usually a small professional staff to direct, train, and coordinate RSVP volunteers.

Paid Employment

The "Foster Grandparent Program," another federally subsidized initiative administered through ACTION, offers a small stipend, as do the other programs mentioned below. This program offers part-time volunteer service opportunities for low-income elderly of 60 years and over to work with children in need of supportive adults; children in hospitals or community programs for retarded or neglected children are included. Working some 20 hours spread over the week, the elderly persons help the youths assigned them—usually two or so a day—with both physical and speech therapy. They help some with their school work and, in general, represent a loving, supportive friend. Such workers receive a number of hours' training before they go to work with these children (Zalba and McVeigh, 1982). The federal ACTION role is to award grants to local agencies providing these work opportunities. The local agency recruits and trains these foster grandparents, who receive a minimal hourly stipend, a daily hot meal, and a transportation allowance. They are also entitled to an annual physical examination at government expense. In 1981 the foster grandparent program employed over 18,000 volunteers, who rendered services to approximately 54,000 children. As Barrows and Smith (1979) report, this program, the first of the federally sponsored volunteer programs, has been successful because it has provided benefits to two different groups: older, lower-income people who want to participate in community life; and lonely, institutionalized or otherwise disadvantaged children who desperately need care, love, and attention.

   "Senior Companions" is another ACTION program funded by the AOA: in this case, the elderly help their peers. ACTION allocates money to local agencies to support part-time employment in supportive services to adults (usually as Senior Health Aides). In the senior companions program, low-income elderly work about 20 hours a week for a minimal stipend. They assist other elderly in nursing homes and hospitals. They visit the homebound who receive home health care, nursing care, or who have special disabilities. The senior companion may do shopping for her clients, refer them to needed social services, or help with housekeeping and cooking. Senior companions read and write letters to those in nursing homes. In 1977 some 2,800 low-income elderly were employed by the program, serving over 10,000 frail elderly.

SCORE gives retired professionals a new chance to apply their talents—in this case to benefit small-business owners who lack the funds to pay for such services.

THE SENIOR COMMUNITY SERVICE EMPLOYMENT PROGRAM

SCSEP of the Older Americans Act gives the Department of Labor funds to provide national organizations with money for programs which hire the elderly. The goal of such programs is to provide work and income to those elderly who want useful work in their communities. Low-income elderly are hired to do part-time work (20–25 hours a week) at state or federal minimum wages. One such program is the National Farmers Union's "Green Thumb," which provides jobs for rural elderly. It employs retired farmers and other rural elderly who live at or below the poverty level to work in parks, soil conservation programs, and highway projects. Green Thumb's goal is to beautify the community through park maintenance, roadside cleanup and planting, and other activities of this sort. Training programs for those involved give instruction in horticulture and environmental restoration. About two-thirds of the employees are over 65. The U.S. Forest Service runs a similar program for rural elderly over 55, employing them in Forest Service activities.

SENIOR AIDES

Another program of SCSEP, developed by the National Council of Senior Citizens (NCSC), utilizes "senior aides." Thousands of aged are placed in community service jobs across the nation; these elderly persons receive a small stipend, working part-time in such programs as homemaking, home health aid, information and referral, and nutrition services.

The SCSEP also contracts with the AARP to place elderly workers (about 8,000 in 1979) in a number of nonprofit and public organizations. It does the same with the National Council on Aging (NCOA). Elderly employees under NCOA sponsorship, if working with the aged, are most likely to be placed in senior nutrition, outreach, referral, senior citizen centers, or other recreation programs. If they work with the general public, they are most likely to serve in social services or education programs.

Other General Volunteer Programs

All age groups are eligible for the VISTA (Volunteers in Service to America) program. It is similar to the Peace Corps, but focuses on community projects in the United States; only a small proportion of volunteers are elderly. Most large cities have centralized volunteer bureaus. Some have one dedicated specifically to recruitment of elderly volunteers, and staffed by the elderly themselves. A bureau of this sort lists a wide range of volunteer opportunities, from Girl Scouts sponsorship to hospital work. Some of the jobs are specifically designed to be with children with the intent of encouraging contact between generations.

Many elderly volunteers simply go directly to community agencies, hospitals, churches, senior centers, or youth organizations. These usually have age-mixed volunteer programs which give elderly volunteers gratifying reassurance that they are still an important part of the larger community. Often these are, in fact, programs in which they have participated throughout their adult lives. Another avenue to volunteer service is the program developed by community or statewide groups. A good example is that of Dade County, Florida, which hires people over 55 as teacher aids for industrial arts and language classes; another is two Michigan counties' use of seniors as tourist guides at fishing and camping sites (Irwin, 1978). A small town in California hires elderly for part-time jobs at minimum wage as parking lot cashiers. In Maryland a group called Senior Home Craftsmen does minor home repairs, including plumbing jobs (Irwin, 1978).

Nonprofit organizations often have their own programs. The NCSC, for example, has a number of projects which employ the aged in a part-time capacity to provide such services as outreach and nutrition. The AARP has developed a free employment service, *Mature Temps,* which has offices in a number of large cities and places elderly with different skills in temporary jobs. Many nonprofit volunteer employment agencies have established service units for older workers. They counsel the elderly on the kinds of jobs available and the training needed for them.

The volunteers and part-time workers in these programs are greatly appreciated by the organizations concerned. The cadre of volunteers and part-time workers in senior centers and other agencies produces the action, the warmth, and the vibrant atmosphere in these agencies, where volunteers comprise the major part of the staff: they are irreplaceable assets. It is only this way that most senior centers and many other agencies can offer their varied programs. A *Senior Center Report* (1981) was on firm ground when it observed "that the monies appropriated by Congress for aging programs through the Older American Act are a mere pittance compared to what would be required if all center volunteers were paid wages appropriate to the services they render."

Benefits of Volunteering or Part-Time Employment

Volunteer work benefits the elderly as well as those whom they serve, for it is a channel for social interaction. A 1975 Harris poll found that 22 percent of the elderly performed volunteer work, while another 4–10 percent would like to participate, given the right opportunity. Volunteer activities serve a number of functions for the elderly. Volunteering gives them a role to play and provides a setting in which to socialize with both young and old in the community. This kind of work gives elderly participants the chance to be engaged in the larger world around them. By volunteering, they have an organizational affiliation—and can enjoy the status, prestige, and power associated with that. They can also take part in the group's decisionmaking and supervision of clients (Ward, 1979).

Above all, volunteer work makes the aged person feel wanted and productive. He is performing a needed service, whether for hospital patients, delinquent or dependent children, or handicapped adults. Volunteer work also provides an opportunity to use the skills he acquired in former jobs, as well as to develop new skills. These meaningful activities make the elderly person feel more capable and competent than might otherwise be the case. As Rosow et al. (1974) point out, membership in such organizations may help cushion the loss of instrumental roles and provide new ones in their stead. Volunteer activities are a means to ensure the integration of older citizens into the community and to give them a role in local affairs. Such activities increase intergenerational contact, while simultaneously providing a vehicle for expanding the circle of elderly contacts, since many other volunteers, especially in government-innovated volunteer programs, are also aged

Problems with Volunteering

A variety of problems exist which threaten to decrease the number of volunteers. One is that the expense of volunteering is increasing. For example, the cost of driving a car to a senior center or of acting as a volunteer chauffeur has increased with the increasing prices of gas and car repairs. The need to eat away from home or to wear fairly new clothes to the job are barriers to those whose incomes are already tightly stretched. Some agencies—and some volunteer programs such as RSVP and other ACTION programs—do cover certain expenses, such as transportation and meals. RSVP has always recognized that volunteer service almost inevitably entails some expense to the volunteer; therefore, it has sought to minimize that expense through appropriate reimbursement. A large midwest senior center's special volunteer program pays from $7.50 to $60.00 a month for the expenses its people incur in their work. These are well worth paying, considering the salaries they save the centers. This large midwest urban city center's director estimated that, if full-time staffers were hired to fill the 30 positions volunteers handled, it would cost in salaries at least six times as much as the total of the reimbursement paid (Lind, in *Senior Center Report*, 1981).

Among other problems is the fact that volunteers simply get worn out: they need relief. Many volunteers in senior centers and other agencies have served long terms. The fun and excitement of the work is gone, but replacements are hard to find. Centers need to recruit new volunteers and find different jobs—or more recognition—for present volunteers. The above-mentioned midwest urban senior center uses a job rotation system that gives everyone a "fair crack" at each position available. Volunteer positions are offered for rotation on a quarterly basis so that everyone who wants to serve has an opportunity to do so. A special committee of the center's advisory council screens the applications and recommends to the director those it judges most capable of functioning as volunteers: the director then makes the appointments. This center reports that in actual practice, only about 10 percent of the positions are rotated in any quarter: the supply of volunteers willing to extend such a high level of service is not as large as one might wish. This midwest center attempts to attract new volunteers through formal job descriptions for each position available. It publicizes this list of positions widely. This center, like many, insists that volunteers undertake training for the job in question, and thus works to improve their quality of service.

Other factors, such as education and social class, are pertinent to interest or lack of interest in volunteering. The Harris (1975) survey found that elderly volunteers usually have higher-than-average incomes, have attained higher levels of education, and are, for the most part, white. Volunteers are largely those who are active, alert, and healthy. The elderly from lower socioeconomic groups often do not volunteer, either because they are still in the work force or are otherwise fulfilling family obligations. Some low-income elderly do not want to volunteer because they fear that they could not cope with the demands of the job and the expectations of the staff. Others worry about their ability to meet the interpersonal demands of the job. They believe that they may have difficulty or experience discomfort—physical or emotional—in attempting to meet what is expected of them; thus they may well decide not to participate in order to avoid threats to their own identity and self-esteem. Finally, many elderly have health limitations that make it hard to volunteer. The 1975 Harris study found that health was the number one reason given for nonparticipation by those who would have liked to volunteer; other major causes of the same result include lack of time or transportation, pressing family responsibilities, absorption in work, lack of opportunity, procrastination, or simple lack of energy. Even if all these limitations were somehow removed, there would still be a number of elderly who would refuse to take on volunteer work. I found (1977), in my study of

Canadian elderly housing residents, that a number of them felt that they had already done enough volunteer work in their younger years. This was a period of life in which they wanted to rest from such obligations. Their feeling was, "Leave such work to the young and healthy." On the other hand, in these same housing developments, some volunteered as "buddies" for their more frail elderly associates, volunteered to lead the tenants association, or took it upon themselves to organize recreation activities.

Conclusion

Social contact services, whether recreational centers, friendly visitors, telephone reassurance, educational, or the wide array of volunteer programs, provide a support system and opportunities for continued socialization. These services help the elderly to keep alert, active, and meaningfully occupied; they decrease the likelihood of disengagement and isolation from the community.

Different elderly may respond to or need different types of social contact programs related both to their interests and to their health status. The human service worker should perceive what best fits their need.

Senior centers, the dominant and best-financed social contact services, can reach a number of different groups with differing needs if the centers move away from their old format as social clubs to the new orientation of serving as multiservice agencies. They can provide outreach; they can be a source of telephone reassurance; they can organize all sorts of volunteer activities. The best of them are doing this; yet they need to do still more. Krout (1983) reports, from his study of a multipurpose senior center, that it served predominantly a social and recreational function. It did meet social contact needs, for participants said that above all they came "for something to do," because "friends invited them," or in order "to be with people/make friends." Centers need to put more emphasis on their other programs. They need to reach out to minorities and the less active elderly. Hanssen et al. (1978) find that senior center users not only have a relatively high level of health, but high social status and support as well. Others, such as Krout (1983), maintain that those involved appear to be members of the stable working- or middle-class group (almost all in Krout's study owned a home). In many areas minorities make little use of the services available. And in general a small proportion of all elderly use the centers—18 percent in the Louis Harris poll, and even lower in the Krout (1983) study. Clearly, the senior centers need to include a larger part of the diverse aged population in their programs. This is not to say that there is no room for the provision of social contact services by other groups. While churches do a good deal of work in this area, the evidence shows that they neglect their older, frail members who are homebound or stuck in nursing homes (Ellor et al., 1983).

Volunteering has great merit, both for the older citizens who give their time to an agency, and for the community as a whole. However, more effort must be made to avoid excessive costs for the volunteer or "burnout" due to agency demands upon volunteers. In general, social contact services are cheap to provide due to the use of volunteers. Thus a wide array of them should be available. Each community should have its telephone reassurance service and many others. The need is to find sources to organize these necessary services.

CHAPTER 7

Meals Services and Transportation Programs

Nutritional Needs and Meals Services

Nutritional deficiencies affect the aging process and may cause various health problems. Thus a nutritionally balanced diet is essential for the health of the elderly. In evaluating an elderly person's diet, one must consider its protein, vitamin, and mineral content, and evaluate the quantity of intake as well, for both undereating and overeating are common. Here I will describe some of the nutritional problems of the elderly and the various programs to provide them with a more balanced diet: these include congregate meals, services to the homebound, food stamps, "brown bag," and food commodity programs.

Nutritional Deficiencies

Various studies show that American elderly have nutritional problems. Ruth Weg (1978) reports that "subacute" or "subclinical" malnutrition is fairly widespread among those over 55. A Department of Agriculture study finds that six to eight million elderly in this country have nutritionally deficient diets (Cain, 1977). Local nutritional assessment programs have found large groups of elderly who need nutritional assistance (Russell et al., 1984).

Poor nutrition makes it difficult for the elderly to sustain the increased stress associated with infection or surgery. Dietary deficiencies may also contribute to the development of diabetes, heart disease, certain cancers, and arteriosclerosis and other coronary diseases. Decreased physical activity by most aged, metabolic changes, and such chronic disorders as diabetes and arteriosclerosis will reduce food consumption and require some restrictions on what is eaten (as, for example, in the case of salt-free diets). Reduced intake will mean a need for higher-quality foods.

Like other Americans, elderly persons have moved away from raw fruits, vegetables, and dairy products to diets too high in cholesterol, sugar, and refined grains. They lack the fiber content derived from raw vegetables and fruits; this is a potential contributing factor to cancer of the colon and of the intestine. The elderly often eat too much food high in the saturated fats of meat: this adds to the lipids in the bloodstream, exacerbating the risk of arteriosclerosis and other coronary diseases. The aged eat too much bread and cake, both of which are high in carbohydrates. The elderly lack adequate vitamin content in their diet. Because, with the exception of the potato, foods high in vitamin C are expensive the aged eat too few of them. Elderly people often avoid milk, with its high vitamin and calcium content, because they see it is as a children's drink. Many avoid cheese because they believe it will constipate them. By avoiding these dairy products they take in too little calcium, which is essential to prevent osteoporosis. In fact, their most common dietery deficiency is calcium, followed by iron (Rawson et al., 1978).

Although these deficiencies are well known, researchers are still uncertain about the aged's minimum daily nutritional requirements, both as to amount and content, partly because each individual's biochemistry is different (Russell et al., 1984). As the American Dietetic Association recommended in 1981, more research is required on the nutritional needs of the elderly. This must be kept in mind when considering the government-suggested use of a Recommended Daily Allowance (RDA) of essential vitamins and other nutrients in the Title III Standard Meals program. To prevent such nutritional deficiencies the officials propose that each meal should represent one-third of the RDA. However, the problem is that the RDA is not age-adjusted, nor can it consider the biochemical individuality of the aged, according to Metress (1981).

Factors Affecting the Quality of Nutritional Intake

A number of factors, both socioeconomic and physical, affect the nutrition of elderly people. These factors include income, education, cultural background, physical condition, stress, and social isolation.

In general, studies find that for the elderly there is a direct relationship between their income and the nutritional quality of their diet; hence many experts conclude that the problems of geriatric nutrition are a function not merely of age but also of socioeconomic position. Protein-rich foods such as meat and dairy products may simply be too expensive for many elderly, who may have to eat cheap carbohydrates instead. They may also use cheaper canned foods—even dog food—instead of fresh meat and vegetables. Some elderly even try to cut food costs by sleeping until noon, thus eliminating one meal.

Cultural background may explain certain eating habits, including over-consumption of some foods and underconsumption of others. For example, the American diet typically includes too much meat and salt and not enough fresh vegetables. First-generation Italian-Americans may eat too many car-bohydrate-rich foods such as various forms of pasta, and some Orientals may eat too little protein. But attachment to familiar foods may serve a psycholog-ical function among some elderly. However, for some, the consumption of ethnic foods, such as pigs feet among black Americans, may be mainly due to their low cost (Nahemow, 1982). Educational level may be even more impor-tant than income in determining nutritional habits. Lack of information on proper diet is commonplace even today. Pelcovits and Holmes (1969) report from their evaluation of demonstration meals programs that there is wide-spread misinformation about food and nutrition among all economic strata in America; this ignorance contributes to malnutrition. Many elderly, for exam-ple, do not know about the effects of overconsumption of saturated fats or of carbohydrates. Many groups, including the nutrition committee of the 1981 White House Conference on Aging, call for more nutritional education—both for today's elderly and for the younger Americans who will make up tomorrow's elderly. It is essential to educate the young because it is difficult in later life to correct nutritional deficiencies which begin early.

Physical problems, too, can contribute to poor diet. The inability to chew food properly, due to dentures or lack of teeth, means reduced con-sumption of meat and fibrous vegetables. Problems with the digestive pro-cesses of older Americans contribute to a decrease in the amount they eat, especially of certain types of food. Another aspect of the aging process, reduction in the acuteness of taste and smell, may also decrease appetite. Disabilities that make the elderly only semiambulatory may affect the type and amount of food eaten. Elderly who have trouble standing up long enough to prepare food often resort to easy-to-prepare foods, such as TV dinners and other packaged foods, which are often low in nutrients and high in carbohydrates. They will also be more likely to have food delivered or to use nearby "mom and pop' stores, compensating for the higher cost per item by buying the cheaper and usually less nutritional foods on the shelves. Stress from physical or mental illnesses may well diminish or increase the elderly person's appetite. For some, stress decreases appetite, while for others it leads to continual nibbling and overeating, especially of carbohy-drates.

Social isolation, especially among the single elderly, decreases interest in food. Eating is usually a social occasion which brings the family together.

When this warm atmosphere is missing, perhaps due to the death of a spouse, so that the survivor must sit at the table alone, there is often a loss of appetite or interest in preparing a full meal: the widow stops making regular meals and substitutes snacks without nutritional balance; the widower has meals erratically because he never learned to cook.

There are, then, many factors, from lack of dietary understanding to cultural biases in foods, physical disabilities, loneliness, and decreased income, which can, and often do, result in the elderly's suffering from inadequate nutrition. Programs are needed to see that these people have a healthy diet. Take the example of Mr. S:

> Mr. S., a widower for two years, had a serious arthritis condition in his right arm that made it hard to use it. He couldn't open cans or easily lift even light objects. His wife had always done the cooking and he lacked knowledge on preparation of even basic meals. In addition he was handicapped in cooking by his arm problem. He stuck to television dinners or bowls of cereal. But using the oven seemed too costly for heating one television dinner so he did that less and less. He didn't enjoy eating alone anyway, so he made less and less effort; he just nibbled or brought in fast foods.
>
> One day when he was getting out of the elevator an older women in the apartment down the hall asked him if he knew about the meals program at the senior center a few blocks away. The next day he decided to try it out and he has been going there ever since. He feels better and has better bowel movement. He now enjoys eating meals and seldom feels despondent.

The Food Programs

In the last decade the federal government and local community organizations have moved ahead to improve the nutrition of the elderly through various food programs. The best known and most widely used is the Title III nutrition program of the Older Americans Act. It has two major parts: the provision of meals in congregate settings, and home-delivery service for shut-ins. Brought in as a 1972 Title VII amendment to the OAA, it has been integrated into the Title III program since 1978. State agencies on aging and the local AAAs administer this service. The staff, including nutritionists, check that local programs meet federal criteria for nutrition. The staff also decide on acceptable sites for the congregate dining facilities.

The Congregate Meals Program

Congregate meals are the major part of the Title III nutrition program. This service follows in the steps of other hot meals programs which have been offered in churches and senior citizen centers one or two times a week (or monthly) for a number of decades. These programs still exist; they are paid for by various non-AOA funds or—with the help of volunteers—are self-supporting. Meals are often available only once or twice a week, whereas the Title III meals programs in congregate settings are available five days a week. Title III programs are available to all elderly 60 and over, rather than to select groups, such as members of a denomination or sect.

The Title III nutrition projects address the basic causes of nutritional deficiencies described above—lack of skills to buy and prepare balanced meals; impaired physical ability to shop or cook; income loss; and isolation and loneliness. The aim is to provide older Americans, particularly those with low incomes, with a low-cost meal in a strategically located center such as a church, community center, senior citizen center, school, or other public or nonprofit agency which is accessible at the same time to other social and rehabilitation services.

The original legislation also required the grantor agency to provide the center with extra support, such as transportation and even escort services. In addition, the legislation mentioned provision of nutrition education, information and referral, health and welfare counseling, and recreation activities. From the beginning, only 20 percent of funding could be used for these; the idea was to integrate users into existing community services, rather than develop a separate social service program (U.S. Senate Special Committee on Aging, 1982). This is why the preferred sites are those with existing community programs, such as senior centers. A fourth of the sites used are senior centers; another fourth of the sites are at churches; many public housing projects are also chosen as good locations. Such sites are preferred today more than ever because the Reagan administration has severely restricted the diversion of funds earmarked for nutrition to recreation, counseling, or information and referral.

Outreach to the isolated is still mandated, as are access services. For most sites, there are regularly scheduled trips to bring in participants unable to use public transportation. Since a large number of the participants are 75 or over and many have low incomes, one can easily see why such transportation is necessary.

Nationwide, the congregate meals program serves over half a million meals annually—580,000 meals in 1980 at over 13,000 different sites—a vital part of 1,200 nutrition programs. Almost two-thirds of the users have low incomes (U.S. Senate Special Committee on Aging, 1982).

A primary problem of this program is that it can serve only a limited number, usually 20 to 60 a day at a site; there are long waiting lists for participation and not enough sites available. With recent funding cuts, some centers are establishing a three- or four-day rotation system of attendance. This situation prevails in spite of the fact that the Rural Mini-Conference recommended to the 1981 White House Conference on Aging that there be no limit to the number served and that meals be served seven days a week.

Another difficulty is that the original aim of serving those of low income and minorities by locating many centers in their areas has not always been followed. Critics claim that there are an inadequate number of sites in ethnic residential areas; for example, the Marin County, California, AAA (1982) complained of lack of sites in Hispanic residential areas. In addition, many minority-group aged do not even know of the sites near them. A third barrier to success is that the site chosen, such as a public housing project or a church, often does not fully welcome those in the neighborhood not affiliated with it; it makes them feel like outsiders when they come for the meals. This is one reason why a housing development for the elderly is often *not* used as a site, even though there is obviously a concentration of those in need of the service there; another reason some nutrition program officials have given is that "elderly public housing tenants are looked upon as a privileged group already receiving assistance," so a community site for nonresident elderly is preferred. However, there are disadvantages in locating the site in the neighborhood rather than these concentrated elderly population centers, since difficult transportation problems often arise. The distance to locations creates a special barrier for those who are handicapped or find mobility difficult, as one elderly user complained. Bad weather, of course, makes this condition still worse. Even if transportation service is available it is often of limited use because of irregular or unreliable schedules.

Even in the face of such problems the program is successful in offering many elderly Americans one nutritious meal a day. Because of the congregate settings it also offers a daily chance to socialize. As Pelcovits and Holmes (1969) report in their study of demonstration congregation meals programs, "Eating habits of the aged depend to a large extent on the atmosphere in which the food is consumed." As one program user in public housing reported (Huttman, 1977):

> The depressing and sickening circumstances of day in and day out eating alone is the true deterioration factor. In my humble opinion a glass of milk and a biscuit in the happy and loving companionship of others could be a more healthful benefit than meals on wheels where one must still eat alone.

Other users stated that their appetites had gotten better from eating with others at the meals sites.

It is an important benefit to provide a warm setting to help the elderly ward off depression on holidays and at other times. Congregate meals programs also help by providing recreational events before or after the noon meal. In addition, the participants socialize while waiting for the meal or do volunteer work in preparing the meal: The chance to serve as a volunteer in running the program can be a morale booster in itself. All this contributes to a healthier mental state for the elderly, especially those who are single.

Home Delivery Programs

Under the OAA's nutritional provisions the government has allocated, since 1978, separate resources for delivery of food to individual homes—a project often called Meals-on-Wheels. The OAA now also allows support for meals programs serving only the handicapped (no congregate part), with the funds channeled through the AAAs to subcontracted organizations. Many other organizations provide home meals without OAA funding. In the early 1980s about 15 to 20 percent of the OAA meals went to the homebound, or to those normally participating in the congregate meals program but temporarily limited to their homes. Often this program works in conjunction with an outreach program for homebound elderly.

This OAA home delivery (Meals-on-Wheels) service, like its volunteer nonprofit community counterparts, prepares, packages, and delivers a nutritionally balanced noontime meal. In many programs the volunteers or paid staff delivering the meal also leave food for a cold supper or even for breakfast. A minimal charge is usually levied. Sometimes the delivery people stay and sit with the client during the meal, although it is more usual for them to deliver a number of meals to different elderly during the noon period. Whichever is the case, it does provide at least a short daily contact with the housebound elderly person. The staff or volunteers can ascertain possible need for other services and then make the necessary referrals. Provision of a meals service often encourages isolated but ambulatory clients to use the congregate meals program and other community activities.

These meals are usually prepared in institutional facilities, such as a hospital, school, church, or senior citizen center, by volunteers—or, more likely today—by paid help. (The congregate meals are also often put together by these sources.) A prime requirement is to organize the complicated food delivery services efficiently, seeing to it that meal routes are well planned, that there is adequate volunteer assistance, and that the food is packaged to stay hot and taste good.

The Title III home delivery service is limited to elderly who are 60 or over, who qualify as homebound according to accepted medical criteria. A large proportion of the participants is aged 75 or over; many of them are of low income. The number of low-income "old-old" actually needing the program is much greater than the number served. Waiting lists are long, and there are still many rural areas which lack the service entirely. The Rural Mini-Conference preceding the 1981 White House Conference on Aging recommended that the conference take "into consideration the uniquely rural problems of physical isolation, as well as the correspondingly high cost of service delivery to rural area residents." It urged the government to "explore alternative service delivery modes appropriate to meet the unique rural needs such as mobile grocery stores."

Nutrition Education Programs

Nutrition education is another area emphasized by the Older Americans Act. Such education may be included as part of the meals program or it may constitute a separate program for the elderly population in general. An example drawn from one AAA indicates the different directions such education can take. In 1981 this agency had a nutrition coordinator for resources related to nutrition and aging within the county; she served as advocate for the nutrition needs of the elderly, provided educational materials to nutritionists and other professionals for distribution to older adults, and provided nutrition consultation to other agencies and organizations. This same county also had a Department of Public Health nutritionist who consulted with community agencies; another group, Nursing Dynamics, offered weekly nutrition counseling at the major meals program administrative center. Yet in this same county the authors of the annual AAA report stated in 1982 that "most of the nutrition programs or services are not comprehensive in scope; they either provide food or counseling/nutrition education, but rarely both services." They also saw "lack of nutrition training for home health aides" as a county deficiency (Marin County, 1982).

Another program in some locations is nutritional assessment of individual diets, recommended by Committee Four of the 1981 White House Conference on Aging. In some areas the county department of health has such a program of screening and nutritional assessment under a health project for persons 60 and over. Clients are screened for under- or overweight conditions, nutritional problems, and chronic disorders (U.S. Senate Special Committee on Aging, 1982).

"Brown Bag" Programs

Another type of community food service which helps low-income elderly with their food costs is the "brown bag." In Contra Costa County, California, for example, four different communities distribute surplus food this way. In the best known—the one in Antioch, California—volunteers, many of them elderly, fill 125 bags once a week for qualifed low-income elderly; there is a waiting list for participation. The volunteers pick up second-day donuts and desirable but discarded supermarket food. Members of the brown bag committee go to farms to pick unharvested crops; some bake trays of cookies. Various local businesses, canneries, and farmers also donate surplus goods. At Christmas many local families donate items such as cakes or candy for the Christmas bag. Various community groups, including the local VFW and the Young People of St. John's Church, provide special dinners for Antioch's brown bag recipients.

In another community, the focus is on local people donating surplus vegetables from their gardens and farms. In this self-help program, elderly individuals go to participating farms and pick the surplus or solicit food from food processors. They then package and deliver what they have gathered to the needy. This "Gray Bears" program distributes free produce and other salvaged foodstuffs to between 800 and 1,200 seniors each week. Another program provides emergency food to the elderly. Local areas may have human concern organizations that provide a two-day emergency food supply to needy persons who are not eligible for food stamps. Many cities have soup kitchens for the needy and homeless.

Cooperative bulk purchase of food exists in some areas. These programs are often called food-buying clubs. Some communities have centers for canning food picked by the volunteers at cooperating farms. In one large West Coast city over 48 food clubs, involving at least 6,000 low-income seniors in 1977, were participating in a Mobile Mini-market program which bought groceries—mainly produce, meat, and poultry—at the best wholesale prices available and then transported them to resale sites or food clubs, some of which were located at senior centers and housing projects (California Department of Aging, 1978). The U.S. Department of Agriculture (USDA) surplus commodity program distributes USDA excess commodities to charitable and nonprofit organizations for use in their meals service. In 1981 legal restraints still made full utilization of this program difficult. The USDA surplus commodity program also distributes specific surplus food, such as cheese, to individual needy through nonprofit and public bodies; recipients include SSI beneficiaries. For example, in a New York rural town local churches had a program in coordination with the town to distribute surplus cheese to qualifying elderly and others.

Food Stamps

The food stamp program, started in 1964 by the Department of Agriculture as a partial replacement for surplus food commodity programs, is another important form of assistance for the elderly. The food stamp program allows low-income Americans to purchase, at less than face value (or if very poor, obtain for free), food stamps that substitute for cash in buying specified kinds of food at the grocery store. The low price paid for the stamps lowers the price of the food. The price of these stamps is based on income; those with more than a certain income are not eligible to buy them. In many states all elderly SSI participants are automatically eligible (though not all use it), but some states use the food stamp "cash-out" practice for SSI recipients. This means the SSI payments are structured to include a "bonus" value—money to which the recipient would be entitled were she in a position to buy food stamps.

Underutilization of the food stamp program is a major problem. A large proportion of the elderly does not use it: these people are too proud to submit to a means test. The 1978 U.S. Senate Special Committee on Aging reports that less than one-fifth of the elderly below the poverty level register for food stamps. Reforms brought in by the Food and Agriculture Act of 1977 and national food stamp program directives have improved accessibility somewhat. These reforms lessened red tape by simplifying the application, introducing application by mail or at local Social Security offices, allowing elderly living in hotels to be eligible, permitting stamps to be used for home delivery meals to shut-ins, and permitting a designated third person to apply for, and shop with, the stamps on another's behalf. However, the Reagan administration cutbacks have made food stamp officials tighten up on regulations and discourage food stamp use.

Summary

Many elderly need assistance in paying their food bills. A number of programs, including food stamps, surplus food commodities, congregate meals, home delivery, and brown bag supplies, help elderly poor reduce their nutritional costs. In addition, many elderly need someone to cook them at least one nutritionally balanced meal each day; when they live alone or have physical impairments, they find it difficult to handle this task without help. Several programs, such as congregate meals and home delivery, serve to alleviate the problem. They also offer opportunities for socializing, for providing nutrition information, and for referral to other services.

Transportation Services

Transportation is the lifeline to independence and to integration into the community. Lack of transportation constricts social life, limits capacity for self-maintenance, and inhibits use of medical and social services. As public hearings and research studies indicate, the elderly themselves consider transportation of great importance to their well-being. For example, in 20 public hearings conducted by one state's department of aging, the elderly mentioned transportation more often than any other single category of need. For many years experts undervalued this service; they were surprised when transportation proved to be a major concern at the 1971 White House Conference on Aging. By 1975 legislators had named transportation as one of the four OAA priority services (U.S. House of Representatives, Select Committee on Aging, 1976).

Health and Transportation Needs

Conventional public transportation poses numerous difficulties for the aged. Riding buses or subways requires a high degree of speed, mental agility, and quick reactions. In recent years, transportation systems have become even more complex, demanding quicker reaction time. Furthermore, some systems have become more crowded or less accessible, requiring longer walks to airport gates or to scattered suburban bus stops. Elderly people who have experienced declines in sensory acuity, strength, and agility often cannot cope with the demands of rapid transit. They have less endurance to walk to or wait for needed services, poorer vision, especially at night, and slower responses. Approximately one-third have physical limitations or disabilities that restrict their use of conventional public transportation (U.S. Department of Transportation, 1977).

KINDS OF NEED

Yet transportation to various services is necessary to the elderly. Visits to the doctor are imperative, although the number varies according to health status. Before or after an operation visits may be especially frequent. Obviously most elderly must also visit the grocery store. The most typical pattern of grocery shopping is once a week, though some go more frequently (Carp, 1977b). Few use taxis because they cannot afford them. Visiting friends or children is another important use the elderly have for special transportation as is participation in community activities. According to the Carp study, dissatisfaction with transportation to the latter was high; many said that they would go to the senior center, to the library, or to various kinds of entertainment more often if it were easier to get there. Travel to church is common among the elderly (one-half attend once a month, according to the Carp study) but again, it is not always easy to arrange.

Present Use of Transportation by the Elderly

Carp's and other studies show how much the elderly are inhibited by lack of transportation. About one-third do not drive a car, in spite of its importance for accessibility in the modern world. Women and minorities are especially unlikely to drive. For example, over half of the elderly white women, half of all black elderly, and almost three fourths of Mexican-American elderly do not drive a car. Women brought up in an age when wives let husbands drive may well have never learned to drive. In addition, a car—with its high insurance and gas costs—is too expensive for many elderly. There are also large groups of elderly who own a car but seldom drive, particularly at night. Vision problems, poor health conditions, slow reaction times, lack of money, or lack of confidence about driving on expressways or in heavy traffic serve to discourage the elderly from driving.

Many urban elderly use public transit. However, problems within the system discourage use (U.S. Department of Transportation, 1980). Carp (1977b) estimates that in San Antonio, Texas, only one in five retired persons usually goes somewhere in a bus as often as once a week and that, in fact, 40 percent never take a bus, although it is the major public transportation system for the city. Bus design contributes to the difficulties encountered by the elderly using public transit. Entrance steps are often too high, and the vehicle halts for too short a time. The *Elderly Market for Urban Mass Transit* (U.S. Department of Transportation, 1980) reports old people have trouble getting in and out of seats, reaching handholds, seeing landmarks out of the windows, finding a place for packages, and standing, if seats are not available. Physical handicaps may make it hard to see or hear location information. Physical barriers in the bus terminal itself include long stairs and walks, poor crowd-flow design, insufficient seating, and poor connections with other modes of transportation. Many transit stops have insufficient shelter and platforms unsuited to the vehicle. Stops are frequently located on hills which are icy in the winter—or in inner-city areas frequented by undesirable types. A shortage of bus stops is yet another problem, one which may mean uncomfortable or impossibly long treks by foot for the aged.

Furthermore, public transit systems are planned for needs of commuting workers, with expanded services at commuter hours and poor services during off-peak hours. Routes are planned to get riders to work in downtown, industrial, or office locations—not to get the elderly to hospitals, clinics, and senior centers. Thus, the elderly often need to make one or more transfers to get to their destinations, and may have to walk long distances from the bus stop. For example, in one Canadian city I studied (1977), the elderly complained that all the buses went downtown—while they had to go crosstown to reach the hospital. If transfers are necessary, the infrequency of the service and poor coordination of routes can make the trip a very long one. For example:

> Mrs. A., who used a cane due to her arthritis, had a medical appointment at 4 P.M. at the local hospital. She had to walk three blocks to the bus stop, which took her 15 minutes. Then she had to wait 20 minutes for a bus and then she had to stand on the bus (even though the front seats were reserved for elderly and handicapped). Children were just getting out of school and crowding the bus and she feared they might push her. When she got off, she did so slowly, hoping the bus door would not close too fast. Then she had to stand in the rain at another unsheltered bus stop 15 minutes waiting for a second bus headed for the hospital area. All this meant 2 hours time to get to the hospital.

In addition to the energy required for these exhausting bus trips, the elderly must always be alert to the threat of crime. At bus stops or on buses in large cities they are easy targets for youngsters hungry for money. The most serious obstacle to the elderly's use of public transportation may be their psychological reluctance to "face the uncertainties, terrors, and dangers of a bus ride" (Lowy, 1979).

Many urban elderly would rather walk to needed social and medical services. Carp (1977b) estimates that a fifth of the aged go somewhere on foot every day; about a quarter usually walks to the grocery store. A sizable group, however, is not inclined to walk anyplace. The ideal length of a walk for most elderly is estimated at about eight blocks. Many important facilities—such as the grocery store, church, drugstore, bank, or hospital—are farther away than that. Carrying heavy bundles or making the trip in bad weather can cause fatigue or be dangerous. Lack of paved sidewalks, designated crosswalks, graduated curbs, and benches on which to rest often causes difficulties as well. Traffic lights may be timed too fast. Some cities are changing these factors so that the elderly can enjoy comfortable, safe pedestrian travel, but much still remains to be done.

Especially the rural aged need transportation. They can seldom walk where they need to go unless they live in the center of a small town. The distances between people, people and towns, and people and services is a unique problem in rural areas (Kaye, 1982). The distance to be travelled has even increased in recent years because lower rural population density has caused the consolidation of services such as hospitals to one county location.

Passenger intercity bus lines and rail service are rarely available to people in towns of less than 2,500. Even where railroad and intercity buses are available, cost and other problems may inhibit their use. As the California Department of Agriculture concludes:

> Because the demand for services [in rural areas] is lower than in urban areas due to lower population densities and generally lower income levels, and because the distances from origin to destination are longer, the cost per trip is prohibitive to most providers of transit service. Yet more rural elderly than urban elderly do not drive or even own a car. This is especially true for minority elderly. In low income rural counties over one-fifth of the households are without private transport; many of these are elderly. (California Department of Aging, 1978)

Lack of public transportation in rural areas has several negative economic consequences. It may force the elderly to move to an urban area where needed resources are available. Often this means a move to a nursing home—and increased costs for the state. Lack of adequate transportation to rural services has another detrimental effect in that non-use of services or out-migration of elderly may mean that resources will be closed down due to lack of clients. Elderly residents, through their government benefits, such as Medicare, Medicaid, and Social Security payments, provide essential funds to keep the local services and community private sector in business (Cottrell, 1975).

Providing transportation to services can actually increase the demand for services. Cottrell (1975) in his demonstration of specialized rural transportation finds that the latter makes it possible for the aged to get more of the medical services to which they are entitled but which they could not use without such special provisions. Cottrell's group, with its assumption that the elderly's transportation needs are not fully met by relatives and friends in rural areas, provided free transportation in this project. Two-thirds of the users had children and other relatives in the area, but the aged hated to ask them for rides, feeling they would be a burden. About a third of them actually had cars themselves, but preferred using the services.

In the suburbs, public transportation is again limited by the low density of the population and by the widespread assumption that everyone has a car. The mass exodus to suburbia began in the 1950s, so that some of the suburban residents who left the cities 35 years ago are now in their 70s and 80s. Some suffer physical disabilities that make it hard to drive a car or even use a bus. It is hard to serve this group with specialized transportation because they are so widely dispersed (Golant, 1976).

Funding of Programs

The greatest impetus to provide transportation for the elderly has come from the Urban Mass Transportation Act (UMTA), especially its later amendments, and from the OAA itself. In the Biaggi amendments to UMTA, the federal government finally focused on the elderly's needs, stating that they and the handicapped should have equal rights to mass transportation facilities and services and mandating special efforts to care for their unique needs.

A major criterion used to qualify for UMTA funds is that local governments provide fares reduced by at least 50 percent to elderly and handicapped riders in non-peak hours. Local governments can receive UMTA funds for urban mass transit facilities and equipment; special needs of the elderly may be included in seeking these federal monies. UMTA also funds innovative transportation services and vehicle adaptations. This includes Dial-A-Ride, experimental coaches (such as "careful coaches" with wheelchair lifts), or retrofitting present mass transit vehicles. UMTA's sections 16 (b), (1) and (2), authorize public agencies and nonprofit organizations to spend capital grants and loan money to meet special needs of the elderly. Over 3,000 special vehicles had been purchased by various agencies by 1977. The Federal Highway Act of 1973, Section 147, targeted on rural public transportation planning and improvement, specifies that project selection criteria must include consideration of the needs of elderly in rural areas. Demonstration grants are available for development of special transportation subsystems to assist the rural elderly and handicapped.

In addition to the above, many services have transportation components. For example, OAA Title III area plans must include transportation provisions for their various programs. This applies especially to nutrition programs in which a number of users are transported to meal sites. Besides provision of transportation to the Title III programs themselves, monies from the model project fund can be used for transportation projects; in fact, in 1977, transportation accounted for the third-largest outlay of the Title III model project fund. The general social service programs, under SSBGs, fund transportation for their constituents. Under the 1973 Rehabilitation Act, handicapped elderly receive transportation assistance; Medicaid pays for transportation to medical appointments when need is documented, and the Public Health Service Act funds transportation to community health centers and emergency medical services. Thus, a number of federal projects, administered by a variety of agencies, provide transportation for the elderly to specific programs under certain circumstances. Individual states also supplement federal provisions. For example, in Missouri the Older Americans Transportation Service (OATS) serves 89 counties with over 125 vans and buses (1978), of which 25 are wheelchair-equipped. Medical trips are given priority in the OATS schedule (Pierce, 1979). Some states use part of their income from gasoline taxes to support special transportation programs for the aged.

Types of Programs

Some services are geared specifically to the elderly, whereas others attempt to make public transportation generally more usable, more comfortable, and less expensive. Most city and regional mass transit systems now have reduced fares for the aged. This, however, sometimes still leaves them with a sizable transportation bill, especially for interregional travel. Another local public transit effort, in response to senior group requests, is to reroute buses to increase accessibility to hospitals and other places frequented by the elderly. Still another is improvement of bus shelters.

One UMTA regulation (1979) tried to improve access to vehicles by requiring new buses to have hydraulic-lift equipment for wheelchairs, or to provide boarding ramps; however, this regulation was rescinded in 1981 due to its high cost. The UMTA now allows local communities which receive their funds from them to demonstrate that they are making reasonable efforts to meet the needs of the elderly. The problem is that most public transit systems do not offer the variety of vehicles and vehicle-design characteristics required by special users, as a California Department of Aging report (1978) points out. They lack such features as handholds, low entrance steps, and special loading apparatus for wheelchairs. However, indications are that there is a continual attempt to improve this situation with each purchase of new equipment.

SPECIALIZED TRANSPORTATION

There should be a variety of modes of transportation available, including the demand-responsive type as well as fixed-route, fixed-schedule public transit systems. Although adequate public mass transit will meet some needs, pilot studies indicate that in some instances more personalized transportation better serves the needs of the transportation-disadvantaged, particularly the frail, ill, or handicapped elderly. This may even need to include door-to-door service.

Specialized transportation services include those provided by agencies: typically, a vehicle takes clients to a specific program, such as that offered by a senior center, or the group might be taken to do grocery shopping. The service may be of the demand-responsive sort, or may use a specific route, scheduled times, and designated stops. An agency may of course provide transportation to a number of places rather than to a single, particular destination. However, even this kind of general, subsidized transportation assistance is likely to be limited as to the destinations for which it can be used. It may have to be used for medical appointments or shopping; this does not help the aged person who wants to go to a local bar or movie, or to visit an old friend.

A community uses three modes of transportation to achieve the goals just described: taxis, minibuses, and private cars run by volunteers. Some are supported by the UMTA as demonstration projects, by the OAA or other federal or state arrangements, while others are maintained by local social service agencies and community groups such as churches and service clubs.

One county's program will suggest the variety of programs possible; this is the small suburban and partly rural Marin County above San Francisco. Its Senior Coordinating Council operates a "Whistlestop Wheels" program with 23 vehicles on the road (including 6 lift-equipped vans). These provide transportation to shopping, adult day care, medical, nutrition, and recreation/education programs. In FY 80–81, they made 103,555 passenger trips (Marin County, 1982). The Council uses OAA funds to provide transportation to nutrition sites (about 2,200 passenger trips monthly), some transportation for adult day care participants (about 1,000 passenger trips monthly), and one-day-per-week medical/shopping assistance for residents in rural areas (about 75 passenger trips monthly). Many other groups in this county provide different kinds of specialized transportation. They may serve as an example of wasteful duplication of services. The county mass transit system has a program called Handi-Wheels, established in FY 80–81, for elderly and handicapped in the sparsely settled rural areas of the county; using 5 vans equipped with lifts, over 4,000 passenger trips were made in the first quarter of that year. A Human Needs Center in another community provides scheduled transportation with OAA funds. "La Familia" receives OAA funds to run not only an outreach program, but also to provide limited transportation and escort services. The American Red Cross has 2 vehicles, which provide medical transport with 6 to 7 volunteer drivers. The American Cancer Society also offers limited transportation for cancer patients (Marin County, 1982).

Many of these programs depend upon volunteer drivers. For example, volunteers driving their own vehicles provide medical transportation (upon professional referral) for elderly and handicapped in a program of the local Volunteer Bureau. About a third of the volunteers (FY 80–81) received mileage reimbursement through OAA funds. One community's Senior Service program has about 40 volunteer drivers who supply transportation or deliver meals to older adults. In addition, 4 taxi companies in the county give the elderly discount rates ranging from 10 to 25 percent. This is not a complete list, for there are many other services even in this one small county of Marin, California (1982), all of which offer some degree of transportation assistance. While standing out as an example of service duplication, this county's varied transportation system does include some coordination efforts; some use of reimbursed volunteers driving their own cars or driving minibuses acquired by their agencies; some use of OAA, some use UMTA funds—and all draw upon a variety of nonprofit resources. Minibuses are acquired in some cases by agencies through fundraising benefits, or they are donated by community service clubs such as Kiwanis. Some agencies supply transportation to special services, including church activities, and some concentrate on general transportation.

The use of subsidized taxis is popular for widely dispersed suburban areas. Most elderly do not have the negative feelings about travelling by taxi that some do about riding in minibuses. Subsidized taxi fares may prove cheaper in many areas than such experiments as Dial-A-Ride, where one calls to reserve a minibus service for a ride. In fact, most programs which operate vans with hydraulic lifts on a call-and-demand basis have proven quite expensive. Without government subsidies they are not economically feasible on a community-wide basis.

ESCORT SERVICE

A still more specialized transportation service is that which offers escorts to accompany frail or confused elderly persons on trips, whether on foot, by auto, public bus, or subway. Escorts may be used when the elderly concerned are very handicapped, perhaps using a walker or crutch; such conditions make it difficult for them to cross streets, get on buses, or climb stairs without help. Escort service may also help persons with language problems: bilingual escorts may well accompany minority-group clients to the place they need to go and interpret for them there.

In high-crime areas, the escort serves as a protection force. For example, during 1977 police in an inner-city area of Chicago provided a bus and driver escort to take elderly from two housing projects to banks and grocery stores on the day social security checks arrived. Police in New York City have organized a teenage volunteer escort service; in one year this program of 1,000 volunteers served 5,000 elderly (Irwin, 1978).

SHOPPING ASSISTANCE

Senior centers and other senior organizations often organize a service to transport the aged to supermarkets and shopping centers. It is usually offered at a regularly scheduled time once or twice a week. By using the large markets, it allows the elderly to buy more economically. In some areas stores feature special senior discount days. On such days they even package meats and other foods in smaller quantities than usual. Such a shopping service, on a door-to-door basis, allows elderly to get larger quantities of goods, shop less often, and save money.

PROBLEMS WITH SPECIALIZED TRANSPORTATION SERVICES

As I mentioned above, the cost of a minibus service is a major draw-back; this is especially true for rural areas. Lawton and Byerts (1977) conclude that such specially designed vehicles are relatively expensive, and the UMTA has rescinded its requirement that cities buy these buses. Many experts question whether mass transit should have these specialized vehicles at all, since it is likely that only one passenger per trip will often need them. In addition, not all the handicapped will be able to use the fully accessible vehicle, continuing to need specialized transportation. However, when such buses are used for specialized transportation staffing is expensive. The door-to-door pickup, for instance, has been estimated to require a minimum of 30 minutes per person (round trip) if assistance is given in mounting, dismounting, and negotiating the route between house and vehicle. Gas, repairs, and insurance are often high-expense items.

Insurance costs are a major problem for specialized services, whether they use minibuses run by agency drivers or rely on private cars. Increasingly, insurance costs have been forcing small transit operators and volunteers to cease providing services for the elderly. While vehicle transportation costs have risen for the population in general, insurance for older drivers, volunteers, and transit for the elderly programs has risen disproportionately. In 1981 the Rural Mini-White House Conference recommended that the federal government reexamine state insurance options and rates offered by individual insurance companies to maximize the utilization of public, voluntary, and religious-group transportation systems. In 1980 the federal government convinced insurance companies to establish new insurance ratings for vehicles owned by a program, employees, or volunteers who transport the aged—a rating halfway between that charged school buses and city buses. The new rates also allow for excess liability insurance at a low premium for vehicle's owner when transporting elderly clients (*Older American Reports*, 1980).

The variety of specialized transportation, and even the variety of funding, contribute to another problem—the need for coordination. As the Cal-

ifornia Department of Aging (1978) states: "A significant point about specialized para-transit services such as those funded under the programs
described above . . . is that they are generally uncoordinated, duplicative
and expensive. In some cases regulations prevent effective cooperation
among different agencies operating in essentially the same neighborhood
with many of the same disadvantaged clients." The U.S. Senate Committee
on Aging (1981) has condemned this fragmentation of programs, duplication,
and unnecessarily restrictive eligibility. The 1981 Rural Mini–White House
Conference demanded greater coordination between the Federal Highway
Administration and the UMTA regarding rural transportation. The different
federal funding sources need to get together.

    To complicate matters further, there are too many sources of informa-
tion. There should be one central telephone number in a community to
provide information about transit service. Many areas have developed coordination efforts which deserve emulation. The Delaware Authority for Special Transportation has been set up by the state legislature to coordinate all
resources for transportation for the disabled and the elderly, for example.

    Many elderly find it troublesome that these specialized services take
them only to certain services, such as medical appointments; even then, the
transportation staff may not want to wait around for them or may try to hurry
them. Agencies themselves have their own problems concerning volunteer
drivers. The mileage payment to volunteers is too low. In addition, volunteers have the insurance problems mentioned above. For these reasons it is
hard to find volunteers.

    These problems of insurance restrictions and diversified funding may
pose important barriers to one suggested method of increasing transportation for the elderly, especially in rural areas. Some seek the solution to many
difficulties in a multiple-use vehicle system, whereby several different
groups of specialized users ride the same vehicle, either at the same time or
in separate time slots. Barrows and Smith (1979), in suggesting use of school
buses and surplus government vehicles on routes accessible to the elderly,
comment that "both insurance coverage and design features limit use of
these vehicles." Only 15 states had legislation permitting school buses to be
used for nonschool purposes in 1977 (U.S. Department of Transportation,
1977). Yet other countries do this. In Switzerland the rural postal bus service
carries school children and regular passengers as well as delivering mail. Lee
and Lassey (1982) point out that in American rural areas many federally
supported vehicles operated by separate institutions pass by the same spot
each day, picking up school children, delivering mail, picking up senior
citizens; they feel this redundancy should be eliminated. To do this, however, considerable behavioral resistance must be overcome: "The reluctance of
the elderly to ride with the young, the well with the ill, the affluent with the
poor and vice versa." Many different social service programs in urban areas,
such as those of charity groups, churches, sheltered workshops for the handi-

capped, and federally funded community programs, should also consider sharing their transportation services.

Conclusion

This chapter has focused on two services essential both to the well-being of the elderly and to their utilization of other complementary services. The existence of a congregate meals program means such services as information and referral and social contact and recreational programs can be provided expeditiously at the same site. The existence of a transportation program increases the elderly's ability to utilize the health clinics, senior centers, and even the congregate meals program. Not only does participation in both these programs encourage contact with supportive services, but utilization decreases the elderly's isolation.

Each of these programs has its special problems and unique pitfalls. A major issue with congregate meals is where to locate the service and how—with what sort of personnel—to run it. The evidence indicates it is preferable to situate these meals programs in a location that welcomes people of all backgrounds. The site must, of course, also be easy to reach. To be successful, congregate meals programs should also utilize the elderly themselves as volunteers and decisionmakers.

Another question is the degree to which service should be directed to homebound persons needing meals as opposed to those able to come to a center. I think there should be more emphasis on providing meals to the homebound; for one thing, the latter are in greater need than those attending the congregate meals program. Providing meals to the homebound allows frail elderly to stay in their own homes. With that in mind, the program must do more than provide meals; it should be part of a larger caretaker team, working with other agencies to supply the whole spectrum of services necessary to function in one's own home. Those serving meals to the homebound should spend enough time with them to observe their health and their overall needs. To do this the program may have to rely heavily on trained volunteers.

The debate will continue over the importance of improving public transportation to better serve frail and handicapped elderly, versus developing a specialized transportation system only for the elderly. The variety of needs involved dictates that this should not be an either–or decision. Special transportation is needed to bring handicapped elderly to services not easily accessible by public transportation, such as some medical facilities. At the same time the special transportation must be given careful and creative thought to decide when such a service is needed and to design ways to provide this service most economically. Duplication should be reduced by greater cooperation between providers under a clear and efficient community-wide plan.

CHAPTER 8

Housing Programs for the Elderly in Their Own Homes

Both poor physical condition and the financial situation of many elderly make it difficult for them to find and afford suitable housing for this period in their life or even to make repairs on their present dwelling.

Those with physical problems often lack the mobility and energy to keep up their house or to move to another unit. They are frequently reluctant to leave the familiarity of their present neighborhood. Last, there is little variety in housing alternatives that would specially suit this varied group of 26 million Americans (Pynoos, 1984).

Yet housing is very important to the well-being of the elderly. It is a major source of self-identification and status for them. Certain types of housing can also be the locus for a variety of needed services. Yet today both elderly homeowners and renters are often living in housing units unsuitable for their needs and substandard in quality although they typically pay a very large part of their income for housing. The federal government barely addresses their needs; it serves mainly renters, while most elderly own their homes; furthermore, it does not provide subsidies for the wide array of housing assistance required by the elderly.

Quality of Life and Quality of Housing

For older Americans quality of life is intertwined with quality of housing. As the U.S. Senate Special Committee on Aging (1965) pointed out:

147

Housing and its immediate physical surroundings influence well-being and the quality of life of people in any age group, but suitable housing is doubly important to the retired person whose home is the center of virtually all of his activities. Few factors have as much potential for promoting the well-being of the elderly as housing of appropriate size which offers safety, comfort, and the opportunity of choice between privacy and contact with the community.

In their older years physical disabilities, lack of energy, and lack of transportation limit the elderly's movement outside the home. I found that a third of the surveyed elderly renters do not get out daily (Huttman, 1977). Many over 65 spend at least half their time in their domestic environment (Hansen in Montgomery, 1977). With shrunken financial resources and decreased energy, many older people limit the physical space they occupy to the neighborhood grocery store, nearby church, and their own dwelling. For some frail aged, life space is reduced to the housing unit, to a single room, or—eventually—to a bed. Therefore, the quality of their housing environment becomes increasingly important in the lives of many elderly.

Independence and Social Esteem

Having a private house or decent apartment also gives one status and a feeling of self-esteem at a stage of life when many other sources for such self-esteem, such as a job, no longer exist. The dwelling symbolizes the self to the outside world. This image contributes to a person's sense of social identity. Furthermore, an elderly person living independently in his own home reaffirms his competency and makes the implicit statement that he is not dependent on others for his personal needs. The elderly's housing units represent places where they still exercise social control. This is personal territory—and for many old people it is the only place where they still have some control over their world and can arrange it to suit their individual needs and tastes. Most elderly achieve their wish to live independently. Only a few live with their adult children—and these are mainly either the ill or very old widows. Only 18 percent of elderly women and 7 percent of elderly men age 75 and over live with relatives (Soldo, 1980).

Familiar Surroundings

Most elderly not only do not want to live with relatives, but they do not like to move from their long-time residences. Relatively few move during their retirement years; in fact, given the choice, most aged—especially homeowners—prefer to remain as long as possible in their own home in the neighborhood where they have developed familiar ties (Regnier and Byerts, 1983). They treasure this dwelling as familiar ground, the site of past happinesses, and a valuable repository of various experiences. Intimate knowledge of a familiar area also provides a large measure of support in daily activities for the aged person, who often has difficulty adjusting to new environments and new ways of doing things.

These, by the way, are some of the reasons why many older people remain in central-city locations, even though a majority of the area's population may have changed to a different racial-ethnic background from their own. The elderly also do not move because they have little energy to pack up their lifetime belongings, sell a house, locate another one, buy it, and then move. In 1976 one in three elderly owner-occupants had lived in their current residences for 25 or more years (Huttman, 1977).

Housing Conditions

At a time in life when housing is particularly significant, many elderly find theirs inadequate. Too often, elderly people live in deteriorating dwellings in rundown inner-city neighborhoods, or in poor rural areas. Many of these homes are substandard. Housing for rural, minority, and poor elderly is particularly bad. One example of the worst housing for the elderly is the transient hotel or boardinghouse in the inner city. In recent years, some elderly do not even have shelter in transient hotels, but wander through city streets without a home, sleeping in public places. Finally, even though housing is often inadequate, the elderly pay a greater proportion of their income for housing than other groups in the population. Their income has steadily diminished as housing costs, particularly in cities, have increased.

Most elderly—about three-fourths—own their own homes (Soldo, 1980). In fact, they represent a fifth of all homeowners. While elderly couples are much more likely to own homes than those who are single, a third of all elderly owners *are* single, and their number has been increasing in the last decade.

The housing owned by elderly is likely to consist of older units, half of them built before 1939. Fewer than 5 percent were built after 1970. The unit may be a big old farmhouse or small-town rambling home, a rural shack or a mobile home, an inner-city house or a suburban home. Many of these are too large for their owners: overcrowding is hardly a problem. In fact, a number of elderly close off some rooms, especially in the winter. The 1974 *Annual Housing Survey* reports that three out of five elderly single homeowners had more than five rooms. Welfeld and Struyk (1978), using that data and later information from the 1977 *Annual Housing Survey*, estimate that 31 percent have one or more rooms without heat—not surprising considering the generally large house sizes involved. They also report that a third of those surveyed said they had no central heating; 59 percent had no air conditioning (1977).

Lawton (1978), using data from the 1975 *Annual Housing Survey* on 25 housing deficiencies, finds that over a third of the elderly surveyed indicated they had housing problems. The elderly, more often than the nonelderly, lacked complete plumbing (1977), even though this proportion was only 3.28 percent (Welfeld and Struyk, 1978). In general, few elderly lacked complete kitchens, and few (2.04 percent) felt they had serious maintenance problems.

Certain groups of elderly—such as the rural and minority elderly, as well as poor elderly (often overlapping categories)—have considerably worse housing than the average. Housing conditions for elderly *renters* in nonmetropolitan areas are especially bad. Fourteen percent in the 1977 *Annual Housing Survey* did not have complete plumbing facilities in their unit. For rural *owners* almost 6 percent lacked these amenities. Around 8 percent of the aged *rural renters* had two or more serious maintenance problems, such as leaking roofs (Welfeld and Struyk, 1978). Elderly in the rural South are more likely to live in deficient housing than those in other parts of the country.

Black renters and owners are both likely to live in units with a high incidence of housing deficiencies. In 1976, 16.5 percent of black single homeowners and 8.8 percent of black husband–wife homeowners lived in units without complete plumbing facilities (Welfeld and Struyk, 1978). Though most elderly had a complete kitchen, a surprising 11.7 percent of black elderly single owners did not. Black *renters* were even worse off; of the single renters, 14 percent did not have complete plumbing and 11 percent did not have a complete kitchen.

Poor elderly, not surprisingly, had many more plumbing, kitchen, and maintenance deficiencies than those with income twice the poverty level (Welfeld and Struyk, 1978). About a tenth of single owners living below the poverty level had incomplete plumbing facilities; for elderly poor renters, this incidence was somewhat higher (Newman and Struyk, 1984).

Transient Hotels and Boardinghouses

Most elderly live in either single-family dwellings or private apartments; some live in the specially designed apartments discussed in the next chapter, and a small proportion in convalescent homes or other institutions. However, some—especially single men—may turn to the transient hotel or boardinghouse as a cheap solution. These hotels serve some of the most desolate of our aged. We must realize that isolated and psychologically disturbed people do grow old and will be likely to constitute some of the clientele of transient hotels. Many are alcoholics or mentally ill but, even in a skid row, many are simply old single men or women with no place else to go.

The rundown transient hotel, often lacking a bath or even a toilet in the room, while cheap, is far from desirable (Erikson and Eckert, 1977). Fires are common, and conditions are often substandard. For example, in San Francisco a group of elderly tenants in such a hotel complained about "sub-human and atrocious living conditions." One disabled tenant said, "I can't take it any more. . . . There's never any heat in the building, the toilets never work, the lights are always burned out, the bathrooms are dirty and the hot water goes out at least two or three days a week" ("Tenderloin Hotel Tenants," 1982). This tenant and two other elderly residents were withholding nearly a year's rent to protest the owner's failure to make needed repairs. In this particular case the city is negotiating a remodeling loan in order to take over and renovate this and three other slum hotels for elderly, disabled, and low-income renters.

Landlords themselves are often unwilling to do much renovating. Loether (1975) describes this situation in relation to boarding houses. These differ from hotels in that they often started out as single-family homes; these big old houses deteriorated with age and are now located in slum areas. Frequently, landlords rent these units at very modest prices during the area's transitional period. Rather than renovating the building, the owner simply rents the rooms as they are, often to the elderly, for whatever he can get; he holds on to the property until there is more demand for the area, whereupon he sells the property for its land value and realizes a handsome profit.

Some elderly are literally homeless. They include the "bag women," who carry their belongings about in one or more bags, or old men with knapsacks and bedroll—sometimes without even that much, just the clothes on their backs. While some are alcoholics, many are not. They sleep in public places such as bus and railroad stations or in any other type of shelter available to them. As Neuhaus and Neuhaus (1982) point out: "Increasing numbers of the urban poor are old people who live in barely minimal conditions: park benches, train and bus stations, or who drift from shelter to shelter with no established residence and no place to lay their heads."

Income Versus Housing Expenses

Elderly live in poor housing accomodations because their low income makes it impossible to pay the current rents for something better. For example, in most major East Coast cities in 1983 the median apartment rent was over $300 a month, while many single elderly had a *total* income of around $400–450 a month. Thus, for elderly renters, the rent–income ratio is often very disfavorable. Today many elderly renters pay more than 35 percent of their income for rent. This is, by all accounts, excessive; in fact some would argue that out of their low incomes even 25 percent is too much. Yet Welfeld and Struyk (1978), using the 1976 Bureau of Labor Statistics for three budget levels, find that on the average for each budget level the aged group paid around 35 percent of its income for housing. Forty-three percent of the single elderly and more than half of female single renters paid over 35 percent (*Annual Housing Survey*, 1974, in Welfeld and Struyk, 1978). Even rural elderly, who supposedly have cheaper rents, were no better off.

The elderly who suffer the most, of course, are the poor. Welfeld and Struyk's (1978) data indicate 41 percent of those elderly below the poverty level use almost half their income for housing and over a fifth of these poor use 60 percent of their income for housing. This problem is definitely due to low income, for in general, the elderly pay lower rent than their nonelderly counterparts. However, in the current rental housing shortage their rents are likely to go even higher. America's pattern of household formation, including an increase in elderly households, and the sharp decrease in construction of new rental apartments, are likely to make this scarcity more severe.

The housing expense burden for homeowners is harder to calculate. Many elderly homeowners (at least 84 percent in 1974) have paid off their mortgages. Even then, however, they must bear substantial expenses for maintenance, property taxes, insurance, and utilities. Fuel oil, gas, electricity, the reshingling of roofs, and insurance are going up in price. Property taxes, even with special provisions for the elderly, are still a heavy burden. These costs, taken together, may easily exceed $300 to $400 a month. Thus, while Welfeld and Struyk (1978), using the 1975 *Annual Housing Survey*, find most homeowners without mortgages do not pay over 35 percent of their incomes for housing expenses, most are close to it. And those elderly who still have mortgages are considerably worse off: almost a third pay more than 35 percent of income for housing expenses.

The irony of this situation for homeowners is that their home has increased in value over recent years. Because it is likely to be in rural or central-city areas and is usually older housing, it may not be as valuable as most other real estate, but since it is mortgage-free for the most part, it is a considerable *nonliquid* asset for the elderly. The problem is that without selling the property itself, it is hard to get the money together needed to pay for its proper maintenance.

In sum, the housing situation of the elderly is far from ideal. One out of every five of our nation's elderly citizens lives in housing inappropriate to his or her needs—too big, too expensive, or too much work to care for (Brody, 1978). And income problems are a major stumbling block to improving the situation. Located in deteriorating neighborhoods, with special needs resulting from decreased mobility, and with income loss, the elderly are at a severe disadvantage in the housing market (Brown and O'Day, 1981).

A major need for the elderly is to reduce housing costs without leaving their own homes. As I stated above, most want to live in familiar surroundings and find it too stressful and expensive to move, although ideally they need a newer unit, one that is accessible and easy to maintain. They also need secure and safe housing in a desirable area near facilities and transportation services.

Programs

Programs for Homeowners

For the majority of the elderly population who do not wish to move from their owner-occupied units, the question is how to help them pay their bills and make the home fit the needs of their older years. Welfeld and Struyk (1978) and Lawton (1978) both believe HUD has emphasized programs for elderly renters and has done too little for this large group of homeowners. Stressing that HUD's programs are misconceived, Welfeld and Struyk (1978) state:

> HUD's current approach to the housing needs of the elderly is inappropriate for large numbers of elderly households. By HUD's reckoning, two-thirds of elderly homeowners—over 6 million elderly households—have low income. . . . Some HUD programs have been geared to ownership, but they have been ill-suited to older households. . . . No present program assists the elderly to move into accommodation suited more to their needs and retain their ownership status. . . . There is also no present program that assists the elderly to remain in an old house and maintain it in a good state of repair.

Although HUD has allocated little money for homeowners, some programs have emerged that are funded by the state or selective local use of city general block grants.

Property Tax Exemption

Many states reduce property taxes for low-income elderly homeowners. Since the average homeowner (1977) nationwide paid a tenth of her income for property taxes and the very-low-income elderly pay a much greater proportion, this abatement is most helpful.

Most states have some type of property tax relief program. An Abt Associates (1975) survey reports that by the end of 1974, 48 states and the District of Columbia had authorized 83 different programs. Most of them are primarily for the elderly. While many receive help, the payments are usually low. An example of such property tax relief is California's homeowner assistance for those who are 62 and over, blind, or otherwise disabled. (In 1981 this was for homeowners who earned less than $12,000.) Assistance is based on the tax paid on the first $34,000 of the home's assessed fair market value and can be as high as 96 percent of this amount. However, since California homes often have assessed values of $80,000 and over, this definitely covers only a small part of the whole tax for many beneficiaries.

Tax Postponement

Another source of help to owners is the postponement of property taxes until sale of the property or until death. In California this program is for seniors 62 and over who had adjusted gross incomes of $33,600 or less in 1981 and at least 20 percent equity in the property. When the elderly owner files for postponement, the state enters a lien on the property in an amount equal to the postponed taxes; 7 percent annual interest is added to the lien. Neither the lien nor the interest fall due until the home is either sold or the owner dies, leaving behind no spouse who continues to live there. While this opportunity to postpone property taxes seems especially appealing—it can raise the California elderly homeowner's annual income by $1,000 or more—many do not want a lien on their home. They want to leave it to their children free of debt when they die.

Reverse Annuity Mortgage

The elderly can get liquid funds out of the equity on their homes through another innovation—and this without selling them. The increase in housing prices in the late 1970s may have made a home worth $80,000–$150,000 or more in urban areas. Many of these owners are thus house-rich but income-poor. There were almost one million elderly homeowners with incomes of only $5,000–$9,000 in 1976; another large group (especially single owners) had even lower incomes. These low-income owners would usually have to sell their home if they wanted to realize any income from it. As Gutowski (1978) reports, they are often reluctant to take on the burden of a second mortgage, much less take the more dramatic step of selling.

The Reverse Annuity Mortgage (RAM) enables the elderly to realize some income from their home without selling. This plan, by loaning the elderly some of their own equity, allows them to utilize part of the appreciation in value of their property (Weinrobe, 1983). These home-equity conversion plans provide additional income (a type of annuity) to senior homeowners while allowing them to stay in their own home. Such programs have been encouraged nationally. The Federal Home Loan Bank Board now permits member institutions to provide such loans on a fixed-term annuity basis.

Many RAMs have a *fixed-term contract*, whereby the homeowner receives payments for only ten, or even for only five years. The homeowner may pay interest on the loan and then begin repaying the principal at the end of the five or ten years. He usually has 25 to 30 years to repay; the house is collateral against this mortgage. An example of the RAM with a fixed-term contract would be a $20,000 ten-year annuity loan on a $30,000 house at 8 percent interest, taken out by a 65-year-old homeowner. The mortgage is for 30 years. The borrower receives $177 per month for ten years. At age 75 the homeowner must start to repay at the rate of $146 a month. If the owner dies before completing his payments, the rest of the money must be repaid from the sale of the house.

The problem with this type of RAM is that after the five or ten years, the period set for the loan, the elderly are required to produce cash to start repaying the loan; otherwise they most likely have to sell the property. Since the household is then again thrown back on its own resources, few lower-income homeowners utilize the program (Welfeld and Struyk, 1978).

An alternative type of RAM allows the owner to draw on the equity of the house through level monthly payments. Lawton (1978) says that in such a housing annuity program (reverse mortgage), a purchase price for the elderly person's home is determined and on an actuarial basis an annuity is established that serves as an income supplement to the owner. This is a true annuity. It is calculated like an insurance policy annuity. The advantage here is that no loan repayments are required until the owner disposes of the property, dies, or the debt exceeds the value of the property.

Either of these plans allows the elderly to stay in their own home for more years than might otherwise be possible by giving them more money for maintenance work and living expenses. However, the annuity amount—especially in the later years of the loan, when inflation has devalued it—may not be great enough to allow much repair work.

To date elderly homeowners have not been eager to use RAMs. This is especially true of the fixed-term contract type. The San Francisco Foundation RAM program had under 50 takers in the first three years of operation. As Lawton (1978) points out:

> While the [house annuity] plan was judged feasible from an economic standpoint, questions have been raised as to whether older people would feel a strong psychological investment in the unemcumbered possession of the deed, and would be unwilling to give up the idea of passing along the property to their children.

All the programs I have discussed in this segment have certain features that affect utilization. The property tax exemption and the tax postponement programs are for low-income homeowners. Many states keep the number of users down by not fully adjusting the income maximum to cost-of-living increases. Thus the number of homeowners that qualify drops as inflation rises. Then too, for these very low income homeowners, the tax exemption or postponement does not provide enough monetary assistance to really help them: the spiraling cost of utilities and repairs is so high that even with these programs giving them tax exemption or postponement, they cannot afford to keep their homes. In addition, many low-income homeowners do not know the details of programs, especially RAM. In many cases the takers are those of middle-class backgrounds, even though they now have low incomes; these are the sort of people who are educated and motivated enough to participate. Even these elderly—better able than the usual working-class elderly person to fill out complex forms and understand their complicated provisions—do not often take advantage of the reverse mortgages because they worry about their ability to pay off a mortgage when the five- or ten-year period is up. They fear the possible loss of their home and consequent lack of a place to live. Again, they are reluctant to take out liens on the home they want to leave to their children. Thus, while these RAM programs sound very sensible, they have not been much of a success. We need to revise the program to decrease the barriers which inhibit their use.

The programs have generated enough publicity about unusable equity in one's home that both elderly and policymakers, made aware of the problem, may come up with more workable ways to handle equity. For example, the new tax provision allowing adult children to rent to their relatives while still taking the usual landlord deductions encourages the elderly to sell their homes to their children, or the latter to build a unit for their parents to live in.

Program Assistance for Maintenance and Repairs

Elderly homeowners often need assistance in paying for repairs and maintenance to their home. They live in older homes that were suitable when the children were at home, but they continue to live alone in this home, even when it is much in need of repair. The old person is often unable to provide for the required upkeep, maintenance and care. As described earlier, the elderly—especially the rural, black, and poor elderly—are likely to suffer from a number of housing deficiencies, and they are not happy about this situation. Those elderly who had serious physical housing defects in the 1974 *Annual Housing Survey* expressed the least satisfaction with their housing (Struyk and Devine, 1977). Yet dissatisfaction does not necessarily lead to action. The same survey found they were less likely to have the repairs done than the nonelderly, even though their homes were older and in poorer condition. Only 31 percent of the elderly, compared to almost half of all owners, had completed repairs in the previous year—and fewer expected to do so in the coming year. The elderly least likely to make repairs themselves were the older singles, those with mobility limitations, and those with low income (Struyk and Devine, 1977).

A major reason for lack of maintenance, of course, is high costs, which mean that, due to the low income position of many elderly homeowners, they are forced to forego necessary maintenance and grossly reduce discretionary improvements (Lawton, 1978). While they cannot afford to pay for repairs, many elderly are unable to perform them themselves due to poor health. Widows often know little about home maintenance, and cannot make minor repairs, do yardwork, or shovel snow (Struyk and Devine, 1977). They may unknowingly neglect routine maintenance procedures. Furthermore, widows may be especially easy targets for consumer fraud.

Because of all these factors, even middle-income elderly need assistance with repairs. As Welfeld and Struyk (1978) put it:

> The nearly half-million houses with multiple structural deficiencies occupied by the elderly represent evidence of an unmet need. Unfortunately, detailed studies of maintenance and repair activities by elderly homeowners indicate that increases in income do not necessarily bring corresponding increases in such activity. Complicating the matter even further is a discrepancy in homeowners' and housing experts' perception of what is a serious deficiency. When a deficiency is not perceived, it will not be corrected.

Given maintenance assistance, however, the elderly would be able to stay in their own homes, improve the existing housing stock, stop abandonment of housing, and contribute to upgrading their neighborhoods.

TYPES OF REPAIRS AND MAINTENANCE

The house may have a leaky roof, an old and inefficient furnace, or peeling paint. It may need weatherization, or help may be needed with routine maintenance tasks, such as shoveling snow and fixing minor appliance breakdowns. Different programs may be needed to meet this variety of repair and maintenance needs. Because there is virtually always some maintenance work to do, help is needed on a continuing, stable basis: it is thus different from the one-shot major repair or renovation–remodeling job.

However, minor renovations are also needed if their old houses are to continue meeting elderly owners' needs. Such houses may have been suitable when they were younger or more energetic, but they may now lack the good design characteristics prescribed for housing for the elderly. Renovation is needed, such as the installation of grab rails to avoid accidents. The bathroom may need to be changed to make nighttime visits safer. Putting in noncombustible floor material and other such improvements can increase fire safety. A program may be needed to provide battery-operated smoke detectors, check for faulty wiring, or make security modifications to prevent crime.

Major rehabilitation may be needed to bring a deteriorated building up to local housing code standards and to halt blight and abandonment of housing in the neighborhood. In deteriorated urban areas with a large proportion of older houses, there are often code enforcement programs or neighborhood conservation programs. These major rehabilitation programs, often semicompulsory, coordinate all activities associated with upgrading a whole neighborhood, including helping to determine the scope of the work owners need done, obtaining financing, and contracting for the work itself. Funds may come from Section 315 of the Housing Act, community block grant funds, city programs backed by the sale of bonds, or the Farmers Home Loan Administration.

The elderly, however, do not usually have much interest in neighborhood conservation and rehabilitation programs. They are often reluctant to participate because they do not want to take out loans, not even at low interest. They want to leave their homes unencumbered by debt for their heirs. For example, when the San Francisco Bay Area Association of Governments (ABAG) attempted to rehabilitate an area of El Cerrito, California, the elderly were very slow to take part in this low-interest loan improvement program, even when the special arrangements with the local bank were explained to them and every effort was made to encourage them.

This particular program is characteristic of the advocacy model (Steinfeld, 1979), in which human service workers encourage residents in a small local area to rehabilitate and maintain their units. In such programs these workers provide the close and continuing client contact necessary for maintenance programs, as well as often providing quick emergency services. Steinfeld (1979) also includes self-help programs in the advocacy model. He says: "The grass roots approach is particularly appropriate for developing self-help competencies and education efforts in such areas as fire safety, accident prevention and security."

These advocacy programs can clearly benefit the elderly. In major *rehabilitation* programs the opposite often happens: the elderly are victims of rehabilitation because they are forced to leave their longtime apartment or home. This often means they have to find another home (Borup et al., 1979). If they can later move back, they will usually have to pay a higher rent. Elderly are also often the victims of *urban renewal* programs: if they live in the older, deteriorating neighborhoods, their homes are frequently scheduled for demolition to make way for "progress." Relocation officers in redevelopment agencies, as I (1981) show, spend a large part of their time with the elderly: because of their limited resources they are likely to have great difficulty finding other suitable housing.

EMERGENCY REPAIRS

The elderly, especially widowed women, may lack both the ability and the energy to make even stopgap repairs in emergencies—such as plumbing breakdown, utility shutoff, heating or hot water cutoff, or severe roof leakage in times of rain or snow. A local service can provide a repair crew that responds quickly to the need before there is major damage to the building or risk to the resident (such as freezing from a heat turnoff); it ought to be a 24-hour service. Emergency repairs should be limited in scope. The problem, as Steinfeld (1979) points out, is to not overtax the service with nonemergency requests, but to refer such requests to other agencies.

EXAMPLES OF REPAIR AND MAINTENANCE PROGRAMS

Many of these are initiated at the local level, with funds from a variety of sources such as federal community block grants, or the OAA's Title III.

As of 1983, the City of San Leonardo, California has a loan program for major repairs and a grant assistance program for minor repairs or maintenance to benefit low-income homeowners. Under the first of these, the homeowners chooses either a 3 percent amortized loan or a 5 percent deferred loan to help pay for a wide variety of repairs. For small emergency repairs or health-and-safety hazards, grants are available. For security the city provides deadlocks for doors and battery-operated smoke detectors. City money is provided to insulate attics or to paint weathered house exteriors. The city also removes debris at reduced costs.

Welfeld and Struyk (1978) report on a Des Moines program focusing on repairs to stem the effects of deferred maintenance, effects such as blight and abandonment. The city's own study showed that abandonment of houses owned by the low-income elderly was likely. Des Moines therefore initiated a project which in the late 1970s gave grants of up to $1,500 to low-income elderly in target areas for emergency repairs of certain code items. Evaluating the program, the city concluded that no participants had abandoned their homes, although one-third of those involved stated that without a grant they probably would have abandoned them within three years.

Welfeld and Struyk (1978) also describe Baltimore's use of the Comprehensive Employment Training Act (CETA). Baltimore hired carpenters and plasterers to work on jobs for very-low-income elderly. Boston encouraged renovation by offering homeowners cash rebates of up to one-half of the cost of improvements, technical assistance, and an exemption from property tax reassessment. A number of cities have set up minor repair programs (e.g., Handy Andy, Mr. Fix-it); usually these are financed through state and local grants under Title III of the OAA or through SSBGs under the Social Security Act.

In looking to the future, we can probably expect to see an increase in repair and low-level maintenance programs. As local governments intensify their efforts to retain the elderly in the community and rehabilitate and otherwise improve inner-city areas, there will be even more willingness to provide funds for repairs and maintenance (Liebowitz, 1978). An added reason for cities to do the same is that such programs also provide work for unemployed youth: they can paint the elderly's houses, repair their roofs, and so on. The elderly seem willing to take part in these repair-and-maintenance programs. The main barrier to wider use seems to be income limitations to participation, wherever such restrictions exist.

Rehabilitation programs have more problems. I believe the elderly will continue to resist participation in them. Their high cost, inability to find appropriate contractors, and the need to refinance or take out a loan to undertake rehabilitation—all are serious barriers for homeowners in old age.

WEATHERIZATION

Elderly people have a major need for thermal comfort—but they often lack the wherewithall to pay high heating bills. In cold climates weatherization projects, centered on repairs and modifications that affect energy utilization, can be a big help. They stop cold-air infiltration by replacing broken windows, weatherstripping, installing storm windows, insulating attics or walls, servicing the heating system—or even sealing off the underutilized part of a large house. In rural areas weatherization programs should also focus on mobile homes: their occupants must not only be protected against overturning in high winds, but—more commonly—from the very high heat losses that characterize these structures (Collin, 1979; Steinfeld, 1979). Funds for weatherization come from the Department of Energy, which has provided grants since 1977 (usually through state agencies) to weatherize the homes of low-income persons, particularly the elderly and the handicapped in this category.

Alternative Housing for the Elderly

A variety of other housing programs help keep elderly people in private units of their own, whether owner-occupied or rental in nature. Included are shared housing, communes, "granny flats," and repair of mobile homes.

Shared Housing

One way to allow the elderly to stay in their own home—or at least in an independent, private unit—is shared housing or senior matching (Mukherjee, 1982). The agency in charge of the program matches owner with renter. The National Council on Aging (NCOA) differentiates between this program—which it calls "senior matching"—and "shared housing," which it defines as what happens when an agency itself purchases and rents a home to seniors who share facilities. The NCOA describes "senior matching" as what happens when a single elderly person invites another single to share housing. This may take the form of a boarder arrangement, whereby an elderly homeowner in a large house takes in a boarder who has kitchen privileges and shares in cooking and meal provision—or it may be that part of the house is converted to small apartments for renters. In most of the pertinent literature, however, "senior matching" is considered a kind of shared housing.

Many organizations working with the elderly, including housing groups, churches, and senior centers, are now actively recruiting them for shared housing under various auspices. For example, Alternative Living for the Aged in Los Angeles in 1983 received state funds to hire housing counselors: they will assist elderly people who presently live alone but want to share housing with other seniors. Widowed persons may find that such sharing decreases loneliness; frail elderly are not alone when emergencies occur. Those who have trouble doing housework or exterior maintenance can share the work In general, those who share housing in this manner can cut back on their costs to a considerable degree.

Pearson (1982) describes, for her shared-housing program, successfully matching a recently widowed 80-year-old in a big house with a young man who had recently moved to the area. He treated her like a mother, becoming heavily involved in household maintenance and in running errands. This type of solution, I fear, will not have much success: elderly owners are likely to worry that their privacy will be sacrificed—or the sharer will have different habits, habits likely to cause friction.

An example of shared housing in which the sponsoring agency buys or leases the unit, then rents it to others, is a program in Plainfield, New Jersey, where the sponsoring group converted a large house into a number of small apartments. The group did this with the help of the New Jersey Department of Community Affairs. However, Lawton (1978), reporting on the program, says it involved important problems: administrative costs, zoning, loan funds—and locating people to undertake this arrangement, either as owners or as renters.

Many shared-housing projects are for the benefit of the frail elderly—those not yet ready for institutionalization, but needing a certain minimal amount of mutual help or supervision. Brody (1978) reports on the Philadelphia Geriatric Center experiment, which made purchases under HUD's Section 236 to remodel older row houses near the center, subdividing them into private bed-sitting rooms with kitchenettes and bath and shared living rooms and entrances. While the intent was to attract the "competent" elderly, those who applied and were chosen tended to be somewhat older, in poor health, and more isolated than the average. Brody (1978) thinks that the project's location near the center was a major security factor. She believes that the experiment had a positive psychological and—social—impact as well as costing relatively little.

When the elderly have to share kitchen and livingroom space, they may hire a housekeeper rather than do the work themselves. In fact, the

National Council on Aging includes in the definition of its "Share-a-home" program that a housekeeper be retained to do cooking and household chores.

I think arrangements in which an agency or group sponsors shared living accommodations will have greater success than arrangements in which an elderly homeowner invites someone to share housing. It almost amounts to an intimate and informal version of congregate housing. As Brody (1978) says of the Philadelphia project, it is likely that groups eager to use this solution will seek it out as they grow older. Barriers—such as those that Lawton (1978) mentioned—may well decrease due to pressures to keep the elderly in the community. The most important thing may now be to be sure that established standards are maintained through regulations and inspections.

Improvement of Boardinghouses and Transient Hotels

Boardinghouses and hotels, if improved, can also provide shared housing. Many single aged persons live in such housing (Erikson and Eckert, 1977). In some cities, charitable institutions have bought such housing and brought it up to a decent standard. Here bathrooms, small kitchenettes, and, of course, the hotel lobby are shared.

The units concerned can also be built as—or converted to—modern rooming houses, so that single men who do not want to cook and do not like—or need—a dining room can be comfortable without excessive cost. Welfeld and Struyk (1978) describe this as a stripped-down accommodation, with substantially lower rent than that paid for regular units. They report that a 13–storey, agency-renovated rooming house in Toronto has single rooms, each with a refrigerator, toilet, and stove. There is no bath in the room itself, but a communal bathroom and shower serves a number of rooms. The building has a laundromat and a small, privately owned supermarket, just off the lobby.

As rents go up and as the number of single elderly men rises along with increased life expectancy, there will be a definite need for more accommodations. A number of existing transient hotels and older tourist hotels, as well as unused hospitals, can be converted to such shelter. Some of the programs for the homeless are beginning to do just this.

Granny Flats and Second-Unit Ordinances

A new idea in housing alternatives for the elderly is the idea of a separate, mobile minihouse, or small mobile home, allowing aged parents to live near their adult children on their children's land. Australia pioneered this concept and called them "granny flats." Here the local housing authority rents units to the old—and removes them when the accommodation is no longer needed. The British have also used this alternative to put the aged near their children. They cluster a few units of council (public) housing for the aged in areas near the parent's children (U.K. Department of Environment, 1976).

However, "granny" units are not always mobile, as is also true of the United States. Many areas will need to redefine zoning laws to allow the provision of these separate granny units, immobile as well as mobile, or permit the addition of a second unit to a single-family dwelling unit. At issue is a small inlaw apartment, usually with a separate entrance. The priority recommendations of the 1981 White House Conference on Aging (Housing Alternatives Committee) were to change local zoning and land-use regulations to allow granny flats, shared housing, and mobile homes.

A number of California towns, encouraged by new state laws, have adopted second-unit ordinances. In some areas, the Gray Panthers and other lobbies are still fighting for second-unit ordinances, which they hope will provide flexible ordinances to allow small-size units. The Gray Panther lobby believes it is possible to have a type of second-unit ordinance that protects the existing neighborhood and avoids misuse by requiring that at least one of the units be owner–occupied. The Gray Panthers believe that the planning commission and design review board can ensure that each unit is compatible with the neighborhood, doesn't encroach on anyone's privacy, and has adequate parking within blanket restrictions against variances. In an article on one Gray Panther project, Xiques (1983) reports that those who are against legalizing second units are usually owners who fear parking problems and a greater traffic flow in their neighborhoods which might change the character. She finds that experience for communities that have adopted second-unit ordinances does not seem to justify this fear: there seems to be minimal neighborhood disruption from the small number of converted units. A Gray Panther leader adds that such ordinances help old people stay in their homes and retain contact with young people—including family members (Xiques, 1983). Future pressure will be great to allow second units due to the high cost of housing and the elderly's income needs.

Mobile Homes

Increasing potential site locations and improving the types of units required makes mobile homes more acceptable to cities and town planning commissions. Mobile homes are popular with moderate-income elderly because they are relatively cheap. Prices for used mobile homes are as low as $27,000, although more than $50,000 is a more frequent figure. Mobile homes are most common in warm states such as Florida and Arizona. They are also a small town and rural phenomenon. Only a third of the mobile homes occupied by the elderly are inside metropolitan areas. The concentration of this new housing is in rural areas—probably resulting in some upgrading in the quality of housing for the rural elderly there in general.

Recent years have witnessed a number of well-designed, neat mobile home parks for "adults only." These are far removed from the common image of the rundown mobile home park. Many have facilities for recreation, pleasant landscaping, a laundry—even a swimming pool, in many cases. The small, tinny structure has largely been replaced by the double-size, bright-looking, house-like structure—often with colorful shutters and awning. Some of the mobile homes now being sold are almost as large and elaborate as houses; they are only marginally more mobile. The adult mobile home park suits many elderly because it provides a community-like, protected environment to persons of the same age—and often of the same economic means. Such homogeneity in a mobile home park community often provides the elderly with security and companionship in addition to low-cost housing. Even the older mobile home parks may fill this function, as Sheila Johnson (1971) reports in her description of elderly residents in a mobile park.

Given its relatively low costs, the mobile home represents inexpensive home-ownership: this is a major reason for federal and state housing agencies to promote it. However, cost estimates are a complicated matter. Depreciation rates for mobile homes are high. Thus the full cost for them is greater than that for conventional homes. At the same time, the low original payment makes the mobile home attractive to those elderly seeking a home for 10–15 years. Weitzman (1976) is somewhat more pessimistic about mobile home living being cheap. Using his data, Welfeld and Struyk (1978) claim that the lower initial cost of the mobile home is offset by site rent, higher financing charges, and higher rates of depreciation. The site rent, which accounts for approximately 30 percent of monthly occupancy cost, is not a factor in areas where the occupant owns the land. But even in a mobile home park, the land cost *should* be cheap because mobile homes occupy little land. This matter deserves further inquiry.

In addition to savings on the initial cost of the unit, the mobile home owner saves furniture costs, since many of the necessary items come with the unit. The mobile home has another advantage for the elderly: a very small yard to maintain; furthermore, its new, efficient interior requires limited housekeeping. Mobile homes, however, do have a number of disadvantages (Collin, 1979). They have a short lifespan—15 years or less—and they may develop a number of structural defects. They may also be improperly installed to begin with. In colder and wetter climates they may suffer from leakage and inadequate insulation.

Furthermore, mobile homes are not really mobile. Moving a "mobile" home to a new location is quite expensive. Mobile home parks are scarce—and some are being closed down. Once installed, 95 percent of all mobile homes never move again, partly because of the difficulty in finding a park that will accept a used mobile home (State of California, *Mobile Home*, 1980). Thus, if one has to move, it is usually necessary to sell the mobile home on site. Mobile park regulations sometimes limit the parks to adults only; this and other regulations discourage prospective buyers. In some states new laws, introduced to make mobile homes more acceptable, also allow trailer park management to refuse to keep older mobile homes i.e., those more than five years old. The difficulty in moving a mobile home may discourage some who wish to spend their 60s—and even their 70s in a mobile home park in a semirural area, but want to move back to an urban area in their 80s in order to be closer to the hospital, shopping facilities, and their children.

Measures are needed to make local authorities more willing to accept mobile home parks. Traditionally they have not looked favorably on mobile home park operators because, reacting in terms of a past stereotype, they see the mobile home park as a blight on the landscape and mobile home-owners as low-income, often undesirable persons. Local officials also dislike mobile home owners because they do not pay local property taxes, only state-imposed personal taxes on their units. For such reasons many towns and cities have zoning laws excluding mobile home parks—or allowing them only in undesirable locations.

Recent laws in a number of states are making mobile homes subject to local property taxes. Another change (in California) is that the state is now requiring cities and counties to allow a person to install his mobile home on his own land, on compatible lots zoned for single-family dwellings; the structure is subject to all the same development standards to which a single-family dwelling on the same lot would be subject. Of course, in rural areas mobile homes have often been put on private lots. It appears, then, that the situation is improving for mobile homes. Over 3 percent of the country's elderly in 1976 lived in mobile homes; Welfeld and Struyk (1978) estimate that the figure will be 8 percent by the year 2000.

While there are problems because of the lack of a clearly specified service role for management, anecdotal evidence indicates that "age-segregated, carefully planned, relatively high-cost trailer parks in a mild climate are an entirely acceptable living environment for the healthy older person" (Lawton and Byerts, 1977).

Section Eight Rental Housing

A HUD-subsidized housing allowance program for rental housing, usually administered through local housing authorities, Section Eight subsidies make up the difference between the rent and a certain percentage (now 30 percent) of the household income. The would-be recipient is means-tested for eligibility; if she qualifies, she obtains a certificate and then looks for a standard unit (as defined by the program) within the range allowable for rent in her category. The successful applicant can usually stay in her present rental, as most elderly recipients do. This program has been used heavily by the elderly, including those in specially designed housing under HUD's Section 202 (called 202/8).

The problem at present is that the Reagan administration (1984) is phasing the program out. It may replace it with a similar housing voucher program, but this will only work if higher rents are allowed than under Section Eight. Such a program has the advantage of keeping the elderly in a private unit, often their own.

Thus it is to be hoped that some kind of housing allowance—whether Section Eight or a similar voucher program—will be kept: it is a major way to help elderly renters meet high and increasing rental costs when their income is low. It may be that the program will be simply redesigned; it could even include homeowners, for example. At present, the low-level income maximum for this means-tested Section Eight program inhibits use by a large number of elderly who are slightly above this maximum. However, if the maximum is raised, fund allocations must also be raised, for there are already long waiting lists in many cities which boast high rents and few housing vacancies. Another desirable change would be more aggressive role played by housing departments in hunting for a unit, negotiating the case, and checking up on compliance with housing standards. Elderly have trouble doing all these things, yet the present program requires them to do so. Many do not participate in the program simply because their limited mobility and energy make it hard to hunt for an apartment; furthermore, their ignorance of landlord–tenant arrangements makes it hard for them to negotiate a lease, as I (1977) found in studying elderly interested in the HUD housing allowance experiment. Section Eight should return to the arrangement under Section 23, the former housing allowance program, which required the housing authority to do these jobs.

Conclusion

The existing trends indicate that some sort of housing allowance will continue into the future. It is also likely that the homeless and renters who are both poor and single will get *more* help: remodeled transient hotels, hostels, or other simple accommodations. Elderly owners will make all sorts of adjustments in order to remain in their own homes, including subdividing their home and renting out the second unit, sharing housing or taking a second mortgage or even a RAM—although the first solution seems much more likely than the others. These elderly may make inventive special arrangements with their grown children to exchange ownership of the home while allowing the parents its continued use. Some elderly are likely to sell their present home in order to buy a mobile home or move to smaller quarters. And of course, as they move into their 80s they are likely to sell their former residence in order to live in congregate or specially designed apartment units, although waiting lists may inhibit their ability to do this. The continual growth of the old-old population leads us to expect a variety of different housing arrangements by the elderly and their families.

CHAPTER 9

Specially Designed Housing for the Elderly

It is, in general, a worthwhile goal to enable the elderly to live in their own homes as long as this is safe and practical. Nevertheless, many of the would-be beneficiaries reach a stage in their late 70s which makes it more humane and sensible to explore the availability of housing designed specifically for the aged.

Specially designed housing, which typically includes a variety of supportive services, can help old people compensate for their decline in physical mobility and can better deal with the special health problems associated with advanced age. Inherent in the concept of "satisfactory" housing is a living arrangement that provides accessibility to desired services and contributes to a sense of well-being and satisfaction; for some frail elderly specially designed housing does just this.

It was this point which I wanted to make in calling my early book on housing for the elderly *Beyond Shelter* (Audain and Huttman, 1973). Audain and I showed that elderly living in specially designed developments were satisfied with this environment. We also reported that more of such housing was called for.

That there is a great need for special housing, including appropriate services, is pointed out by Donahue et al. (1977), who declare that in the United States:

> It has been amply demonstrated that there is a need for specially designed housing with a variety of associated services for scores, if not hundreds of thousands of older people who must now live under growing apprehension of

having too soon to seek refuge in long-term medical care facilities as they progress through the later years of their lives. These are the impaired but not ill, noninstitutionalized, often low-income older people who must struggle against rising odds to maintain themselves in the community.

Types of Special Housing

The services provided in special housing vary. There are three main types of specially designed housing for the elderly. First, there are the various types of apartment complexes, including public housing projects for the elderly and nonprofit and even privately owned housing complexes. Such apartment developments provide a varying number of services and facilities; however, the tenants usually do their own cooking and housekeeping. A second type, for the more frail elderly, is the *congregate* development where staff takes care of meals, heavy housekeeping, and numerous other personal and recreational services. Limited health services and an infirmary are often available. Residents usually live in hotel-type rooms; in many cases they share them with other residents. Such rooms, except in luxury developments, usually lack kitchen facilities. The International Center for Social Gerontology describes congregate housing, Carp (1975) reports, as "assisting impaired, but not ill, elderly tenants to maintain or return to a semi-independent lifestyle and avoid institutionalization as they grow older."

Some developments are hard to classify as belonging to either the congregate or apartment type because they combine the two: that is, they provide meals, houskeeping services, and even limited health services, but residents live in apartments with full kitchens rather than in hotel-type rooms. This is true of the luxury "life care arrangements" that one buys into for life. In some developments, both in North America and Europe, there is a congregate wing and an apartment wing.

A third type of special housing is the retirement community planned and built specifically for the elderly: Leisure Worlds in California are good examples of this. Instead of an apartment or congregate building, there is an age-segregated community, often isolated in a rural area. Residents either buy apartments or free-standing homes. A variety of services—with emphasis on recreation—is offered in this adults-only community for the middle class.

As the 1972 U.S. Senate Special Committee on Aging emphasized, all these types of developments fit a special concept of housing:

> It is essential to point out at the start that housing for the elderly is a very special concept—one that should relate to every aspect of living. To the elderly person in search of better shelter, the question of "bricks and mortar" is secondary to the question of total living environment. The number of supportive services available is as vital as the convenience of the location. The atmo-

sphere of activity and interchange is more important than square footage or closet space.

By filling the gap between independent living in one's own home and complete medical care in a nursing home, such housing arrangements, especially congregate living, avert premature removal to an institution (Newcomer and Frise, 1979; Lawton et al., 1980). Carp (1977a), in her restudy of a Texas elderly public housing complex, reports a lower level of institutionalization and a lower death rate for this population than for a comparison group not in specially designed housing. She concludes that better housing increased both length of life and the quality of those extra years.

Congregate housing, as a more supportive environment than apartments, has been especially recommended for deferring institutionalization; a move to it from even specially designed apartments may be the best course to prevent transfer to a nursing home (Chellis et al., 1982; Byerts, 1982). As one public housing director interviewed by Donahue et al., (1977) said, "Every year, a large number of our tenants must leave our elderly housing projects and go into nursing homes. . . . I am convinced that if we had a congregate housing project under management, we could extend the number of years of independent living for our elderly tenants."

Provisions for the Needs of the Elderly

Whatever their type, these special housing developments fill a number of needs. They eliminate some problems, such as maintenance, that are barriers to continual independent or semi-independent living. In specially designed housing the aged are freed completely of outside—and most inside—maintenance. To varying degrees they are freed of even minimal cleaning. In our (Audain and Huttman, 1973) survey of Canada's specially designed housing, the second-most-often mentioned reason for coming to the development was "to get away from maintenance problems." Moving to such housing, of course, means living in a smaller unit, one that is probably easier to maintain. Specially designed housing meets the desire for a modern, efficient home. Most elderly have lived many years of their lives in old and deteriorating units. Women especially welcome an easy-to-clean, modern place to live. In our Canadian study (Audain and Huttman, 1973) many of the elderly we interviewed said the main reason they had moved to the housing development was to have "comfortable modern housing."

Such housing developments also meet the need for different types of security—security from crime, such as burglary or even a violent attack in one's own home. The developments under discussion often have staff in their lobbies, assigned to watch out for suspicious persons. Another type of security provided in times of emergency deals with sudden illness or accidents: staff, other residents, and perhaps even (in congregate housing) medical help can be found on the premises (Lawton, 1980, 1982). These developments fill vital needs for inexpensive housing: this is possible only because public housing and many nonprofit projects are subsidized by a government program, so that their rent is below market value (see pp. 184–185). In our Canadian study (Audain and Huttman, 1973) the most frequent reason for moving to the development was this need for cheap rent. The move not only guarantees a subsidized rent but, for homeowners, it means the end of many house expenses, such as those for insurance, heating, and repairs. More important, it allows them to sell their houses and live on the proceeds.

Above all, these housing developments ease physical tasks for frail elderly who have energy limitations and mobility problems. They cater to those who can no longer climb stairs, easily walk down a long corridor, or open heavy doors. They provide elevators, grab rails in corridors, ramps, and other special design features for the semiambulatory. The apartments themselves are designed with a view to the physical limitations of their users. They are efficiently organized, have low shelves, unique bathroom features, and special stoves ("Architectural Design," 1981).

Services, Facilities, and Staffing in Specially Designed Housing

The major attraction of specially designed housing complexes for the elderly is that they offer a variety of services, a number of useful facilities, special design features, and, in many cases on-site staff. Congregate housing, more often than apartments, has meal service, housekeeping service—and recreational and sometimes even medical services. Congregate housing usually includes a dining room and recreation rooms—such as a library, television room, or an arts-and-crafts room. It may have offices for medical and social workers, a small kitchen on each floor, physical and occupational therapy rooms, an infirmary, and sometimes a chapel and/or swimming pool (Chellis et al., 1982).

Apartment complexes, especially public housing and Section 202 apartments, are often more limited in their facilities. Public housing developments for the elderly usually have a communal room and possibly an adjacent kitchen, an office, and a reception area in the lobby. A varying number of services are brought in from the community. These complexes, like the congregate type, generally have a laundromat and adjacent sitting area.

Some nonprofit apartment developments go far beyond this: they have most of the facilities mentioned for congregate developments. Some have a dining area where a midday meal is served by an outside agency or by volunteers. This is true of Satellite Central, an apartment complex funded by Section 236 with rent supplements (see p. 180). Satellite Central serves two meals a day on weekdays; these are provided by staff, with outside funding. The Oakland project, with 151 studio and one-room apartments, has extensive facilities, including a library, a large activities room, and an arts-and-crafts room which is also used for special clinics. The lobby acts as a small lounge. There is also a tenth-floor sitting area, an outside roof garden, and a ground-floor patio. Many services and activities are provided by the community for residents and often for the neighborhood. In an earlier book I described this situation (1976):

> Satellite Central has a variety of activities going on in its facilities. It serves as the meeting place or center for a number of community activities. Tours for Oakland seniors, run by the city Recreation Department, also operate out of the development. The recreation coordinator for the development, paid by the Recreation Department and school district, spends considerable time there. . . .
>
> A wide variety of classes and programs are held in the development. On almost every weekday afternoon and some evenings there are classes: such as ceramics, weaving, painting, crochet, creative writing, English lip reading, history, religions of the world, dress-making. The instructors come from different educational and recreational resources in the area, including the local junior college adult education program. There are bingos weekly, bridge games, and such.
>
> Special events include a monthly birthday dinner party, holiday parties, and movies. The development's Tenant Association holds a monthly meeting, at which time there is a special event arranged by residents of a particular floor of the development. The development's central location means easy access to city as well as to religious services. (Huttman, 1977)

Many other apartment complexes, especially those designed for the middle-class elderly, include the life-care facilities described below. When a congregate wing and an apartment segment are combined—as in subsidized Canadian housing developments and some Dutch subsidized housing developments—a number of facilities and services in the congregate part are available for use by residents of the apartment wing (Huttman, 1982).

Retirement communities are, of course, even more likely to have such facilities and services, as described for Rossmoor–Leisure World.

Types of Services and Sources of Provision

Recreational and educational programs are a natural adjunct for most developments. For public housing and for subsidized, nonprofit complexes such services are often provided by outside groups, including voluntary organizations affiliated with the complex. The tenant association is usually organized by the development or headquarters staff; it may offer special events and parties. In addition, midday meals service may be available: funding may come from AOA monies (see Chapter 3) with neighborhood elderly encouraged to use the program as well.

Social contact services—such as a buddy system, whether by elderly residents joined in pairs to look after each other, or by floor contact persons (alert elderly) who check on the health and needs of the frail elderly on their floors—are usually initated by the development's staff, by the public housing authority, or by the tenant association itself.

Information and referral services may also be provided by either on-site staff, an AAA or, for public housing by the city's general housing authority staff, usually called community services staff.

TRANSPORTATION

Many developments have a minibus that takes residents to local shopping centers, medical appointments, to church, or to various special events. In some cases volunteer drivers provide this service; in others, community organizations provide transportation to certain services. The location of the development influences the need for transportation services: they are a true necessity for outer-area locations.

MEDICAL SERVICES

More of a problem is involved when it comes to the question of the degree to which the development should supply medical services. Most provide at least weekly or monthly visits from certain medical personnel, such as public health nurses, podiatrists, and physicians. Some—especially if they are congregate or luxury housing complexes—go far beyond this: they have staff nurses or even part-time doctors. They often have an infirmary where residents can stay in cases of minor illness, after return from a hospital, or in an emergency. Some retirement communities have a complete medical clinic, and if they are life-care facilities, they may even have a permanent nursing home.

Lawton and Byerts (1977) discuss the difficulties involved in centering medical services in the development itself:

> Medical care is a somewhat different proposition [than other community services being centered in the housing project]. Economic factors, state licensing regulations, and the aversion of some tenants to the sight of relatively sick people in the housing have caused most housing to avoid imbedding any medical care into the service package. Research shows, however, that tenant need is very strong for a doctor's office on the site, with regular hours by physician and nurse. Housing combined with a physically separate, long-term care facility has been successful in other situations, though infrequently for moderate cost.

Community Versus Development Provision

Should a complex depend on local community agencies for the most part—
or should the development provide the services itself? Utilization of community agencies is the path usually taken by public housing authorities. This is
obviously the least expensive course. However, there are a number of drawbacks. First, there may not be community agencies available to provide
some of the needed services; even if such agencies do exist, their quality of
service may be poor, or they may not want to concentrate their limited
resources on a housing development for the elderly which they believe
already receives enough attention (Moos, 1980).

Of course some community agencies think that, because the development has a concentration of aged, that is where to focus their efforts. Consequently, they locate their senior center, meals program, or other services in
the development. Lawton and Byerts (1977) regard this provision of medical
services in the development as difficult to bring off due to licensing requirements, high costs, and the aversion of tenants to sick people. They consider
it economically desirable for most on-site services to broaden the consumer
base by including community users, in other words, to be community services. This has the advantage of intermingling community residents and
housing residents. All the same, centering community services in the housing development does not always work well—development residents tend to
monopolize the services and often do not welcome area neighbors to the
facilities.

An alternative solution is to transport elderly residents in need of
service, such as a medical clinic, directly to where they need to go. Many
developments have minibuses or other vehicles to do just that. However,
some residents may not be ambulatory enough or well enough to travel
comfortably. Another course is for the development itself to provide the
service for exclusive use of its residents. Many congregate and luxury apartment complexes do this. It is expensive—both in terms of building the
facility and for staffing. For certain services, moreover, there may be few
users. Some apartment developments do not have enough users to justify
homemaker assistance or part-time nurses, referring the few cases they do
have to community agencies which will provide for their needs. Funding is
not often readily available: developments often have to solicit from a number
of different sources (Gutowski, 1978; Thompson, 1978).

On-Site Staff

Some think that the same criterion, namely, the degree of need, should be
the deciding factor as to whether on-site staff is needed. However, many

other experts, including the author, feel it is imperative to have at least a minimal staff on the site, regardless of how healthy the elderly residents seem to be. Some of them are likely to have emergency needs: important to them is the security involved in knowing staff members are on hand to help them or that trained staff will respond rapidly should the development be penetrated by criminals—something which often happens in inner-city housing developments (Harel and Harel, 1978).

Location

High crime rates often result from siting developments in such undesirable areas as a skid row or in sparsely developed urban renewal locations. Public housing authorities have been especially remiss in this field. In such cases not only the development's own halls, but the nearby bus stop and parking lots are a danger: muggings are frequent.

Earlier it was popular to locate these housing complexes in outer area or rural area park settings. While these are at least picturesque, with their broad green lawns and landscaping, such sites are isolated from community activities. Elderly who live in these Edenic places lack access to needed services, the chance to walk about a shopping area, or to even have a bus available. The best site is one away from slum areas but close to the services needed, to a shopping area, and to public transportation.

Life-Care Facilities

A special type of congregate development is the life-care facility. Users must pay a large sum to buy into the development, usually to buy a specific apartment. Residents usually live in apartments or townhouses; they receive a variety of services, including meals, housekeeping, recreational programs, and above all, comprehensive medical care. The complex usually has a well-staffed infirmary, and occasionally a full-scale nursing home. Well-to-do elderly are attracted to such life-care facilities because of an agreement whereby they are assured of care in specified quarters for the rest of their life, or a specific number of years, upon payment of a large, nonreturnable sum, sometimes called a "founder's fee," running from $30,000 to 150,000 or over. Life-care contracts are like an annuity, whereby the providing organization gambles on the recipient's life expectancy. The usual practice is to pay an entrance fee, perhaps $1,000, and then, after a trial period of several months, decide whether to stay on—which requires payment of the large founder's fee to get a specific apartment. Besides the founder's fee, one makes a monthly payment labeled either as "maintenance fee" or as rent. Common sponsors of such developments are churches—the Episcopal church has been especially active in this area—or service or professional associations. In Sunbelt territory a number of developers of life-care facilities are private corporations (Chellis et al., 1982).

Both federal and state governments have been concerned about developers' willingness to meet the lifelong obligation to residents stated in the life-care contract. In 1963 the Housing and Home Finance Agency (now HUD) issued a regulation requiring sponsors to offer life-care contracts to residents, thus providing legally enforcable guarantees. Some states have made their own provisions to assure that life-care facilities meet their obligations. A number of private life-care facilities have gone bankrupt: Wishard and Wishard (1981) report that even well-regarded groups have failed. Loether (1975) shows that in the past, residents who put their life savings into founders' fees have been left high-and-dry—with neither their money nor their supposed life care—when homes without sound financial backing failed. It follows, then, that the applicant must learn as much as possible about the sponsors—including a check with nonprofit housing groups that are likely to know more than she.

Retirement Communities

Retirement communities involve more than apartments for the elderly or congregate developments: a whole, planned community is at issue. It is defined by Heintz (1976) as a "planned, low density development of permanent buildings . . . offering [not life-care but purchased] 'moderate–high' cost housing, designed to house 'active adults' over a certain age (45 or 55) and equipped to provide a wide range of services with an emphasis on leisure activities." From her study of a retirement community in New Jersey, Heintz (1976) concludes that the primary focus is a leisure-oriented environment. She adds that the residents of these retirement communities are moderately affluent, have the physical capacity to take care of themselves, are younger, and more frequently married than the elderly nationwide. These retirement communities are usually located in the Sunbelt near metropolitan areas (Longino, 1981).

Retirement communities are often described as an outgrowth of the postwar mass-housing movement. Developers or independent builders who had already pioneered large tract developments saw a housing need for the growing group of affluent elderly who were faced with early mandatory retirement, with an "empty nest," no further need for a large house, and an interest in accommodations with leisure facilities (Pastalan, 1983).

Rossmoor Walnut Creek, one of the three "Leisure World" commercial retirement communities developed in the 1960s, serves as a good example of the characteristics of such planned, security-patrolled retirement communities. The case study done by Dale Romberg (1982) illustrates the discrepancy between the developer's focus—a community for active older

Americans desiring leisure activities—and the reality of a residential group aging over the years and increasingly in need of supportive medical and in-home services. What happened in Rossmoor is also occurring in many specially designed elderly housing developments.

The Rossmoor retirement community is situated in a suburban setting of about 700 acres near San Francisco. In 1982 it had over 5,000 housing units and 8,000 residents. The owner-occupied units include early, less expensive cooperative townhouses and more recently built—and more expensive—condominium units. Residents are assessed a monthly fee for maintenance and for programs and services, and a separate optional fee for use of the medical clinic and its many services. Community facilities include four clubhouses, the largest of which has a wide variety of weekly activities ranging from card games to crafts or sewing. There are many recreational facilities for active adults, including a golf course, riding stables, or swimming pools, and tennis courts.

Services for elderly with physical limitations or health problems, by contrast, are quite limited. In 1982 Rossmoor did not have a daily noon meal program for residents but relied instead on Meals-on-Wheels or on the Rossmoor homemaker service affiliated with its medical clinic. The clinic included a home health agency.

This medical facility does provide a wide variety of services. It is a fee-for-service clinic with a staff of full-time and part-time physicians covering a variety of medical specialties. It offers a number of specialized facilities—such as physical therapy rooms, a pharmacy, and an optical and hearing aid shop. It has a 24-hour emergency service. Residents are provided with "Lifeline," whereby those who need help can send a signal from a small transmitter; a city hospital's emergency center notifies Rossmoor security, who follow up on the call. In other communities with "Lifeline," the hospital notifies a relative or the police. Other services for the frail elderly include a friendly visitor service and "Telecare," in which volunteers call residents daily or weekly.

Transportation services are also available at Rossmoor, although the community is adjacent to a large shopping center that fills many needs. Besides a local bus system, Rossmoor operates its own four-route bus system within the community, as well as providing a Dial-A-Ride service on weekends.

Such supportive services are especially necessary because the population is rapidly aging. While recruitment to the development is geared to an active adult group desiring leisure recreation, this group's needs change over time. When it was founded in 1964, Rossmoor fit the description traditionally given to a retirement community population. However, because of external social change, low resident turnover, and a resultant, quickly aging population, Rossmoor has changed in the past 18 years in several respects.

By 1980, widowed women and men made up over half of all Rossmoor households. The average Rossmoor population has become appreciably older. In 12 years the percentage under 65 declined by almost half, and those 75 and older doubled—to 52.6 percent of the population. A high proportion has low incomes—possibly due to this very same aging of the residents—which means diminished resources compared to the 1964 entry period.

LOW TURNOVER

Part of the reason for this rapid aging of Rossmoor's population is low turnover. Over half of the existing units were sold during the first four years of Rossmoor's existence; a large proportion of this group, now some 20 years older, is still there today.

Even newer residents are now fairly old. Most of those now entering are already retired; over a third are already widowed. These new residents differ from the rest of the Rossmoor population in that many have quite high incomes and buy the new condominiums that start at $189,000 as a minimum. Their high income may be a negative asset to the rest of the population because they can afford to pay for services longer-time tenants—with their lower incomes—cannot pay for. They may demand expensive services such as more security patrols which will mean that the monthly fee paid by all must be increased.

The long-term residents, however, dominate—and they are those who are shaping the present environment at Rossmoor.

IMPLICATIONS OF LOW TURNOVER AND AN AGING POPULATION

Since most of Rossmoor's population consists of long-term residents now in their late 70s, their needs have changed somewhat from the time they signed on. An aging population will definitely have an effect on services offered, survival of the development, and the capacity of Rossmoor to maintain a high quality of life for residents.

At Rossmoor some indications of an aging population are a decline in resident participation in cleaning and weeding of the small gardens outside the townhouses; a decline in active sports, most noticeably golf; an increase in the number of resident requests for staff assistance; a slight increase in the use of Rossmoor's clinic; and a 12 percent increase in requests for homemaker service over the last three years. There has already been a small increase in monthly payments, after adjustment for inflation, to meet these rising service demands (Romberg, 1982). Given the present demographic trends, Rossmoor's management expects increases in bus ridership, in sedentary activities, and in the number of townhouses for sale because of death or relocation to a long-term care facility.

The future of services at Rossmoor will depend on the size and age of its population. Based on present trends, all existing services will probably have to be augmented, especially bus, managerial, social service, mainte-nance, and health services. Rossmoor's clinic has hired additional doctors and medical services in the past several years as the population aged and grew; it is now planning a congregate facility, which will provide meals, housekeeping, and medical services.

The example of Rossmoor shows some of the major problems of these retirement communities; it shows how a full-service retirement community undergoes change due to the increasing age of many of its residents. Rossmoor still attracts some newly retired to the development, especially in the new condominiums, but given the low turnover rate, the older group is dominant, contributing to a shift in activities and services. Rossmoor's man-agement is better than many retirement-community developers in respond-ing to changing demands. However, as a profit-making enterprise it must worry about the increased costs and ability—or in this case, lack of ability—to increase fees drastically. The Rossmoor solution at present is to try to increase the size of the younger age-group by building more condominiums and building and advertising more facilities, such as tennis courts, for this group. They have also lowered the entrance age. Other developments, with less land and more limited resources, may not be able to follow Rossmoor's lead. This means that the elderly person entering such a development should be aware that maintenance fees may drastically increase over time—or that services may decrease. They are ill-advised to enter a development focusing on such leisure activities as golf at an age when their ability to participate is decreasing and they are in greater need of the kind of suppor-tive services which may well be in short supply there. Lower-middle-class elderly must be aware that a down payment on a condominium may be only the start of their housing costs; there will be continually rising maintenance costs and other, separate fees—such as those for medical services, use of leisure facilities, various supplies, and so on.

Subsidy Programs

The federal government has gradually moved to give support, through vari-ous subsidy programs, for different types of specially designed housing. In fact, a large proportion of federal subsidies for aiding the elderly in their housing needs are for special rental housing and Section 8 private rental allowances. Three-fourths of the elderly are homeowners, so that subsidies to this group would seem more logical (Welfeld and Struyk, 1978; Struyk, 1983).

Government assistance to special housing for the elderly has taken two forms: a program designed especially to encourage construction of public housing for the elderly and aid to nonprofit and limited-profit housing devel-opments under the Section 202, Section 236, and Section 231 programs. Section 8 housing allowances have in many cases been a rent supplement to those elderly in Section 202 housing who are poor enough to qualify. The Section 202 program, which subsidizes interest on development mortgages, and the Section 8 program have been run together as 202/8, a doubly subsidized, specially designed housing program. The Section 236 program, now terminated, had a below-market-interest subsidy for mortgages for housing for the elderly and for families.

Section 231 is a program whereby the government protects lenders against losses on mortgages taken out by nonprofit or for-profit developers to construct or rehabilitate rental-unit housing for the elderly 62 and over.

Public Housing

The public housing program produces the largest number of special housing units for the elderly, but they are unequally distributed. Local housing authorities must design such programs and then obtain citizen approval through voter referenda. Some towns have been much more vigorous than others in doing this. Some have built only housing for the elderly. Subsidies under this program take two forms. First, the federal government—i.e., HUD—authorizes the acquisition, construction, or rehabilitation of units specifically designed for the elderly and provides the loans for them, just as it does for multifamily housing for the poor of all ages. Second, HUD subsidizes the rents of tenants in such public housing; tenants pay 30 percent of their income for rent and the federal government covers the difference between rent and income. Provision for the elderly started in 1956, when HUD allowed public housing units to be occupied by singles over 65, at first in multifamily projects where they were mixed with families. The unsuitability of mixing poor families with many children together with the elderly was recognized as early as 1965. The next move was to provide one floor per building, or an entire building in a project, for the elderly. Such arrangements still exist; in the last decade, however, it has become common to build separate housing complexes for the elderly, some of them with very good design and landscaping. Indeed, the whole public housing authority building program has been increasingly directed to building for the elderly, with over half of the public housing units constructed in recent years designated as housing for the elderly, mainly in separate complexes.

These public housing developments for the elderly vary as to the facilities and staff available. Some older complexes for the elderly, and some converted from family housing to elderly units, lack communal rooms; but most have them, and sometimes a kitchen as well, for serving special meals or for the AOA meals program. They may also have an office for visiting professional staff such as nurses and social workers. A few projects have on-site facilities for other agencies. The New York City Housing Authority was an early pioneer in providing such facilities.

An example of an early model public housing project for the elderly is the Victoria Plaza project in San Antonio, a nine-story facility with a community center on the ground floor. This center includes rooms for counseling, television, high-fidelity record players, a pool table, and a room for parties. Victoria Plaza also has a number of special design features such as bathrooms containing buttons to call help in case of emergencies (Carp, 1977a). Some developments, including Victoria Plaza, have on-site staff. These can be managers or tenants; the latter is the case in California's Marin City housing project, where tenants have been hired to do maintenance or office work. Some public housing projects for the elderly have solicited students to take a rent-free apartment in the project, who thus provide an on-site night staff. British public housing (council housing) commonly provides wardens—usually a couple who get a rent-free apartment. The wife provides daytime emergency aid when needed, and the husband, who often works in the community, provides some maintenance. Some wardens are paid a modest amount. Many American and Canadian public housing projects do *not* have on-site staff but do have staff, including maintenance men, who serve the development from a central downtown office.

Provision of services may be secured by a Community Service Office in the downtown Housing Authority. The central staff, while serving all tenants, often center much of their effort on tenants in projects for the elderly. Besides securing services from other agencies, they may provide a newsletter, organize a tenant association, or initiate a telephone contact service. Services often brought in include public health nurses and voluntary groups for special entertainment, such as Thanksgiving and Christmas programs. In the mid-1970s, a HUD official reported that AOA meals programs were provided at over 700 public housing sites. However, at a number of elderly public housing projects there is no meals program and only a minimal recreation program. Lawton (1975) found that in 1971 only a quarter of public housing developments had medical services. They rarely had dispensaries or dependable on-call emergency services.

PROBLEMS OF PUBLIC HOUSING

Because many of these public housing projects have a fairly ambulatory, independent population one might claim that a heavy provision of services is not necessary. However, this is, at best, only part of the story. Because a large number of these projects have been in existence for many years, some of their residents have been there a long time and have developed some physical limitations. In fact, this situation presents a real crisis for public housing. As Marie Thompson (Donahue, Thompson, and Curren, 1977) points out:

> Many tenants now in public housing have "aged" in their present quarters, as have those in private housing in the community. As could be anticipated, an

increasing number of public housing agencies are faced with the fact that either they must evict the more frail or impaired who cannot sustain the shopping, cooking or heavy housekeeping chores designed for the hale and hearty, or they must develop on a crash, and perhaps, ill founded basis—some semblance of the services these aging occupants need to maintain at least semi-independence in a residential setting.

Donahue, in her study of public housing for the elderly, found that many of them had limited mobility; others indicated problems of frailty, chronic disease, crippling arthritis, visual impairment, and mental confusion, in that order (Donahue et al., 1977). Lawton's surveyed elderly public housing tenants also seemed to have physical limitations, since two-thirds of them complained about the lack of on-site medical service (Lawton, 1975). There have been some moves to turn public housing projects into semi-congregate housing or to obtain more community services. In recent years HUD has given some support for this. More effort needs to go into supplying on-site staff for emergency help when there are many frail residents.

Housing authorities have problems in getting these frail elderly to move out. Then, too, there are not enough nursing homes willing to accept these low-income elderly. As a Manchester, New Hampshire, housing authority reports (Huttman, 1977):

> We have in our (elderly) projects at least 50 persons that probably should, now or in the near future, move into congregate housing. We estimate that approximately 25 persons, per annum, move from our program into nursing homes. Even the nursing homes have waiting lists, and cost is a major factor. Unless the elderly applicant has assets, he or she is not even considered for a bed.

As another housing director in Richmond, Virginia, points out, "The scarcity of nursing home facilities is another obstacle to local housing authorities. Without them the low-rent housing development for the elderly itself may soon become a nursing home" (Huttman, 1977).

Another problem that many public housing projects have is difficulty in providing security from crime. This is due to their being located in deteriorated areas, inner-city ghettos, or skid rows, especially in large cities. Some projects are actually former family projects which have been converted because of vandalism and crime, or because they are high-rise structures; such projects, too, are usually located on undesirable sites. Even if the site is in an acceptable, middle-income area, the elderly housing residents may be victims of crime if they are housed on one floor of a building that is otherwise devoted to family housing, with many restless teenagers. An example of this was a White Plains, New York, project in a pleasant area surrounded by single-family homes on tree-lined streets. Here the elderly tenants occupied a top floor of a high-rise public housing project inhabited mainly by single-parent families: teenagers had no supervision after school. The elderly dared not use the elevators during those hours, and feared crossing the lobby where the teenagers loitered about.

Of course, even with all these problems in public housing, many do desire a unit in these projects; there are long waiting lists for these cheap accommodations. Many projects, especially in smaller cities and towns, are attractive and do not suffer from these problems. In recent years they have often been architecturally pleasing buildings with well-landscaped green space, standing out in sharp contrast to traditional public housing. They are on acceptable sites in decent areas of town. They have been serviced by a number of community agencies, especially when SSBG and Older American Act monies were more available.

These projects do suffer from another problem, however: they can house only those of very low income. Many elderly, even those called the "near poor," have income too high to qualify. Unfortunately, they also have incomes too limited to cover the costs of other kinds of adequate housing. Other subsidized housing—under sections 202, 231, or 236—is very limited in number of units. And retirement communities and life-care arrangements are available only to the well-off. This is true even though all these programs have grown at such a phenomenal pace in the last decade.

The degree of assistance the government provides to help house the elderly is very limited in comparison to need. In 1981 only 3 percent of all American elderly benefited from any of the HUD programs. Demand for subsidized housing far exceeded the supply. The U.S. Senate Special Committee on Aging (1982) received reports estimating that 32,000 elderly in New York and 12,000 in Chicago were on the waiting lists for public housing. Even the demand for nonsubsidized, owner-occupied, specially designed housing with appropriate services was estimated by HUD at a half million or more units, and HUD sources guessed that if subsidies were included, the demand might be much higher.

While the supply of elderly housing is limited, the government has provided more of this than of other kinds of housing. Historically, because of the need for local approval of public housing the federal government has to some degree accidentally fallen into this heavy emphasis on building housing for the elderly versus building or subsidizing housing for families. For example, the public housing program focused on families almost entirely until 1956, when it was amended to include single persons over 65. One reason the program moved to greater constructions of such units was because family public housing, full of poor families with many children, developed such a bad reputation. Since a local voter referendum was needed to build new public housing, the local housing authority in many cities designated it as housing for the elderly because it was easier to get voter approval for such projects.

The family-rental nonprofit complexes built under Section 236, which provided below-market-interest rates on project mortgages and gave rent supplements to low-income residents, also ran into trouble due to poor upkeep and rent delinquencies by families; the 236 elderly projects had a better record. The eventual slowdown of this 236 program helped provide more interest in Section 202 housing for the elderly (Willlamson et al., 1980). Elderly were easier for management to work with—they paid their rent, kept their units clean, and were more cooperative. They actually appreciated the housing and expressed their gratitude to management. Thus it is not surprising there was a new emphasis on housing the elderly in the late 1970s.

Of course another reason for the increase in elderly housing was the power of the elderly lobby in the 1970s. It had been a long fight: not until after the moratorium on subsidized housing ended in 1976 did Section 202 start to receive large appropriations. Lobbying for congregate housing, including meals and other services, has indeed gone on almost interminably. So, for example, there were hearings before Congress in 1975 and 1978; they supported the value of housing with services for the frail elderly. But Congress has given only minor financial support to *services* in Section 202 housing; it covers primarily housing costs. Brown and O'Day (1981) report that at least up to the mid-1970s, HUD discouraged the development of on-site supportive services (meal or medical facilities) and intended Section 202 projects to be occupied only by fully independent aged.

While the federal government—that is, HUD—has changed its attitude somewhat about providing for housing with services, it has never fully changed its earlier position that its main job is to provide housing, not services. HUD's response to this issue in the mid-1970s was to persuade other government agencies that normally provide services, such as Health and Human Services (HSS), to provide them in public housing. They made a number of agreements with these agencies, including the AOA and the Department of Transportation. However, many experts on housing the elderly criticized HUD's efforts as consisting of superficial, vague agreements. Some feared that reliance on outside agencies to provide basic services was unrealistic—and that these agencies' commitment to the elderly housing project was often merely short term.

SECTION 202

Section 202 is a major federal subsidy program to encourage nonprofit and limited-profit groups to build housing specially for the elderly. It provides direct federal long-term loans, with below-market interest rates, for the full cost of construction of rental units or rehabilitation of structures for housing the elderly or handicapped. Though started in the 1960s, it is from 1977 onwards that this program has really been expanding. In 1977 construction of 50,000 new units for the elderly was planned. In 1978 the appropriate level for the program was set at $750 million (HUD, 1979). From 1974 to 1982 almost a third of a million units were subsidized. (The program was cut somewhat under the Reagan administration.)

The large appropriation for Section 8 rent subsidies specifically for tenants in housing under Section 202 has also been a boon to the program. In

1982 when it was decided to cut back and revise Section 8, this 202/8—that is, new Section 8 subsidies for those in Section 202 housing—was slated for termination or a major cutback. As mentioned in Chapter 8, Section 8 is a program in which the user, after proving he or she is of low income according to the program criteria, receives a rent supplement from the government to cover the difference between the unit's fair market rent and 30 percent of the participant's income.

Section 202 subsidies are used by churches, service clubs, and other nonprofit as well as limited-profit groups that want to build housing for the elderly. To obtain this below-market-interest loan the sponsor must receive HUD's approval of the cost components and the architectural specifications as to type and size of the facilities.

HUD intends this program to serve limited-income elderly—those with incomes somewhat above the level which qualifies for public housing, but insufficient to secure standard housing on the private market. However, Section 202 housing has been inhabited mainly by middle-income persons up until recently. However, the move in the mid-1970s to earmark some Section 8 rent subsidy funds for those in Section 202 housing has meant there are now more low-income residents. By allowing use of Section 8 in these developments, the government gives assistance in two ways: to the building itself through the low-interest loans that decrease mortgage costs; and to the users, or at least to the income-eligible users, through rent subsidies.

Section 231 is a program specifically addressed to building or rehabilitating rental housing for middle-income elderly. Of all the housing subsidy programs, it has the most liberal upper income limits. The government simply insures the mortgage with the private lender, as it would in the FHA program, for housing built by either profit or nonprofit groups. Brown and O'Day (1981) report that numerous retirement centers (some offering supportive services) have been sponsored under this section; a number of them are congregate housing complexes.

STATE SUBSIDIES

Many states now have their own housing agencies which issue notes and bonds as a means to finance developers willing to build affordable housing, including that suitable for the elderly. Through such tax-exempt financing the state agency can provide developers with mortgage money at somewhat below-market rates; this in turn allows the developer to build housing for which he can charge below-market rents.

None of the various subsidy programs discussed has been very large so far. While some religious and service clubs also sponsor developments, the total constructed under Section 202 from 1974 to 1981 is less than 300,000 units (U.S. Senate Special Committee on Aging, 1982). Most cities have at the most three or four such developments and many smaller cities, except in the Sunbelt, have only one.

Satisfaction with an Age-Segregated Environment

Special housing for the elderly means they live in a homogeneous rather than integrated community. Some sociologists and gerontologists oppose age-segregated housing because they feel the elderly are better off integrated into the community, mixing with the young and those of middle age. They believe living in a segregated community tends to narrow one's social world (Harel and Harel, 1978).

Some elderly dislike special housing developments because of the overemphasis on organized social and recreational activities. Some residents "criticize the constant round of activities and feel that there are more important and more profitable ways to make use of their time than card parties, shuffleboard games or ceramic classes" (Huttman, 1977). However, researchers do point out that these age-segregated communities offer more likelihood of services and greater chances for social contact. In a homogeneous community the elderly mainly interact with people with similar problems, common interests, and common perspectives. These other aged can serve as a support system (Pastalan, 1983). Hochschild (1973) describes this for the elderly apartment building population she studied. For example, when one of them was robbed, a collection committee solicited contributions for the victim.

Age-segregated communities are also popular with the many elderly who feel uncomfortable around children or are irritated and annoyed by young adults' noise and manners. Many elderly perceive an age-segregated community as a safe haven, away from the threat of violence and criminal behavior of some young people (Longino et al., 1981). They like luxury apartment complexes with a doorman and secure entry system. For these reasons and others, many of the elderly living in such special housing are happy with their lot. Montgomery (1977) concludes that age-homogeneous environments appear to increase the number of friends and the extent of social interaction, to improve morale, and to contribute to a normative system in which the aged are spared competition and possibly conflict with the life-styles of the young. One example of the popularity of these developments comes from M. Powell Lawton (1975), who describes his Philadelphia Geriatric Center elderly congregate housing project as being almost totally occupied for years, with long waiting lists. He adds that Elaine Brody (1978), in evaluating the impact of such housing, reports that no one has moved out for other than health reasons. In my own study of elderly in age-segregated housing complexes, over three-fourths, when specifically asked, said they wanted to live in an age-segregated building instead of a building with a mixed population (Huttman, 1977).

These studies, however, are not as comprehensive as one might wish because they deal only with elderly who decided to go into an age-segregated development and do not include comparative groups still residing in age-mixed communities. Two studies with such control groups are the Bultena and Wood study (1969) and the one by Carp (1977a). Carp contrasted the life satisfaction and morale, as well as housing satisfaction, of a group of community elderly with a group of elderly in Victoria Plaza, an age-segregated development with many services and facilities. She also studied her group at two points of time, shortly after entry and a number of years later. Using standard tests of life satisfaction and morale, she finds that her elderly public housing development residents, even after a number of years of residence, scored higher on these measures than the community group and express higher satisfaction with their living conditions. Carp also finds that living in this special housing has a positive effect on health and life expectancy. Bultena and Wood compare a sample of retired men in four planned, age-segregated communities in Arizona with retired men in normal Arizona communities. They find morale, as measured by the Neugarten Life Satisfaction scores, considerably higher for men in the retirement community than in the age-integrated community. Second, a smaller proportion of residents of the retirement community than of the age-mixed community experience a decline of close friends and dissatisfaction with their environment.

A somewhat different picture comes from some other studies of age-segregated communities. Sussman and Steinberg (1971) (in Williamson et al., 1980) find that in a New York public housing complex for the elderly—one with fewer services and facilities than Carp's Victoria Plaza—the inhabitants of this age-segregated environment dropped former life-styles and self-images of being active adults, adopting instead those of senior citizens in an old-age home where life trickled along at a slow pace. Another example of a development where residents did not develop a cohesive community or support system is provided by Jacobs's (1974) residential community in a rural isolated area. It lacked some medical services and public transportation. Jacobs's opinion of his residential community population is that two-thirds were low participators when they came, and that they became more withdrawn with residence. Age homogeneity did not seem to prove an asset, for these residents lacked common interests. Some complained that all they ever saw were other old people and that they wanted more frequent, easier access to activities for mixed age groups. They did seem to enjoy freedom from the quicker pace associated with younger neighbors, however. It appears the problems of these two elderly complexes do not provide a condemnation of specially designed elderly housing per se; dissatisfaction was largely due to lack of services and—in the case of Jacobs's (1974) community—lack of transportation from an isolated location. Jacobs feels use of staff to promote social activities could have combated the feeling of loneliness many residents had.

In sum, some elderly prefer an environment with fewer frail aged present and some do not want organized recreation; on the other hand, study after study show that elderly in special housing express high life satisfaction, morale, and housing satisfaction. If they are frail elderly, they are more likely to stay in the community instead of being institutionalized (Longino, 1981).

Conclusion

This chapter has shown that housing can be much more than shelter; it can provide a total, supportive environment for older Americans. For those with health problems this special housing provides a type of security and a variety of services not available in their own homes. While such housing serves only a small proportion of the elderly, it has its place in the continuum of care for the aged. With the increase of the old-old in our society we can expect more focus on this solution.

Specially designed elderly housing takes several forms. There are specially designed apartment complexes with varying degrees of services and facilities. A large proportion are public housing rental complexes designed for use of the elderly; others are nonprofit rental apartment developments sponsored by churches, service organizations, and other groups—often under HUD's Section 202 funding or the limited insurance guarantee assistance of the Section 231 elderly subsidy program. (In the past some Section 236 funding was involved as well.) Residents in these Section 202 or Section 236 developments, if their income is low, may also qualify for Section 8 aid or rent supplements, respectively.

Special housing can also consist of congregate developments—projects with meals service and housekeeping assistance as well as some degree of medical assistance, all covered by a monthly comprehensive charge. Such developments often have hotel-type rooms (sometimes shared), rather than apartments. Congregate developments, because they usually service older, more frail elderly than apartment complexes, have more services and facilities than the latter as a general rule.

The retirement community is another type of special housing for the elderly. In this case units are usually for sale instead of for rent. Such housing is for those of an upper-middle income. A final category of special housing is the life-care facility; it differs from the retirement community in that one buys into the development for a large sum of money and is guaranteed the unit for life or for a fixed period; in addition, one pays a monthly maintenance fee.

Issues concerning these specially designed elderly developments include the relative merits of provision of service by the community or the development by on-site staff; proper location; and whether government and other sources of help should favor congregate developments—with their meals service and housekeeping assistance—or apartment developments. Today apartment developments dominate and funding for congregate housing is quite limited.

In evaluating these issues I nevertheless recommend congregate housing because it serves a frail elderly population that cannot cook or do housekeeing well, and cannot in general "fit in" with regular apartments; it is a group "at risk" for institutionalization. To keep expenses down, innovative developments that concentrate on essential facilities and services are needed. Such developments might provide only one meal a day, twice-weekly housekeeping, and use a minimal number of staff. They would still be better for the frail elderly than many present apartment complexes. Savings on staff by provision of one meal a day does mean the need to provide at least minimal kitchenettes (though this is something all elderly seem to like). The formula of one meal a day is found in Dutch residential homes (often called the "Hiltons of Holland").

These Dutch developments have another benefit: they are often *multi-level housing facilities*—that is, they have either three wings (apartments, congregate housing, and a nursing home right there or next to the development) or congregate (residential) homes and nursing homes adjacent to each other. Denmark also has a congregate wing (service flat) as part of the more traditional service to the frail elderly, the nursing home; this makes for a very attractive, pleasant community facility, as I found in my 1977 WHO research (Huttman, 1982). Elderly in these multilevel facilities have the benefit of being able to move to another wing instead of move out of the development as their health gets worse; their spouse can be in one wing and they in another, according to health needs. If the development is multilevel there is emergency staff and medical services on the premises. Another advantage to such developments is that they can cut costs by having one central kitchen for all wings, one administrative, and possibly even a single medical staff (though this is not true in Denmark and Holland), a single heating plant, and a common maintenance and housekeeping staff.

In these countries it is assumed that services will be provided in the development. I also feel this works best but, because of the costs involved I can see the need for modifications, especially for services little used or of an extravagant nature. Transportation services seem essential if the development is not immediately adjacent to services; of course the best location is one in a central but nonslum area rather than in a parklike, isolated area or a deteriorating inner-city area (Moos, 1980). Other services that seem necessary are at least a minimal health staff and an infirmary and doctor's office for congregate housing, and at least the latter if apartments are involved. Some degree of organized social life, either worked out by the development itself or by community staff, is also needed. Resident councils are essential to preserve morale and encourage active feedback. Residents should take a greater part in developing recreational programs and, in general, in running the development as a whole. In Danish developments residents water the plants, care for the hamsters and other animals, and do other minor tasks. In the newer shared housing programs we see the elderly taking greater responsibility for cooking, housework, and receptionist activities; we need to do more of this in our specially designed congregate and apartment developments—both to save costs and to make the elderly feel more wanted and useful. In too many of our developments staff adopt a patronizing attitude toward the residents; they may even treat them as sick patients. In some developments staff at the reception desk wear nurses' uniforms. This creates just the kind of atmosphere which should be avoided.

Besides self-help measures to keep costs down, limitations on elaborate facilities are necessary; this means that entry fees, rents, and such can be lower, and that more low-income elderly can use such facilities. Beautiful lounges, their use by residents often discouraged by staff, golf courses, or even little-used swimming pools—all these should be given low priority in comparison to infirmaries and nursing staff. In evaluating retirement communities and life-care developments we must recognize that they suffer from these problems all too often. They are oriented toward the active elderly while, as the Rossmoor example indicates, their population is aging and is more likely to need supportive services than all these activities. One can also criticize private life-care facilities on another ground: they make the resident pay a large sum at entry for a long-term commitment the resident might not want or upon which the development might renege. Close monitoring, financial bonding, and such for life-care developments are needed in all states to ensure that the elderly's investment is not lost. I believe that rental arrangements in specially designed housing are probably the optimum solution, allowing retention of liquid assets.

As far as subsidy programs are concerned, I strongly recommend improvements in public housing for the elderly. Some developments are adjacent to family housing with the result that the housing project is dominated and sometimes terrified by teenage youth. Location problems still exist since slum sites are still in use. Some slum-area, high-rise public housing has been converted from family units to elderly units due to its unsuitability for families with young children. All these conditions need to be improved.

With the Section 202 subsidy program the problems are different. Nonprofit sponsors have often been biased in favor of middle-class tenants; even under Section 202 with Section 8 subsidies they take the "cream" of the Section 8 eligibles. These developments are sometimes poorly managed by nonprofit groups such as churches, who have little understanding of the need for services—although other projects are excellent in this respect. With the Section 202 program a major problem is the bureaucratic paperwork required by HUD. This often means years of consultation with local authorities such as planning commissions, architects, and HUD regional personnel before construction can be started—a situation that often discouraged potential sponsors (HUD, 1979).

    In spite of all these problems, specially designed housing has a vital place in the continuum of care; it is especially needed by the frail elderly.

CHAPTER 10

Adult Day Care Centers

Adult day care centers fill a gap in service for older Americans, often in their eighties, who are ambulatory but physically or mentally limited. Many services, including the senior citizens centers, are aimed at the active and alert elderly. Other services, including meals services, homemaking assistance, and transportation assistance, serve the ambulatory with minor problems. These services are in short supply and do not fill all the needs of some frail elderly who are ambulatory but suffer from physical and mental impairments. A stroke, arteriosclerosis of the brain, arthritis or rheumatism, mental impairment, deafness, and vision problems limit these persons' ability to function independently. They may live alone in their own homes unattended, with a spouse who must bear the burden of care 24 hours a day, or with adult children who may have their own children to care for as well as working for a living.

Because these living arrangements do not fully meet the needs of limited ambulatory persons, family members may resort to the nursing home, even though the older person's condition does not dictate such a drastic change to 24-hour institutional care. These semiambulatory elderly, if moved to nursing homes, are separated from relatives and thrust into a hospital-like situation that limits their freedom of action and their privacy. Furthermore, the nursing home is an expensive way to meet the needs described above.

Yet, alternative solutions for the semiambulatory, in the form of more suitable community care services, have seldom been available. One alternative, the congregate housing development, can serve some: it has meal service, housekeeping assistance, recreation activities, and limited nursing help, as described in Chapter 9. However, such housing is often not available, is expensive, and is not suited to some of the ambulatory with mental or physical limitations. Many semiambulatory aged would rather stay in their own home or live with an adult child.

Another alternative is the use of a full-time companion, but many elderly in this category have trouble finding one they can both afford to hire and whom they trust.

The adult day care center seems a fitting solution for the elderly "at risk" for institutionalization. It can provide assistance to many semiambulatory and impaired elderly, while they continue to live with a spouse, an adult child, or even alone. For part of the day, in a group setting, such a center can provide maintenance, custodial care, and social activities; in addition, it can supply limited medical assistance and rehabilitative/restorative services, such as physical, occupational, speech, and reality therapy and social stimulation, as well as provide family counseling (Adult Senior Center *Report*, 1978). As one day care center administrator commented (Huttman, 1977), "Most of our clients fall through the cracks of available agencies in the community. They need more than homemaker services, county health services, yet do not need the 24-hour a day nursing care. Counseling on how to cope is a major need."

Target Population Served

Day care centers may vary in program emphasis and in affiliation, but they are all designed for the broad population of ambulatory, chronically ill, or disabled adults who do not require 24-hour-a-day inpatient care. Without such services, many of these elderly would be hospitalized for a prolonged stay in acute-care or in long-term care facilities (Brown and O'Day, 1981; Robins, 1976).

However, proponents of day care centers do not agree that these centers serve simply as alternatives to nursing homes. They may provide a respite for caretakers as well; two-thirds to three-fourths of the users do not live alone (Weissert, 1975; Mahoney, 1978). Many experts point out that these centers logically come at an earlier stage in the continuum of care than the nursing home. (In the Mace and Rabins [1983] study a fourth of those leaving the center did so to go to a nursing home.) Some in day care will never go to a nursing home. But others will experience deteriorating health, may become almost immobile, incontinent, or severely confused; the job the centers can do is prolong the stay in the community until the nursing home becomes essential. Thus, day care can be either *prevention* or *postponement* of institutionalization—or some of both, even for the same individual.

The degree that a day care center can serve as an alternative for the nursing home depends on the level of care given in the center, as Von Behren (1981) points out. The level of services determines the center's place in the continuum of care. But in comparing day care centers to nursing homes, we must remember, as Rathbone-McCuan and Levenson (1975) note, that the day care center provides a level of institutionalization itself: "Participation eight hours a day in an institutionally-based day care center can be defined as a 'marginal' form of institutionalization."

Development of Adult Day Care

The adult day care center as a service in the continuum of care is fairly new in the United States; it has not settled in one particular mold of activities and goals but varies from place to place. In Europe, where it has long been in existence, especially in Denmark and Britain, it is more well defined.

In the United States the first day care center was started in 1947 under the sponsorship of the Menninger Clinic, but the movement did not catch on for quite a while. Our first government-sponsored demonstration projects were not developed until 1972 under the auspices of the U.S. Health Resources Administration and the Administration on Aging. Although the 1971 White House Conference on Aging recommended development of day care centers, these are still in the beginning stages in the United States. However, there are hopeful indications that they will become part of the continuum of care package all over the United States. While Robins located only 226 centers in her *Directory of Adult Day Care Centers* in 1978, by 1981 she could report that more than 600 programs were in operation—and a sizable number more were in the planning stage.

Adult day care centers have various titles, suggesting a variety of functions. As the National Institute of Adult Day Care Centers brochure (1979) points out, the varying terminology includes day care, day treatment, day health care, psychiatric day treatment, partial hospitalization, and day hospital care. In the past titles also included "geriatric day care hospitals," "daily living centers," and "senior health service centers."

As the titles indicate, some of the early centers were called day hospitals, a concept developed in Britain. These day hospitals, serving as adjunct to acute care hospitals, focused on medical treatment and rehabilitation for chronic conditions or functional impairments, while the day health centers which have developed later provide a wider range of services, including recreation and social activities, along with mental or physical treatment and rehabilitation. As Koff (1982) states, in either setting they provide a wide range of social and medical services—and thus should really be called "adult day health services."

This name now applies mainly to the group offering numerous medical services. They are usually affiliated with a more formal health facility, such as a hospital or nursing home. Some well-known examples are Levindale Hebrew Geriatrics Center and Hospital, Baltimore, described in Rathbone-McCuan and Elliott's book (1976–77) on day care, the Mt. Zion Center in San Francisco, and St. Otto's Nursing Home Day Care Center, Minnesota. In Denmark most are connected to nursing homes (Huttman, 1982).

Other centers, however, follow what we now call the social model, which has only limited medical services. As Monk (1979) found, these are located in multiservice senior centers, homes for the aged, and even social service departments. In Oakland, for example, a Chinese Social Day Care Center was established as an affiliate of the regular Chinese Senior Center.

Many centers are independent; some serve a particular ethnic area of the community, such as the well-known On Lok Senior Day Health Center in Chinatown, San Francisco. On Lok serves Chinese, Filipino, and Italians of the North Beach area. It was established as one link in a planned chain of services for the elderly. This day health care center provides health care, physical and occupational therapy, social services, and nutrition with services available seven days a week (Lurie et al., 1976; Von Behren, 1979).

Types of Services and Service Models

Medical Models

Some detail on the types of day care models—whether medical day health care or the social model—will be useful at this point. Medical day care centers (Rathbone-McCuan and Elliott, 1976–77) or restorative model centers (Holmes and Holmes, 1979) provide medical and rehabilitative services for those recovering from acute illnesses. Participants need intensive, time-limited rehabilitative care. Emphasis in these centers is on restoring clients, many of whom are stroke victims, to normal functioning. One good example is from my own nationwide survey (1979). According to a director:

> One participant [in our center] was a serious stroke victim with depth perception helplessness and also incontinency. His mind was sharp. His wife was a frail diabetic. Both would have needed nursing home care shortly [if the day care program had not existed].

Medical day care centers emphasizing rehabilitation are best operated under the sponsorship of a long-term care institution, such as a skilled nursing or intermediate-care facility, rather than a hospital. Hospitals tend to have high overhead rates, which inhibit the development of day care. Health facility sponsorship grants the center eligibility for Medicaid reimbursement if day care is a specified element of the state's Medicaid plan.

A second type of medical center may be termed the "Health-Related Day Care Center" (Rathbone-McCuan and Elliott, 1976–77) or the Health Maintenance Center. These centers serve mainly chronically ill individuals who require continued nursing and other health supports. Since they provide health supervision for indefinite periods, they are alternatives to nursing home care. Primary emphasis is on maintenance to prevent further deterioration. This type of center is most appropriately located in a health setting; the staff include a high proportion of nursing professionals, rather than rehabilitative therapists. In reality the two types described so far are often combined; in addition, the hospital-based center may take cases classified under the social type—that is, psychiatric cases.

The biggest distinction today relates to whether the center is certified for reimbursement by Medicaid as an adult day health care center. To qualify as such it must have a medical staff, including a part-time doctor and a registered nurse, and must meet certain standards as far as the facility itself is concerned.

Social Types

Two basic social types, sometimes combined into one model, are the general social type (described below) and the kind which serves mainly people with histories of psychiatric disorders who might suffer from mental deterioration if supervision were not available (Rathbone-McCuan and Elliott, 1976–77). For the latter type the center is a alternative to a psychiatric institution. Centers serving cases of Alzheimer's disease and other kinds of senile dementia could also fit in this group.

The more common, general social day care center serves cases in which individuals need assistance with the activities of daily living: they are incapable of independent social functioning; they have cognitive learning problems; they are not in rehabilitative care; they usually have few major physical impairments. The center provides such people a social experience and helps them cope with the activities of daily life.

Here is an example of how the staff in a social day care setting help, as one center administrator described it to me (1979):

> Social interaction at the center aids in less negative attitudes at home. Better sleep habits follow from physical and social activities. Capabilities increase, and the participants are able to help more in daily home chores and independent maintenance.

This "social" kind of facility may be attached to a senior center or be located in a variety of community buildings. It usually has a small staff and a number of volunteers.

Today this social type of day care center predominates. In Robins's (1978) *Directory of Adult Day Care Centers,* half were of the social type; when I (1979) surveyed Robins's listed centers by mail the result was the same. In the my study only four out of ten centers classified themselves as belonging to the medical/rehabilitative/restoration type. This situation continues (Robins, 1981), partly due to the heavy cost of providing a medical model. Medicaid's demands for a medical staff greatly increase expenses. Calculations are that the qualified medical model of adult day health care centers cost from two to three times as much per user as the social model (Huttman, 1979). Centers are also reluctant to try to qualify in this category because of the lengthy paperwork Medicaid requires and because many users will not meet Medicaid's income requirements.

Mixed Type of Center

In reality many centers not certified as an adult day health care center are not strictly of the "social" type; they also offer varying degrees of medical care. This is because, as Mace and Rabins (1983) find in their large study, the. client population is a mixed one with diverse health conditions: Mace and Rabins show that, in general, centers serve a moderately impaired population. The center is often the only one in town, so it takes a variety of cases; it must offer some degree of medical help to some, at least, of its users. My (1979) study shows that in over half of the 114 responding centers the administrator considered that the functions of his facility classified it as being of both the social and the minor health care (maintenance) types. Staff in many centers also indicate that while they may not be medical professionals, they engage in some health care activities. Mace and Rabins (1983) report that almost a third of the centers are directed by either a nurse or a rehabilitation therapist. In 1979 my own study revealed that three-fourths of the centers had a staff nurse; many also had a physical therapist.

Regardless of whether the center is of the social or medical type, its clientele generally includes a number of elderly with physical limitations. In my survey most of the centers had at least a small, and often a fairly large, proportion of clients with health problems. Rogers et al. (1982) report many adult day care recipients have trouble feeding themselves, taking medications, and managing finances. They are considerably more likely than home care cases to need assistance with 13 of the 15 basic activities of daily living and have more emotional and cognitive problems than those receiving home care. Weissart's (1975) sample of 10 centers shows participants had between two and five diagnosed medical conditions each. Some centers have patients with Alzheimer's disease (Winogrond and Fisk, 1982), though they usually constitute a fourth or less of the patients (Mace and Rabins, 1983). A few centers specialize in treating this group (Kretz, 1983), while a few others concentrate on serious cases of the mentally impaired. My 1979 study shows that most are reluctant to accept such clients: I found only eight centers who saw their main role as serving psychiatric or psychiatric/social cases. Most would not take "wanderers" or those characterized by aggressive behavior.

A number of centers made it clear they would not accept elderly who were physically impaired to a serious degree, saying that they could not accept those who need one-to-one care or a life-support system. At the same time many do give assistance to their handicapped clients and have vans to pick them up, recognizing that their mobility is often very limited. Almost half of the centers in the author's 1979 study said a fifth or more of their clients were semiambulatory—many said a third or more were.

Thus, data from various sources show that these centers do have many mildly impaired cases, but are unlikely to serve the most serious cases or for the seriously impaired to make up more than a fourth of the clientele.

MEDICAL SERVICES

Although services vary by type of center, all centers offer some degree of medical service. In my (1979) survey a large number not only offered physical therapy but conducted blood pressure checks, dispensed medication, performed routine examinations, and met other normal medical needs. Some included a public health nurse, a podiatrist, a nutritionist, or a part-time doctor as staff. Medical model centers offered more extensive services in the affiliated hospital or nursing home and included many medical personnel. For example, one of them had three full-time physical/speech therapists and four part-time doctors plus a full-time nurse. The famous medical type in White Plains, New York (Berk Day Hospital), is likewise very well staffed.

Services may include assessment of need and development of a care plan; administration of medication; rehabilitative and restorative treatment; monitoring of health condition; teaching self-help skills to the aged person and her family; and referral to other services.

PHYSICAL THERAPY

Other rehabilitative services include therapies designed to maintain or improve functioning to optimal level, such as exercises for the activities involved in daily life, and advising the person and his family about appliances and ancillary equipment.

SOCIALIZATION SERVICES

Social interaction activities popular in day centers include parties, games, and sing-alongs. In the day center these activities are more passive and uncomplicated than in senior centers. Recreational activities help keep the elderly socially alert and lessen social disengagement; they provide mental stimulation and opportunities to use interpersonal and communicative skills. Social interaction with other impaired elderly helps the person adjust emotionally to her own physical condition. If she is living with adult children, it gives her respite from family tension and opportunities to vent her problems among peers.

SOCIAL SUPPORT AND COUNSELING

The staff often have social work or sociology backgrounds and consider this kind of work a part of their job (87 percent of Mace and Rabins's [1983] centers had family counseling). Counseling may be with the aged individuals, with their families, or with groups of elderly or families. It may center on the illness involved, mental deterioration, family relations, or on other problems. Individual counseling may be offered to increase ability to cope with illness or arrest feelings of depression and uselessness. The social worker also provides an information and referral service, giving advice on available community resources to both clients and their families.

Among other services the center may provide are personal care (such as assistance in grooming), nutrition counseling, and transportation services to the center, to medical appointments, or occasionally to special community events. Adequate transportation is crucial to the operation of the day care center: it makes it more likely that enrollees will attend regularly (Solomon, 1976). Many centers use either their own van or volunteers in cars for such transport. The driver plays an important role in helping the elderly get to the vehicle and then helping them get home, especially if they live alone. The driver must be well aware of the problems which beset these impaired elderly.

The center is usually open from 9 or 10 A.M. to 3 or 5 P.M. to provide the above-mentioned services. Some permit elderly to come at 8 A.M. if their caretakers leave for work at that time, even though the program does not start until 9 or 10 A.M. A typical center serves from 11 to 30 elderly each day. My (1979) survey finds that most clients attend only three to four days a week; less than a third of the centers said most of their clients attended five days a week. Thus, total enrollment at a center is typically higher than daily attendance. A large group of centers report enrollment between 11 and 30, and another large group report it at 31 to 50 (Huttman, 1979). Few had more than a total of 50 enrolled.

Benefits of Adult Day Care

Both practitioners and researchers in this area see many benefits to adult day care programs; these include the fact that they provide medically supportive environments which can improve functioning and provide greater security to the impaired. Another major benefit is the assistance they can give to the family; this includes respite for the caretaker, relief of family tension, help to the caretaker who must work, and counseling and other psychological support for family members. In addition, adult day care centers provide transportation and nutritious meals.

Medically Supportive Environment

The role of the adult day care center (especially in its "medical" form) in helping the impaired person to function has been verified in a number of studies. Kaplan (1976) finds that three-fourths of the day care participants had the same symptoms usually found among nursing home patients. This certainly indicates importance of the day care center as a part of the continuum of care. Centers in many cases supply the otherwise missing links between the options of staying at home without a supportive service of this type or of being forced prematurely into a nursing home. The impaired person can get supportive and restorative services from the day care center. Researchers have found day care participants have improved their functioning after several months' use of the center. Weissart et al. (1980) find this to be the case, just as do Weiler et al. (1976). The Weiler group reports that day care users, when first examined, functioned at a lower level than those in the community control group, but after five months in the day care program they were functioning at a higher level.

The day care center can provide a special benefit through its ability to provide rehabilitative and restorative services such as therapy for stroke victims and others after they have left the hospital where they received their initial care. The medical support in general is at a level high enough to keep many from the nursing home (Huttman, 1979). In fact, in at least one case the person could leave the nursing home altogether. A director reported that, "A man who was in a veteran's hospital could come home and come to the adult day care while his wife worked."

The availability of such centers means a solution is at hand that does not completely separate children from their aged parents and does not burden the children with the guilt that putting parents into nursing homes does. It allows children to continue taking some responsibility for their parents. In the author's study (1979), one director commented: "Daughter frustrated. She sees the nursing home as the only solution. Day care provided. Daughter able to accept and live with this arrangement." Another said: "The son doesn't want the guilt feeling of putting his mother in a nursing home."

Even in cases where people must eventually go to a nursing home, the day care center facilitates a longer stay in the community and a longer period that relatives can care for them. This benefit is mentioned by Mahoney (1978), who reports that only a fourth of the day care subjects in the three centers he studied lived alone. This care, then, really did help the family to be caretakers. In my 1979 study one administrator cited the following case:

One 68-year-old client was a wanderer. She had two grown children, one in Ohio and one local, a daughter with husband and two little girls to care for. The daughter works as a secretary and cannot care for her mother. Subject was so confused that grandchildren did not enjoy her and resented her coming into their home. No sitter could be found. We [the center] kept the subject for five days per week for 11 months, thus giving the family relief. Finally they had to put her into a home as it had become too much for us [at the center].

A period at the center may, incidentally, also prove useful in cushioning the transition to a nursing home environment.

Safety

Centers can provide safe, secure places for the confused elderly or "wanderers" during the period when the caretaker is away from home working, as one center administrator explained (Huttman, 1979): "Our frail clients would have difficulty remaining home alone during the day because of physical or mental limitations. In most cases where our clients live with adult children the adult children work out of the home and need safe care for the parent while gone." Another director gave this example: "We have one [adult daughter] who works now because she has a place for her mother during the day. This woman wanders and is a severe diabetic. She could not be left alone."

The day care center, of course, also provides a place where aged people get some social interaction with their own age group and receive the type of stimulation that works against isolation and passivity.

Respite for Caretaker

A major role of the center is to relieve the caretaker of 24-hour care of the frail elderly person. Rogers et al. (1982) find providing such respite a major benefit. Winogrond and Fisk (1982) report that it helps caretakers to function. In my 1979 study a center director reported, "In most cases with adult children and spouses, the family members need the relief to help them cope with a 24-hour situation 7 days a week." Such help is needed not only when the caretaker works outside the home, but also when at home with the aged person. As one director stated, "In two instances, the adult children don't work, but still need a break from the parent to allow for their own activities and shopping. The Day Care availability allows freedom for both the parent and adult child, therefore improving the relationship at home between them." When both husband and wife are ill the center can provide support for their efforts to help each other in their own home. One center director gave as an example of this: "Wife confused and husband has bad back. They are unable to manage 24 hours a day."

Relief of Family Tension

Substitute or supplemental care for the elderly in cases when they live with relatives relieves the family of the tension and strain between members caused by having the care of a chronically ill person on a 24-hour basis (Robinson and Thurnher, 1979). It helps avoid situations in which friction in the family becomes so bad there is a breakdown of relations, a situation Rathbone-McCuan and Elliott (1976–77) describe. How the center can improve such situations was put succinctly to me (1979) by one director: "Mr. H. lives with his daughter and son-in-law. Friction in the relationship between these people almost caused a divorce. Since Mr. H. started at the Center, a more relaxed atmosphere is noted." Another director cited a case involving the problem of double care—i.e., of both children and parents:

> Adult daughter has four youngsters age 2–7 who are active and noisy. Father twice victim of stroke with paralysis, is depressed and dependent. She cannot provide complete needs of family and father. She now has time for family alone and for father alone, as well as more time to schedule needed medical appointments.

Caretakers Who Work

The provision of day care may also allow caretakers to work (Robinson and Thurnher, 1979). Many caretakers have to be in the labor force. The center therefore is an essential service to the family if it is to carry on its caretaking job (Rathbone-McCuan and Elliott, 1976–77). An example from my 1979 study involves "[an] adult daughter [who] works 8 to 5 and is relieved that aged mother 79 with whom she lives is not alone during the day. Mother when left unsupervised wandered. This is preventing full-time nursing home placement of mother. Daughter was even going to quit her job."

One center, however, reported that the hours of the program inhibited full-time work by the caretaker: "Our hours (10–3) don't permit spouses to be employed. However, ours are all retired or semi-retired. One husband puts in part of a day at work while the wife is with us." The limited hours a center is open can be a definite drawback. However, some centers do open at 8 in the morning and stay open until 4 or 5 in the afternoon.

Some centers resent the role of facilitator in allowing the spouse or adult child to work. According to one respondent, "We do not consider ourselves a baby-sitting service for adult children who work. However, it has made for familial harmony where once there was tension."

Family Support

The day care center plays an important role in family counseling. It can counsel families on how to work with their impaired relatives and what plans to make for their care as well as what medical assistance and medical equipment is needed. Families very much require this counseling, as Johnson and Bursk (1977) report. As one center head told me (1979):

> We see a great need for direct counseling available to the family on a 24 hour a day basis. Most therapists, doctors, etc., will not take the time to explain in detail what to expect, why certain things happen or advise families of adaptive equipment available to make home care more feasible.

Many physicians and nurses will not take the time to give details on the different stages of the health problem. In addition to not taking time, these sources lack the understanding of the tensions and stresses that arise in the family due to the elderly relative's impaired state; day care staff usually can and do fulfill this need for counseling. This counseling can take many forms. As one center's directors said of the program (Huttman, 1979): "Family interaction is built in; family conferences, one-on-one counseling, social functions, and home visits. Very often the clients live with adult children who need counseling to cope with the impaired parent." Some centers use counseling to help the family deal with mentally impaired relatives and learn to use the proper approaches with them when they are at home.

Some centers also use their counseling "to help children make plans for aging parents when the day care is not enough" or as "counseling with the adult children regarding guilt, separation, and possible nursing home placement." Caretakers have continual psychological problems over feelings of guilt and of burden (Zarit, 1980; Huttman, 1979).

Transportation

Centers provide transportation to medical appointments. This, too, is of great assistance to the family. For instance, the family with an elderly member needing physical or speech therapy can be relieved of taking them to treatment if the older person attends the center, for it will provide for this.

Nutritious Meals

Centers fill another important function by providing hot, nutritious meals. This is especially needed by the clients who live alone, but it also relieves working relatives from fixing a special noon meal. Most centers serve such meals—and even have special dietary meals for those who need them.

Summary

A concise statement of the benefits centers provide would emphasize that they help the somewhat mentally and physically impaired elderly to be more independent and satisfied while also easing the psychological and time burdens upon the families who continue to care for their elderly.

Funding of Adult Day Care Centers

While many gerontologists consider day care centers for the elderly an excellent addition to the continuum of care, legislatures and other funding sources have not come forth with adequate financial support, which is why these programs have been slow to develop in the United States.

Funding is not only sparse, but it is often fragmented: centers may have to make use of three or more sources of funding. Some money has come from revenue-sharing programs; other sources include foundations or in-kind donations. The major public resources are Medicaid (subject to the same narrow eligibility criteria as in-home services) for the "medical" model or OAA and SSBG (Title XX) social service funds for other, "mixed" types. Koff (1982) reports that Title XX funded 135 programs in 35 states in 1978. Even with all these sources, the total amount of money spent on adult day care is small—but the situation has improved somewhat from the past in that more centers are being developed and are receiving increasing attention from the media. The 1981 White House Conference on Aging stressed the need to increase day care services, giving the idea an important imprimatur. While the AOA's initiatives, sent to AAAs, have previously stressed the importance of developing day care services for the physically and mentally impaired aged within multipurpose senior centers, Congress has helped by authorizing experimental and demonstration programs relating to health care (P.L. 92–603, Section 222).

Medicaid

The move to allow use of Medicaid funds for day care health programs was a major breakthrough. This came after a tough fight by day care advocates in different states. Robins (1981) reports New York, Massachusetts, New Jersey, and California in the 1970s were the first states to utilize Medicaid for this service.

Medicaid funding has recently expanded to include more programs. Robins (1981) reported that eight states had 128 programs under medical day care that were designated as optional Medicaid services.

For a state to fund day care as an optional service under Medicaid, adult day care must be included in the state's Medicaid plan. Then the day care program needs to apply for the state Medicaid agency's approval. This approval is only given to "medical model" centers with sufficient health staff and an extensive enough health program to meet the federal guidelines for Medicaid funding. In addition, the state makes up its own standards and eligibility requirements, though the federal government mandates that applicants must demonstrate medical need, and of course be of low income to qualify for Medicaid reimbursement.

Reimbursement is made for the health care program and for parts of the social program directly supportive of medical services. In reality this covers most of the center's services, including physical and occupational therapy, transportation, dietary services, most social services, even personal care, as well as medical and nursing services.

Centers fitting into the social model usually do not qualify for Medicaid funds, although individual users may receive some health services through them that qualify for repayment as individual Medicaid services. These Medicaid regulations have split the day care movement into two semiantagonistic groups: those centers qualifying as the "medical" model and all the others, many of which do not want to apply for certification because of the paperwork involved or because they do not want to meet the expensive Medicaid medical staffing requirements.

Cost-Effectiveness

Advocates of day care, as mentioned earlier, have heralded it as an alternative to the nursing home, either preventing the frail aged person's use of it or at least delaying this turn to a haven of last resort. This is not only more humane, they argue, but also a more cost-effective solution.

At the 1981 Western Gerontological Society meeting, Dr. Ruth Von Behren, then head of the adult day care division of the California Department of Health Services, pointed out that in 1981 the average Medical (Medicaid) payment per month for senior day care in California was $265, while for nursing home care it was $776–$788. However, as Weissert et al. (1980) point out, because of variations in services offered, costs differ greatly between centers, with of course the greatest differences between the "medical" adult day health care center and others. Thus as Weissert et al. show, the degree of cost difference from nursing homes varies.

The issue of "cost-effectiveness" is far from settled. Experts argue vehemently about it because "cost-effectiveness" is so central in winning legislative support to underwrite increased funding for senior day care. Holmes and Hudson (1975) claim that some planners have been fairly naive in their approach to this issue and have merely compared institutional care with day care on a cost-per-day basis. The major issue, which is considerably more complex, is how to compute costs of the day care program against those of the institutional program when the latter is so inclusive, including medical treatment and room and board, whereas the day care center uses so many services from other agencies. Researchers at San Francisco's On Lok Center and at the State of California Department of Health Services have puzzled over this. For example, should one include in the computations the day care client's costs of services, such as housing and meals *outside* the center, even when an adult child or spouse shares in use? More important, to compare day care cost with institutional care, should one include the day care client's medical bills? These obviously may be substantial. Another problem in computing cost comparisons is whether one includes capital expenditures—they may be very extensive in the first year of operation compared to a nursing home program that has been in operation many years.

A different approach focuses on the degree to which the day care center substitutes for the nursing home. How many clients would have to go to a nursing home if the day care facility were not available? Weissert et al. (1980) show how a center improves the elderly's functioning over what would happen if they were left in the community without one, but that is not the issue here. The question is, How high would the institutionalization rate be if the center were not there? Holmes and Holmes (1979) note that some think calculating some rate of this kind is crucial in computing cost-effectiveness. They give an example of a day care center that was not cost effective when it "saved" approximately 20 percent of its participants from institutionalization. If it could "save" approximately 50 percent of its participants per year, it would be cost effective.

Cost-effectiveness may, of course, not be the best measure of usefulness of day care centers. How does one measure the decrease in tension for a caretaker when a day care center is used? How does one measure the pleasure it gives the elderly person to still be living in the community, often with a spouse or an adult child? Some would say that even if only 10 percent of the clients of a day care center were saved from use of the nursing home, with its institutional atmosphere and often abusive care, the day care center would be worth the price. As Holmes and Holmes (1979) summarize:

> It should be noted that the reliance on a determination of relative cost effect has at least two negative implications. First, it implies the existence of an antagonistic relationship between day care and institutional care, in the sense that one must be "better" than the other, as measured by cost. This is at best an invidious comparison, which should yield to a more rational determination of appropriate levels along a continuum of available care. Second, the reliance on cost-effectiveness as a major criterion of program desirability overlooks both humanistic concerns and the rights of the older persons to a spectrum of care and services appropriate to their individual needs.

Problems of Adult Day Care Centers

Because adult day care centers are so new, many are still struggling with a number of problems. The continual need to concentrate on funding and prove cost-effectiveness is a major distraction. Many directors spend most of their time applying to funding sources. Most use a variety of sources, and this means continual problems arise in managing and accounting for funds (Von Behren, 1981).

A related problem is the cost of services if one wants to qualify to receive Medicaid reimbursement as an adult day health care center. The cost of providing the required medical component can mean the facility will run at a deficit. The bureaucratic red tape involved in becoming certified as a medical-type center of this sort might be too much for staff to handle. And last, even after meeting all the other requirements, the center might find it does not have enough clients who qualify for Medicaid reimbursement.

Centers are also plagued by the rising cost of transportation to and from the facility. Some of them encourage community service clubs or churches to run special benefits to raise money for vans. But even if these are supplied by an outside source, there is the cost of the drivers; some centers get around this by using volunteer drivers, only to confront high insurance fees and expensive reimbursement for gasoline. A few centers contract for available community transportation sources, such as the vans used at noon for the community meals program; some contract for use of commercial transportation such as taxis or privately owned minibuses. Some use volunteer auto transportation. Many encourage relatives and friends to bring the user to the center. The majority refuse to accept clients who live at a distance of half an hour or more from the center unless the family or user can provide transportation.

Von Behren (1981) also reports that fluctuation in daily attendance and seasonal ups and downs is a cost problem. She also finds that some centers are large enough to serve more clients but are too limited to do so by the funding available.

Acceptance by, and linkage with, medical and other services can be a further problem. Von Behren (1981) holds that, while social service agencies have largely accepted the idea of adult day care, physicians have not; doctors do not refer patients to the centers as often as they should and, in general, these facilities are not used adequately by the medical community. Close linkage with other services has not been established. For example, for patients to make use of the centers they depend upon referrals from agencies which handle these matters for mental health institutions or nursing homes. Mental health institutions, for example, could incorporate day care into their discharge planning—but too few of them have done so to date. Day care centers also need to form links with home health agencies and home nursing groups. If these agencies are used in conjunction with senior day care, even the impaired elderly person living alone may be able to stay in the community longer—and in greater dignity and comfort—than is now the case.

Conclusion

The adult day care center is a program for frail, semiambulatory elderly, many of whom are considered "at risk for institutionalization." Clients spend a number of hours a day, three-to-five days a week, at this program.

An innovative addition to the spectrum of care for the elderly, adult day care brings together a variety of services in one setting: social, recreational, and educational programs; meals; information and referral; transportation; and medical services. The degree of medical services provided is often determined by whether the center is patterned on the medical model, which qualifies for some Medicaid and Medicare funding—or on the "social" model, which does not. The former usually has a nurse, physical and speech therapy specialists, and other medical personnel on staff. It is often affiliated with a hospital, nursing home, or other medical facility. The "social" model usually focuses on a recreational–socialization program, although it may also utilize a community health nurse or other community medical services on a weekly or monthly basis. The social model comprises the largest group of day care centers. It obtains its funding from a vareity of sources ranging from OAA money to SSBG and community block grant funds to private foundations.

A persistent difficulty with adult day care is the increasing distinction made between the medical type ("adult day health care center") and the rest of the centers. Since many sponsors find it too costly to meet Medicaid qualifications for certification, a wide variety of centers are not classified as adult day health care centers. Yet these other facilities badly need funding. They do supply medical services to varying degrees—and should be required to follow strict standards. As early as 1979, Trager clearly saw the problem inherent in separating day care centers into medical versus social types. She said the classification might mean the social type of center would ignore the essential health-related services and restoration needs of many users (Medicaid's rejection of reimbursing such centers encourages just this). On the other hand, Trager felt labeling some centers as designed for physical restoration and for treatment might exclude users who needed some—but not all—of these kinds of service. Perhaps worse, facilities designated for medical and treatment purposes might become institutional or hospital-like in character, treating the users as mere "patients."

Adult day care centers provide an earlier stage of care or a substitute for placement in a nursing home (Lund, 1982). They supplement the adult child or spouse's caretaker services to the aged person. Use of a center allows the caretaker to work away from home—or at least to be freed from 24-hour care. A center can thus play a role in decreasing tension between the care-taker and his family. The adult day care center staff may counsel the care-taker as well as the elderly client on family problems and available communi-ty services.

While many experts see these centers as extremely useful in filling these roles, the day care movement has been slow in developing, primarily because of a lack of funds. Small amounts of money have been allocated for demonstration projects, but continuous funding remains a problem. Fund-ing from such sources as SSBG (Title XX) and AOA fluctuates from year to year. Even the medical model centers qualifying under the narrow Medicaid eligibility requirements receive only partial funding from this source.

This innovative program of adult day care fills a major gap in the continuum of care—but it has yet to reach its potential. One reason for this—besides inadequate funding—is that it directs itself to an impaired elderly population that often does not *want* to be in a setting with other impaired persons, and whose relatives do not want to force them to do so. The caretaker often takes action for change in service provision only when the circumstances dramatically deteriorate: when severe impairment of the aged person or incontinence set in, for example, or a hospital stay ends and special new services are needed. At that point the family may feel forced to insist that the elderly relative use alternative care. By then, a nursing home rather than a day care center is likely to seem the more suitable; the family caretaker no longer wants a partial solution. If the change is in the care-taker's rather than the elderly person's situation this is doubly true; for example, if the caretaker is forced into retirement or falls ill. If the elderly person lives alone and this dramatic change in her health condition occurs, those counseling her may also insist on a full-care solution. This, at least, is my own best guess as to the reasons for relatively low interest in adult day care among those most vitally concerned: it needs to be tested by careful research.

CHAPTER 11

Long-Term Care Services in the Community and Nursing Home

Our population of over 7.6 million old-old elderly suffers from chronic as well as acute disorders. One survey showed that in one state almost a third of those 85 and over was unable to carry out major activities; and almost a fifth of the 75–85 age group was unable to do so (National Center for Health Statistics, 1977). Almost a fifth of those 85 and over and a tenth of the 75–85 group needed help to get dressed. This steadily growing chronically ill population of the incapacitated elderly demands a wide range of health-related services to ensure a higher quality of life.

This chapter will accordingly focus on home health care and home-maker services in the community, nursing home care, and hospice care.

Chronic Illness and the Delivery of Health Care

Care for the chronically ill has never been a major aspect of our health care system. The system focuses on diagnosis of acute, rather than chronic, medical problems. Younger Americans usually have *acute* medical problems that need crisis treatment by a specialized physician. The diagnosis, treatment, and cure of an acute condition rewards doctors in many ways. It is therefore not surprising that it is the focus of most medical training in this country.

However, the health problems of many elderly do not fit this model of care. The elderly are more likely to suffer from chronic long-term health problems for which no real cure is known. Such conditions can often be only controlled or stabilized, not cured—and this is discouraging for physicians. These prolonged health conditions of the elderly include arthritis, diabetes, Alzheimer's disease, and many others. In most cases these degenerative changes in the elderly are irreversible; in fact, they may well be progressively debilitating. Furthermore, since the frail elderly are likely to have multiple health problems, doctors whose expertise and experience is limited to one specialty may have trouble diagnosing and treating such multiple disorders.

Chronic conditions—such as Alzheimer's disease—have vast psychological and sociological implications. Whatever the particular illness, it causes the chronically ill, more than the acute crisis patient, to develop the self-image of "a sick person." It increases dependency on others. Indefinite confinement to bed threatens the patient's psychological well-being.

The drugs used to treat chronic disorders may in themselves further incapacitate the patient. For example, such drugs often cause the patient to be weak and off-balance; this in turn leads to use of a wheelchair and restraining devices. The very existence of a chronic disorder means the older person is "at risk" of removal to a nursing home, where the institutional nature of the facility may cause his subordination to a rigid routine and grave modifications of his normal life-style.

Such are the devastating effects of chronic illness that one would think services ought to focus on this group. However, medical professionals, seeing no cure in sight, and society, seeing this group as nonfunctional, have historically "warehoused" the chronically ill elderly. When unable to care for themselves in their own homes or in those of relatives, they have been placed in institutions: first in almshouses, then in county homes for the aged and in mental institutions—and now in nursing homes.

The Continuum of Care Concept

However, policymakers and gerontologists today are pressing for alternatives to institutionalization. The definition of "long-term" care now includes community-based services as well as institutional care. The new concept of "continuum of care" stresses the need of chronically ill elderly for different levels of care as health conditions and degree of illness vary. The term "continuum" suggests abandonment of the idea of simply providing one service (the nursing home) for all functionally limited persons, regardless of their own preferences and actual support needs. Instead, "continuum" implies a choice of the most appropriate services—with the nursing home the last resort. Increased provision of community alternatives helps the impaired, less-than-fully sufficient elderly function at a maximum possible level of physical, psychological, and social well-being in the least possibly restrictive setting. For example, intensive physical therapy for patients suffering from a broken hip may prevent the onset of total immobility.

Whenever possible, the chronically ill are cared for in their own homes. The idea is to foster as much self-sufficiency and independence as possible and to preserve dignity and positive self-image, while allowing the family to carry part of the responsibility for care.

This new interest in a community-based long-term care system also broadens the base of *who* is covered to include the large elderly population "at risk of institutionalization." The 1977 data from the National Center for Health Statistics show that in one state, almost a tenth of those 85 and over needed help in bathing and 7 percent needed toilet assistance.

Home Health Care and Homemaker Services

Home health care and homemaker assistance are important community supportive services that offer an alternative to the nursing home or other institutional care. With medical and personal support, hospitalized elderly may return to their homes more quickly or may never even need to be hospitalized. These community services are oriented to the person's individual needs but are not 24-hour nursing services.

Benefits of Home Health Care

Providing home health aid and homemaker assistance means that elderly users can remain in familiar surroundings where they can perform at least some duties and family members can offer humane care. Another advantage of being in such home surroundings is that the sick person is more psychologically receptive to care and therefore likely to be more cooperative with medical treatment personnel such as visiting nurses. There are economic savings to the government as an additional advantage, since home assistance is cheaper than nursing home care. (It is given for only a few hours a day.) By offering some relief to family members it encourages them to participate in caretaking. A GAO study estimates that 15 to 25 percent of the institutional elderly could live elsewhere if home health services were available (U.S. General Accounting Office, 1979). A reduction of 15 percent of the nursing home population each year could mean a saving of at least $1.5 billion to the government, which pays the bills for many of these patients.

Furthermore, every reduction in the number of days a person spends in the hospital or institution means fewer hospital and nursing home beds are needed—a further saving, since there is less need to construct hospitals and new nursing homes. Bryant et al.'s (1974) study of two groups of 25 stroke victims illustrates how homemaker care cuts cost. They found that the stroke patients who had in-home services required an average of 24 days in the hospital, while the 25 stroke victims without in-home services spent an average of 34.9 days there. Looking at the groups after nine months, Bryant et al. found that eight persons without in-home help were moved to skilled nursing facilities, compared to only one person in the in-home service group. This suggests that in-home services can mean not only lower costs but less chance of transfer to a nursing facility.

Some states, in this period of fiscal austerity, are turning increasingly to use of these in-home services in order to save money. For example, New York City's in-home service program, funded mostly under Medicaid, increased from $40 million in 1974 to $300 million in 1981–82 (Crystal, 1982). However, under the recent Reagan cuts, other states have reduced the allowable hours of service (Estes, 1983b).

Types of Home Care Services

The need is accelerating to provide community services in addition to traditional nursing homes as our number of old-old Americans increases. In 1977 an estimated 2.5 million elderly required home health services but were without them.

DEFINITIONS

Under the Older Americans Act, in-home services include preinstitution evaluation and screening, and services in the areas of home health, homemaker assistance, escorts, readers, and others designed to assist older individuals to live independently in a home environment. The combination of services varies according to a patient's needs, of course. Coordination of services and reassessment of the patient's condition are necessary to cover individual conditions.

In-home services can be described in three descending levels of intensity of nursing and personal care. The level most likely to qualify as medically necessary under Medicare regulations is that of *skilled nursing services* ordered for patients with acute medical problems. Examples of these problems are bone fractures, cardiac seizures, or terminal illnesses requiring nursing care to adminster intravenous feeding or catheters. The services include nurses' visits, physical therapy, or other medical services ordered by a physician. *Personal care with some medical services* is a lower level of in-home care. In this case the person's medical condition has stabilized; it may be an acute or long-term care condition. The main need is for assistance in daily activities, such as bathing, such minor health aid as supervision of medication and blood pressure tests, and aid in physical therapy exercise.

The last level is *homemaker chore services,* such as housekeeping, meal preparation, and laundry service.

There is considerable overlap between these levels: care needs to be flexible and personalized according to the individual's often multiple needs. Problems in terminology also exist because, historically, the health departments developed home health aide programs and the welfare departments developed homemaker services. The jobs overlapped to such a degree that in 1965 the Department of Health, Education, and Welfare developed standards that established a home health–homemaker category, with both tasks performed by a single individual. However, confusion still exists because Medicare will fund only home health aides while SSBGs also fund homemakers.

Agencies

It may be a good idea to describe the agencies offering such services. These are often called "multiservice agencies certified for participation in Medicare programs." They meet the Medicare requirements that the home health agency must have as its primary function skilled nursing services and at least one additional therapeutic service. Because of Medicare funding regulations, many clients are acute-care patients who have short-term needs after hospitalization.

The multiservice home health agency is likely to be part of the public health department or the visiting nurse association. Sometimes it may be a unit of a hospital or HMO: in such cases it utilizes hospital medical staff and serves primarily the skilled nursing care needs of its discharged patients. In other situations, it is part of a multiservice nonprofit agency such as Catholic Charities. It may also be a private agency. Well over half of these home health services are provided by multiservice agencies.

Some agencies fill only the home health care–homemaker functions; they may be nonprofit entities or private, profit-making enterprises. The latter are greatly increasing in number as the population able to pay their fees grows.

Homemaker agencies, whether public, nonprofit, or private, sometimes provide no home health care. Public departments of social services, funded under SSBG money, have long offered homemaker services. Some homemaker services are also funded by OAA funds.

Staff

Ideally the home health agency should include nurses (RNs and LPNs), physical therapists, possibly occupational and speech therapists, home health aides, and medical social workers. However, many agencies have only one or two nurses on staff.

SUPERVISORY STAFF

Agencies specialized to offer in-home services have a nurse, social worker, or other professional take on the role of supervisor. Part of the supervisory job is to assess the patient's needs. The supervisor, especially if a social worker, will work with the discharge department of the local hospital(s), preferably consulting with the family, to plan for the client's care in her own home. In such cases the supervisor or staff social worker will visit the client's home or have an office interview with her. The supervisor reviews the person's health status and level of functioning. She develops a treatment plan and coordinates services. Such a professional understands that because the illness is usually a chronic rather than an acute one, it will be a long-term problem and that she therefore needs to develop a treatment plan that takes this into account. For example, she may suggest that the family modify its home to facilitate use of a wheelchair in it.

VISITING NURSES

These make up the most clearly defined group on the home health team. They visit the sick in their homes and provide some medical services, such as injections, medication, and restorative nursing. The nurse is often the one who reassesses the patient's needs. Visiting nurses who have received additional training as nurse practitioners may be even more likely to give extended care, and may work with little supervision from the doctor. These nurses—particularly those trained in geriatrics—are more likely than most doctors to look at a case in its totality, with its multiple problems, including social and psychological dimensions.

Such nursing services are generally obtained through a public health agency, visiting nurse association, or separate home health care agency. Costs can be covered by Medicare if clients meet the qualifications for care. The time allowed is limited. If the patient is covered by Medicaid or SSBG funding, visits are made in accord with need as spelled out under the treatment plan.

HOME HEALTH CARE AIDES

The same team which includes visiting nurses usually includes homemaker–home health aides; their number is far below what is needed. Although they are a growing group, they are not yet clearly defined. Often the term "homemaker–home health care aide" is used because the two jobs are done by the same person. The home health care aide receives training in health and related problems before being certified. Standards are set by their own association, the National Council for Homemaker–Home Health Aide Services. The National Council (1976) defines the homemaker–home health aide role as follows:

The trained homemaker–home health aide, who works for a community agency (which could be a hospital), carries out assigned tasks in the family's or individual's place of residence, working under the supervision of a professional person who also assesses the need for the service and implements the plan for care.

Home health aides are trained to visit the aged and check on vital indicators of health problems, including physical and mental deterioration or progress toward improved health. They instruct the patient in self-help. They change dressings and, under supervision of professionals in the agency, check blood pressure, apply ointments, and assist in self-administration of prescribed medicines. The aide can also supervise exercise, perform oral hygiene, and bathe the patient. The aide may also do household tasks essential to health in the home, such as changing beds and doing personal laundry.

An example of one particular home health aide's duties may prove of interest. This aide works at a nonprofit home health service that also has a counseling component. This home health aide is assigned to two or three patients. In the initial period of care, she sees the patient five times a week for two hours; when the patient has improved, this is cut back to three days a week, and later to two days a week. Help is given as long as the health professional supervising the case feels it necessary. On each visit this home health aide charts the patient's temperature, measures blood pressure and weight, and takes samples for urine tests. She gives baths and encourages the patient to take the prescribed medication, but is not allowed to administer the drugs. Sometimes she fixes breakfast and even lunch, although this agency runs a Meals-on-Wheels program that the client can use. The aide puts the patient in the wheelchair if necessary, and assists with restorative exercises. She helps her client use special medical devices, cleaning and storing them afterwards. Finally, the aide occasionally accompanies the patient by bus or taxi to a medical appointment. She often provides homemaker services, even though this part of her work is not eligible for payment by such sources as Medicare.

Only homemaker services may be provided if the aide lacks home health aide training. Some agencies pay only for homemaker services. The homemaker job includes doing chores, housekeeping, and attending to personal care. It can be a combination of shopping, preparing meals, doing laundry, and providing general housekeeping services. This kind of homemaker may also provide some personal care services, such as bathing, dressing, and even feeding patients.

MEDICAL SOCIAL WORKERS

Frequently members of the home health care team, medical social workers may even administer the program itself. These social workers identify psychological needs and counsel patients, helping them adapt to stressful circumstances and to cope with their illnesses and disabilities. They try to locate the patient's strengths and build on them in order to help the person live an independent—or at least semi-independent—life. The medical social worker also helps patients connect with the variety of services in the local community. He helps family members to integrate their efforts with these homemaker–home health care services. He may locate funding sources for these services and assist families in filling out applications for aid. Finally, he may make the necessary arrangements if the client has to return to the hospital for tests or further care.

Funding

The most complicated aspect of homemaker, home health care, and nursing services is funding. Critics have complained that Medicare's tight regulations seriously limit the availability of these services at a time when gerontology experts are stressing alternatives to institutionalization. Medicare does not fund homemaker services; it reimburses home health care for a limited amount of time—and then only if the client has an acute health problem requiring skilled nursing care or physical, occupational, or speech therapy. Thus Medicare coverage does not apply to the chronically ill person; it covers only short-term care and only the home health services component, not homemaker services, of home care.

Medicaid has the severe limitations of being only for the poor elderly; it covers SSI recipients and, in some states, the "medically needy"—those whose incomes are large enough to cover daily living expenses according to income levels set by the state, but insufficient to cover the costs of medical care. Since Medicaid is partly a state-funded program, each state varies somewhat in coverage. Some states focus on home health care while others provide little if any such service. The federal restrictions of homemaker services or personal care services do not exist to the same degree as with Medicare, but states usually follow the Medicare model of providing nursing services, home health aide services, physical and speech therapy, and not simply the maximum allowable personal care. Medicaid can be provided on a long-term basis. One of its goals is to offer a variety of services in order to prevent or delay deterioration of health and subsequent institutionalization.

In reality, neither Medicaid nor Medicare has provided much funding for homemaker or home health services to date. In 1981 home health services received only 2.8 percent of Medicaid funds for the aged. However, this situation is improving somewhat under the new Omnibus Reconciliation Act of 1981, which amends current medical regulations and allows states to provide a wide range of home and community-based services by requesting

Medicaid waivers in order to fund certain noninstitutional long-term care projects or services.

Nursing Homes and Other Long-Term Care Facilities

Most of the services described in this book allow the frail elderly to stay in the community. The nursing home, however, as a long-term care facility, typically isolates the elderly person from the community in an institutional setting.

There has been a growing concern about this institutional solution, not only because it is felt many elderly users could manage well enough in the community with adequate support services, but because the quality of care offered by the nursing homes has been so poor. Many are the complaints about deplorable living conditions and serious abuse of patients: those concerned maintain that the nursing home is more of a warehouse for dying patients than a medical care facility dedicated to reversing or stabilizing the physical and psychological deterioration of these frail elderly. The elderly often fear going there, considering it a prison; many would rather turn their faces to the wall in their own homes and die in dignity. Adult children usually feel extremely guilty for sending their parents to such places.

Yet some type of 24-hour nursing supervision facility is needed for frail elderly with serious long-term physical or mental problems, especially those lacking able caretakers who can look after them around the clock. In fact, laudable long-term care facilities are possible. We have examples of this, both in the United States and in Europe. For example, in Denmark, local municipal authorities have built and maintained shining monuments of good nursing care that they proudly exhibit to gerontology experts from all over the world.

To improve nursing homes is important to every American because there is a chance—one in five or even one in four—that one of us is likely to spend some of the time in her later years in a nursing home. Thus, while only 4 or 5 percent of the elderly are found in nursing homes at a particular point in time, studies show that 20 percent or more of the elderly die in nursing homes (Palmore, 1976; Lesnoff-Caravaglia, 1978–79). In total, over 1.3 million elderly of 65 and over are currently in some 23,000 nursing and personal care homes (including those without nursing, such as domiciliary facilities and board-and-care homes).

Types of Nursing Home Facilities

In this chapter the term "nursing home" refers both to skilled nursing facilities and intermediate-care facilities. The skilled nursing facility (SNF) provides 24-hour-a-day nursing care under the supervision of a registered nurse (RN) on day shifts and/or a licensed vocational nurse (LVN) on afternoon or night shifts. This kind of facility accepts those needing extensive care, both bedridden and ambulatory patients. It provides the emergency and continuous professional services of a physician, nursing care, and rehabilitative assistance. The facility often has physical therapy programs for stroke victims and others. An SNF is usually certified as a Medicare facility; it therefore must meet federal and state requirements regarding staffing, visits by doctors, regular programs of activities, use and preparation of drugs, patients' rights and visiting privileges—and it must allow scrutiny by an omsbudsman program. Such requirements obviously make this kind of facility more expensive than others.

The intermediate-care facility (ICF) has less stringent nursing supervision requirements. It is a "health" model rather than a "medical" model, and its patients are more likely than SNF patients to have stabilized, if chronic, health problems and are likely to need health supervision, but not full-time professional attention. The ICF provides 24-hour service and supervision of patients, but requires that a nurse *or* a licensed vocational nurse be on duty only during the day (eight hours), seven days a week (California licensing requirement). It is assumed patients will be ambulatory, although some will use walkers or crutches. Personal care is provided; patients receive assistance in the activities of daily life, such as dressing, bathing, and even eating. Some forms of social and recreational care are provided.

These two levels of care may be found even in the same facility—but they must be kept in separate wings. Another type is the "domiciliary care" facility, also called boarding home, rest home, home for the aged, sheltered-care facility, and, in New York, adult home. Such facilities provide food, shelter, and personal care; they are often used for former mental institution patients although such patients are also found in SNF and ICF facilities. They serve people who have no health problem or injury, people for whom 24-hour nursing services and medical supervision are unnecessary. They need a protective environment which provides assistance in daily living. Although our discussion focuses on the first two types, the SNF and ICF, domiciliary care facilities have similar problems. In fact, loose regulation of domiciliary care facilities by state and local authorities has led to many problems; they are often substandard and run by unqualified staff.

Medicare and Medicaid Regulations

Medicare and Medicaid make payments to certified SNFs for qualifying patients, and Medicaid reimburses ICFs. In 1965, when Medicare and Medicaid were brought in, the government payments looked so attractive that chains of privately owned nursing homes sprouted up. Because of their new source of support as well as their new role as a locale for former mental hospital patients, nursing homes increased from about a third of a million beds in 1969 to almost one and one-half million beds in 1983.

Medicare regulations allow hospital patients to convalesce for up to 100 days in a certified SNF (20 days full subsidy). However, because Medicare administrators have always wanted to avoid funding long-term care cases, they have made regulations for reimbursement very stringent. The care must be medically necessary skilled nursing care for acute cases with a rehabilitative potential. Thus a very small proportion (less than 4 percent) of nursing home bills are paid by Medicare.

Medicaid, the federal–state health coverage program for the poor, is more involved in reimbursement to skilled nursing facilities. By 1971 Medicaid, concerned with the costs of care of the chronically ill in skilled nursing facilities, and believing a lower level of care was possible for such patients, agreed to cover payments for poor elderly in the intermediate-care facility, with its lower nursing staff requirements and lower costs. Medicaid has now become the main financial support for the nursing home industry, making at least one-half the total payments for nursing home patients (U.S. Bureau of Census, 1976); the main recipients are the long-term chronically ill. However, few are the traditional poor or minority elderly, for nursing homes accept very few poor or minority applicants. Those who qualify for Medicaid are usually "conversion" cases; they enter the home with adequate assets, but *become poor* after being in the facility for months or years. In some nursing homes, a person, after using up her assets, is asked to leave—because that particular home refuses to carry Medicaid cases!

In many nursing homes, the management allows a certain proportion of the total to be Medicaid cases; the rest are private patients. The private patients pay more, and their higher fees help to cover the low Medicaid payments. Thus we have a complex situation in which Medicaid and Medicare money stimulated the growth of nursing homes—but the low Medicaid payments now contribute to the industry's negative view of these patients and restrict their use of nursing homes. The low Medicaid payments lead to another problem: the attempt to curtail costs in private facilities. With low Medicaid reimbursements, the profit-seeking private facility can usually realize a profit only if it cuts back on staffing and other costs. This in turn reduces the *quality* of care in nursing homes.

The main problem in this whole situation is the profit motive; over three-fourths of American nursing homes are proprietary enterprises. In most other industrial countries municipal governments or nonprofit groups operate the nursing homes. Of course Americans *do* help the sick elderly in nursing homes through their tax dollars for the Medicaid and Medicare payments—but in most cases these payments are made to a profit-making corporation. The present reimbursement systems are neither able to produce adequate incentives for quality care nor compelling motivations for keeping serious cases regardless of their income brackets.

Description of Nursing Homes

ENVIRONMENT

American nursing homes usually differ from specially designed housing for the elderly, whether congregate or apartment-style, in that nursing homes look more like hospitals and are "total" institutions whose patients seldom leave the premises except for medical treatment. As a hybrid between old age homes and hospitals, they have not been able to break away from the medical model of the hospital, even though staff often have little medical training. White uniforms and hospital beds, usually two-to-four to a room, contribute to this hospital-like atmosphere.

FACILITIES

In many nursing homes the 60- to 100-or-more-bed accommodations are on several corridors or wings. Each wing may serve a particular type of patient (e.g., the severely mentally disturbed). Some facilities, however, mix types of patients in order to fill whatever bed is available when someone leaves or dies.

The nursing home includes a dining room, although those confined to their beds or wheelchairs often eat in their rooms. Physical and occupational therapy rooms, recreational facilities, and lounges or lobby areas where the residents congregate are often part of the nursing home's layout. There is usually at least one nursing station where the RNs and licensed practical nurses (LPNs) are likely to spend most of their time doing administrative tasks.

The facilities, in many cases, have small, unpleasant lobbies crowded with wheelchair patients and uninviting dining rooms. Another complaint is lack of adequate space and the sharing of hospital-like rooms, usually with one to three other patients, plus lack of one's own furniture. This situation disorients the patient by placing him in a new, unfamiliar environment. The lack of privacy alienates him. Frequently the facilities are also not well maintained: they are often dirty and smell of urine. One New York State adult home (a domiciliary care facility) had over 50 violations, mainly in building deficiencies and equipment. In the 1983 California Commission on Nursing Homes hearing, one spokesman described the nursing homes visited as filthy and roach-infested, with dirty sheets on the floor.

PROGRAMS IN THE HOME

A wide variety of recreational activities is usually included: occupational and physical therapy, exercise classes, and in some cases, reality orientation for the confused. There may be a recreation director, but often many of the programs are run by outside agency staff from a junior college or adult education program.

THE PATIENTS OF NURSING HOMES

Most residents are among the old-old, aged 80 and upward (average age 82), often lacking relatives to care for them. In one survey, half the patients lacked such relatives (Moss and Halmandaris, 1977). Some patients are there for a short rehabilitative stay after hospital care, but many of the chronically ill stay until they die. The average length of stay is around two years (Moss and Halmandaris, 1977) but there are wide variations. Some die shortly after being put in the facility (in one study half died within 30 days); some stay on for years.

Patients suffer from a wide variety of health problems, including strokes, broken hips, arthritis, Alzheimer's disease, or long-term psychological problems—from psychoses to functional disorders. Gottesman and Bourestom (1974) found in their large study some 25 percent of the observed patients confused and another 28 percent "moderately alert." Only half were "alert." Most patients needed primarily personal care assistance rather than nursing care. Gottesman and Bourestom found that about half the residents needed such personal care assistance as help in dressing, bathing, and eating. Crystal (1982), criticizing overuse of the nursing home, reports that at least a third of the nursing home patients in one study could be placed in a lower level of care facility, since their needs were mainly for personal care. On the other hand, Moss and Halmandaris (1977) found one-third of the patients to be incontinent. Many do need 24-hour nursing care, since their health conditions make community and family care difficult.

Today medical assessments are used more and more to screen out those elderly who do not need this intensive care, but who could instead be better served in the community (see Chapter 2). It follows that the family needs more education on the available community alternatives. There is also interest in screening out the mental cases who so often set the tone for today's nursing homes. In some homes these patients are put in a separate wing. In some countries (such as Denmark) they are usually put in separate facilities (Huttman, 1982).

Other ways to improve the atmosphere of the nursing home include redesigning the setting as a more homelike place, less like a hospital. In general the treatment should move away from the medical model. A multipurpose service and multidisciplinary team approach is needed because, as the World Health Organization stresses, there is a social as well as a medical dimension to the proper care of these elderly ill persons. Gerontologists increasingly emphasize treating the whole self—that is, working with the social and psychological, as well as with the physiological aspects of the problem. They say therapeutic regimens are doomed to fail if they do not recognize that effective treatment of the individual means meeting all these needs.

To be able to carry out such a task the whole staff situation of the nursing home needs to be overhauled. The characteristics of the nursing home given above—such as use of the medical model, coupled with a desire to cut staff costs in the interest of profit—have led to a situation in which nurses' aides are far overrepresented. In addition, the large number of mentally ill patients—many of them incontinent—has combined with another disincentive, low wages, to make the nursing home one of the least desirable of all employment locales.

THE STAFF

Staff is the ingredient that sets the tone for the nursing home. It is the staff that determine whether the home exhibits a caring, warm atmosphere, one responsive to client needs.

The training and general quality of the staff in most nursing homes are major sources of the American nursing home's negative image. First, there are too few highly qualified staff and, second, such staff spend little time with individual patients. These facilities usually have a doctor on call; patients usually have their own private doctors as well. Doctors on staff are seldom trained in gerontology and, as Mitchell finds (1982), they view elderly patients negatively as cases with little chance for improvement in their physical and mental conditions. Butler (1975) remarks:

> Many states do not even require a principal physician, let alone a medical director, for a nursing home . . . doctors seldom conduct rounds. . . . Family doctors tend not to visit patients in nursing homes if they are too far away. Other doctors do "gang visits," seeing a number of patients quickly.

Nurses often complain of these "gang visits" of doctors. For example, in a 1975 U.S. Senate report on long-term care, New York State reported that such complaints tally; doctors often provide vague diagnoses, rely heavily on tranquilizers to manage patients, and maintain inadequate records. Many doctors deal with their patients' needs by telephone or prescribe drugs vaguely—such as "use as required"—thus allowing the nurse excessive latitude to do as she sees fit.

Long-term care facility administrators, unless they are nurses, also usually have little experience working with older people or in nursing homes. As Koff (1982) reports, many are not affiliated with any association of long-term care administrators; therefore they are unlikely to be exposed to the association's code of ethics. Many represent the facility's owner, and their main jobs are to keep costs down and deal with families and the licensing regulators as necessary.

Registered nurses make up only a small part of the staff. RNs are usually on staff in SNFs, but in ICFs there may be only licensed practical nurses (LPNs). Harris and Cole (1980) report only about 65,000 RNs, divided into three shifts per day (or about 23,000 per shift), caring for approximately 1 million nursing home patients. Highly qualified nurses are hard to hire and retain because nursing home jobs have a low status in the medical profession. These professional nursing personnel serve the patient mainly by dispensing medication, giving injections, and looking into emergency situations. Their main jobs, however, are usually administrative; sometimes a nurse is even the head administrator of the facility. They order supplies, hire staff, and handle people seeking admission or talk to their families. These administrative responsibilities limit the nurses' time available for patient contact. In the Gottesman and Bourestom (1974) study of 40 Detroit nursing homes, the researchers found that residents received nursing services from either professional or nonprofessional staff in only 2 percent of the time they observed.

Nurses' aides or orderlies usually have most of the contacts with patients and perform 80 to 90 percent of the nursing care. These aides often have no real medical training (Dennett and Mullins, 1982). In the Handschu study (1972), half of the nurses' aides surveyed had received no formal training for this type of job, and only half were high school graduates. Many of these aides had previously held only marginal jobs—and some had arrest records.

Even in the same private nursing home, the staff–patient ratio may vary between private patients and those under Medicaid. Gottesman and Bourestom (1974) report that the patients who get the best nursing care are those who pay their own nursing costs and have at least a monthly visit from relatives. Nonprofit nursing homes had a better staff–patient ratio than privately owned nursing homes (Kart et al., 1978). The minimal amount (two to three hours) of nursing care per patient per day required by some states is often inadequate.

Because nursing homes are undesirable places to work—with their dying patients, mentally ill, and incontinent cases—some of the personnel willing to take the jobs have "spoiled identities." These include former mental patients, alcoholics, drifters in need of temporary work, and those with prison records.

A high rate of turnover and excessive absenteeism are typical of the staff, especially among the nonprofessionals who comprise the bulk of the personnel. The turnover rate of aides/orderlies is estimated at about 75 percent a year by Harris and Cole (1980). In many areas nursing homes are desperately understaffed. Nurses reported to a recent Commission on Nursing Homes that wages are so low and working conditions so bad that most nurses give up hope of having competent aides (California Department of Health, 1983). Since the work of aides includes emptying bedpans, changing soiled sheets, and taking verbal abuse from disturbed mental patients, it is not surprising that aides often stay only a short period or are marginal workers at best. High turnover may even be encouraged by management in order to save money. Leaving positions unfilled for a week or more reduces costs. Turnover makes unlikely staff getting benefits offered after a period of employment. Turnover also decreases the likelihood of unionization—another factor in the profit equation. Sometimes only one-half of the "official" staff is on duty at any one time, as positions are left unfilled or workers take days off. In California's 1983 hearings on nursing homes, one nurse director described a day when she had only one aide for 36 patients (California Department of Health, 1983).

Insufficient staff means that patients are fed in their rooms instead of being wheeled to the dining room; they are left undressed and, if incontinent, left in dirty sheets for hours. Patients' calls for assistance are not answered. High absenteeism and turnover not only contribute to *less* service for patients, but also to *worse*. High turnover means that the patient is continually handled by different staff. Instead of being helped by two or three familiar personnel year after year, the patient is assisted by a continual stream of nurses' aides and others who know little about her condition and may make little attempt to learn about it, because they regard the job as a fill-in until something better comes along (Solomon and Vickers, 1979).

Underpaid and dissatisfied staff are likely to take out their hostile feelings on the patients, especially when the latter are disabled, poor, or mentally confused. Since the patients are powerless, staff need not respond to their requests, and can even be abusive. Overworked staff may get angry at patient requests and verbally—or even physically—attack the "overdemanding and difficult" patients. The aides may define acts of mentally ill patients, such as defecating on the floor, hitting the wall, or kicking an aide, as deviant behavior that should be punished. Since the aides are usually isolated from the nurse at the nursing station, or even from other aides on a particular wing, their abuse often goes unseen or, if seen by other aides, goes unreported.

Overwork and the nature of the job can also cause an impersonal attitude toward patients. *Lack of a caring attitude* is a serious problem in many homes (Vladeck, 1980). While many nurses and aides are sincerely concerned with their patients' well-being, others simply want to get the job done. They may be efficient, but seem indifferent to their charges' physical and emotional health. For example, Curtin (1972) describes the shower-time routine in one home, in which persons who felt they could bathe themselves were showered instead by aides who wanted to get a room's duties done quickly. Curtin reports that these aged had their skeletal bodies picked up by two aides, put into the shower chair, and pushed under the shower. Aides then removed the blanket, and showered the patient down, using soap. Then they rubbed the patient off with a towel and went on to the next. It is easier for the staff to do the personal care of the frail aged than wait for them to do it more slowly themselves—but it is counterproductive and inhumane as well.

Patient Dependency in the Nursing Home Environment

In this staff–patient relationship, then, the staff have power over the patients' private activities, such as bathing; patients must beg for assistance to go to the bathroom or to be fed. Unfortunately, this dependency is usually a major feature of the institutional atmosphere. Unlike the congregate housing resident, patients are treated as if they were sick persons in a hospital. They are often forced to stay in wheelchairs, complete with their physical constraints, and are then wheeled away to their meals.

Heavy use of drugs (chemical constraints), especially by mental patients, also ensures this dependency. Drugs weaken the patient's ability to function in an alert, active way, keeping him drowsy and off balance. The staff may then feel that it is dangerous for the patient to walk about, constraining him in a wheelchair to avoid accidents—thus making him a very dependent person, almost a prisoner. As stated in the U.S. Senate hearings (1975), "Excessive use of tranquilizers can quickly reduce an ambulatory patient to a zombie, confining the patient to a chair or bed, causing the patient's muscles to atrophy from inaction and causing general health to deteriorate quickly." While physical restraint in the case of some mentally ill patients may be necessary, it is not needed for those who are merely confused. One patient who ran away from a nursing home said that he did so before they gave him drugs that would make it impossible for him to carry out such an independent action, and before they restrained him as a prisoner, incapable even of using the bathroom alone. The overuse of drugs includes use of multiple drugs without understanding the reaction of one drug with another. Moss and Halmandaris (1977) charge that "the flow of drugs through America's 23,000 nursing homes is almost totally without control" and is "extremely haphazard."

Guidelines for use of physical restraints should be one of the concerns of any patient rights' group or omsbudsman program. Such use should be a very last resort, and should be approved by an outside source. Restraint on contact with the outside world is also a characteristic of the institutional environment. Many nursing homes require the patient to remain within the home. In the absence of an official policy, staff try in every way to discourage residents from going outside. They may be rightfully concerned about confused wanderers or serious mental cases who try to leave the nursing home, but the staff extend this restriction on outside movement to all patients. Even if relatives wish to take the patient out to lunch, the staff may discourage it. Most of these homes qualify as strictly closed institutions—even though there are no barred windows or locked doors. The price of admission includes the patients' surrender of his contacts with the larger community and his freedom of action.

This lack of contact with the outside world makes the person more vulnerable to the effects of total institutionalization: the nightmarish quality of the situation is accepted, and progressive withdrawal and depersonalization set in. The patient increasingly responds to a machinelike routine in an automatic way. Since new roles and meaningful social activities are lacking, the patient relates only superficially to other patients, many of whom are seriously ill and remain there only for a short period before dying.

Thus because of all these factors—lack of communication with the real world, lack of privacy, extreme dependency on staff, and the routinization of daily living—the nursing home, instead of promoting rehabilitation, has become a place that in every way can hasten the patient's deterioration.

Improvement of the Nursing Home Situation

Complaints about nursing home conditions have been so numerous that many groups, such as the Gray Panthers, have demanded action. Consequently, many legislators have held hearings and have enacted new legislation on the subject.

The new laws include provisions for: (1) increased regulation and monitoring of nursing homes for facility deficiencies and failure to meet staffing requirements, (2) patients' rights, and (3) a nursing homes' omsbudsman program. I think creation of a noninstitutional, more independent atmosphere, increased contacts with community and family, and improvement of staff ought also to be high priorities. Whether these could bring about the reform needed is questionable—but they all represent moves in the right direction.

Deinstitutionalized and Independent Atmosphere

Dependency of patients on the institution staff can be decreased by providing aids to independent movement for the patient. One means to this end is the design and installation of furniture which enables the patient to help himself more easily; for example, toilets can be designed to make it easy to move to them from a wheelchair, and grab rails should be provided at difficult access points. Decreased use of drugs can keep patients more alert—and out of wheelchairs. Reality orientation sessions geared to identify the day of week and planned activities, for example, can also increase alertness. Greater attention to the incontinence problem, such as bladder training and use of incontinence control drugs (Michigan, University of, 1983) or new mechanisms, such as the "fecal incontinence collector," can decrease the existence of this unpleasant handicap.

Deemphasizing the institutional environment of a nursing home will improve the quality of life there. This can be done by allowing the residents to furnish their own rooms, by making the lobbies and corridors more "homelike," by allowing some kinds of pets, and by taking staff out of uniform. Deemphasis on routine would also help. Use of the nursing home for community activities and involvement of volunteers in the program serve to integrate the center into the surrounding community. All of these "reforms" already exist in the Danish nursing homes the author (1982) visited. The atmosphere there was in sharp contrast to that of American homes. Our closest counterpart to the Danish exemplar is the hospital-connected hospice described later in this chapter.

Upgrading Staff Quality

Staff deficiencies also need to be corrected: this is definitely an area where drastic reform is needed. In Denmark many young girls are eager to give service to the aged in a nursing home. We need to recruit this segment of our population into nursing home work. One possibility is to provide funding to encourage nursing home internships for nurses, social workers, nurses' aides, and even doctors. A very worthwhile program would be to train nurses' aides more thoroughly and professionally. Increasing the pay of nurses' aides and improving their working conditions could ensure that nursing homes will not remain employers of last resort. The integration of volunteers and families into care provision activities would also improve the morale of the workers as well as help put an end to abuse of the elderly.

Improvement in State Regulatory Supervision

State regulations for licensing nursing homes have existed for a long time. The state board or department of health inspects and licenses homes; the license must be renewed as often as once a year. When patients, their families, or local agencies file complaints, state inspectors visit the facility in question. The emphasis so far has been on building and equipment standards and safety factors. Although some states do have staffing, service, and patient care standards, many of them pay little attention to such matters. Nurses in homes in such states complain that health departments find trivial violations—inadequate charts, a burned-out fire escape light, an unclean kitchen facility—yet overlook the high absentee rate of staff and other serious problems mentioned above. Inspectors and regulators themselves often consider the regulations to be a poor method of ensuring quality care in these facilities.

A major problem is that whatever the regulation, it is seldom enforced (Pear, 1982). A U.S. Senate Subcommittee on Long-Term Care report (1975), in a chapter entitled "Nursing Home Inspections: A National Farce," reported that the threat of license revocation is about the only weapon available to the enforcers. Even when steps in this direction are taken, judges are reluctant to close a facility if the owners say they will try to correct the deficiencies. If a new owner steps in, inspectors will give him a grace period to deal with the violations. Thus the situation can stay in limbo for a long time.

Enforcement is also difficult because finding another facility for the patients is no easy task: authorities are therefore extremely reluctant to close a nursing home. Most homes even have waiting lists. Should space be available in another facility, the move may be traumatic at best for the patients, again making the authorities reluctant to take decisive action.

Enforcement is also hampered by outright collusion between nursing home owners and inspectors (Mendelson and Hapgood, 1974). The nursing home owners, including physician-owners, may be able to pressure state officials to be lenient. The nursing home industry, through its powerful lobby, can see that regulatory provisions are watered down substantially. Finally, the lack of adequate funds to staff inspection units diminishes enforcement efforts.

Mandatory patients' rights can improve this situation. Patients' rights are now written into Medicare and Medicaid agreements with nursing homes. The homes must prominently display the written statement. The patient has the right to be free from mental and physical abuse and from chemical and (except in emergencies) physical restraints, except as authorized in writing by a physician for a specified and limited period of time, and (when necessary) to protect the patient from injury to himself or to others. Other rights obligate the nursing home to ensure that the patient is:

— fully informed by a physician of his medical condition and may participate in the planning of medical treatment (unless medically contraindicated) and may refuse treatment (ICF resident only);
— able to exercise his rights as patient and as citizen, free from restraint, interference, coercion, discrimination or reprisal;
— allowed to manage his personal financial affairs or to be given at least quarterly accounting of financial transactions made on his behalf if the facility accepts this responsibility;
— kept fully informed of services available and charges for services

This statement enumerates many other rights in addition to those listed above. But "statement" does not necessarily mean "enforcement."

The "exemptions" in each clause of the statement just outlined may be necessary in the case of certain very sick elderly, but such wording allows an easy out for any nursing home that violates patients' rights. It is hard to enforce such a loosely worded regulation. Even when violations are so blatantly evident that a case for enforcement can be made, the penalties involved are too light to worry most nursing home owners. Heavier sanctions are needed, such as higher fines, or even injunctions. Perhaps owners who are continual violators should be sent to jail. Within the nursing home administration itself, a mechanism should be set up to penalize those personnel who violate patients' rights.

An ombudsman program is another promising remedy for this nearly intolerable situation. Such a program designates a public official (and her office) as the body to mediate and investigate complaints about mistreatment and other violations in nursing homes. A mandatory long-term care ombudsman program has been instituted federally through the AAAs. Individual states have enacted their own ombudsman programs and, within these programs, have a local ombudsman in AAA offices. "Ombudsman" is a Swedish term referring to a neutral, independent person who investigates complaints made by private citizens against government abuse or caprice. In the last few years the ombudsman's ability to investigate nursing homes has been strengthened in many states by laws giving the ombudsman rights of access to patients' personal and medical records under specific circumstances, protection from civil liability for the ombudsman while performing his duties, and a civil penalty for willful interference with an ombudsman's legitimate actions. These measures make it harder for nursing home owners and their adminstrators to interfer with the local ombudsman's ability to investigate. However, the ombudsman's power is still quite limited, for he has little ability to impose solutions or fines. As Holmes and Holmes (1979) report, if the nursing home administrators and the government regulators don't want to cooperate, it is hard for the nursing home ombudsman to move ahead with a given case. In fact, the nursing home industry often puts pressure on the ombudsman's office to tread lightly in reprimanding nursing home administrators. In addition, his office is usually poorly funded, understaffed, and unable to conduct extensive investigations.

This does not mean that violations are not recorded when complaints are made to department of health nursing home inspectors; they are—and this means that there is a record on file to which knowledgeable agencies, such as the National Citizens Coalition for Nursing Home Reform or local reform groups, can refer. In addition, newspaper reporters may look at these records and make the public aware of violations.

All this leads to the question of how to increase the *accountability* of nursing homes. Some experts suggest there is need for greater community involvement. Local advisory boards could be set up to oversee nursing homes. Some recommend a more drastic step: to create community-based and -sponsored nursing homes in towns where there are bad facilities. The municipal-owned nursing home is common in Denmark and Britain as well as in other European countries. While many public commissions and federal hearings have publicized the problems of the nursing homes over the years, they have not been able to change the situation substantially. One extreme suggestion is to phase out government support through Medicare and Medicaid and instead provide government subsidies to some other, more humane program, using the hospice concept, while at the same time increasing support for community-based long-term programs such as home care and adult day care services.

The Hospice Movement

The hospice movement manifests an attitude very different from that in the typical nursing home. Its whole orientation is towards providing a setting which offers hospitality, friendship, comfort, and familiar possessions as well as relief from pain for the person in her last weeks or months of life, whether in her own home or in a hospice unit. As Robert Butler (1978–79) states, this is an attitude that could well be utilized by all hospitals and nursing homes. While the type of treatment embodied by the hospice movement is presently directed to the terminally ill, many components of this approach can be used in the whole nursing home system. Hospice experts already report that hospitals, physicians, nurses, social workers, and others are beginning to recognize and respond differently to the needs of patients and families confronting death as a result of their movement. Now, with its acceptance for Medicare reimbursement (and the hospitals' greater willingness to discharge patients to this care source due to Medicare's DRG payment limitations (see Chapter 2), the hospice movement and its philosophy will have even more influence on the whole health system.

"Hospice" refers to a *philosophy* of care rather than to its provision in a certain locale. While the early British model for hospice care was St. Christopher's, London, a free-standing inpatient physical facility, many American hospices offer primarily home care services, though there are also inpatient hospice units in hospitals.

The hospice movement is meant to give people all the comfort from pain they need by proper regulation of drug dosages while allowing them to be with family members and friendly, caring people during their last days. Hospice care allows death with dignity. It is especially appropriate for those who are incurable and hence cannot be aided by modern hospital technology, people who need not be continually in an acute-care setting (Stoddard, 1978).

The aim of hospice is to provide a loving community of caregivers from both the formal and informal support systems, with heavy use of volunteers (Jenkins and Cook, 1981), yet with due respect for use of professional staff. Staff serving the person in the special hospice hospital unit or in the home are trained to understand the person (usually a cancer victim), his special problems, and to deal with the whole individual in a sympathetic way. In whatever setting it is, hospice is a community operating on its own principles: these clearly differ from conventional medical attitudes in America, attitudes which largely determine the atmosphere in hospitals and nursing homes. Hospice believes not only in serving the whole person—that is, his psychological, social, and health needs instead of just his medical needs— but in this last period of life, believes in serving his family and indeed making it an integral part of the care-giving team. As a leader of Hospice, New Haven, S. Lack (1977) writes, "the care of the terminally ill is incomplete without counseling. . . . to help the patient/family cope with the reality of impending death, supportive relationships during the illness are necessary." The hospice program believes in frankly facing the person's condition of terminal illness and making the dying process a humane one. The hospice movement, while offering another option of a place to die, considers itself mainly in terms of facilitating a wider, more personal support system for the last weeks of life. Families are encouraged to take on tasks if it is a hospital setting or work with the hospice team if they are primary caretakers in the home.

There are several basic hospice models: (1) the more common hospice unit in a hospital; (2) the free-standing hospice unit, with bedrooms and lounges and other needed facilities, similar to a hospital; (3) a house where a terminally ill person can go for counseling and medical visits; or (4) a home care hospice. The hospice program, such as the famous one in New Haven, may have hospital-like or hospital-connected hospice facilities as well as home care. The home care type includes the "coalition" model, in which the hospice agency coordinates services from other agencies.

The hospital or hospital-like hospice differs from the regular hospital unit in that it tries to create a homelike atmosphere and to provide the chance for extensive family visiting. It tries to create a more personal atmosphere than that of the usually grim acute-care hospital facility. Generally the patient is encouraged to retain her own life-style as far as possible. Regulations and hospital routine are kept to a minimum. The person can bring her own possessions. Comfortable, homey lounges are provided; rooms are decorated in bright colors; plants are plentiful. Family, including children and even pets, are encouraged to stay for long periods during the day, to eat with the patient in the hospice dining space, even (in some hospices) to stay overnight and to take part in personal care of the patient.

The British St. Christopher's Hospice welcomes families, often spending as long with family members as with the patients (and later helping them through bereavement). They make the family and the patient feel that St. Christopher's is like one big family. Nurses bring their babies in and bring their families for patients' birthday celebrations. Families take part in festivities. As Saunders (1977) says, hospice occasions are a salute to courage.

Facilities are designed to incorporate family members and staff. For example, in the New Haven hospice, each of two patient wings has a livingroom that doubles as a dining area where patients and family share meals together. In the New York City Calvary Hospital hospice program, the family can visit eight hours a day. Instead of the busy, impersonal ward system of a modern hospital, with its detached approach to the dying patient, here close monitoring of the patient's needs is advocated. The staff works as a team. In the Calvary Hospital hospice this includes medical and nursing staff, chaplains, and social workers, with the goal of providing for the physical, spiritual, and psychological needs of the dying. The New Haven program boasts a specially trained nursing staff, clergy, social work, psychiatric and pharmocological consultation, and volunteers as integral parts of the care-giving team. Because pain management or control is such a major focus of the hospice program, especially for their many cancer patients, many of the staff are trained in this. Monitoring the drugs needed to kill the pain is a very specialized job.

The free-standing hospice facility can be seen as a compromise between the absence of specialized medical facilities and equipment in the home and the availability of virtually the whole array of modern medical technology in the traditional hospital (Osterweis and Champagne, 1981). Because patients usually have certain types of terminal illnesses such as cancer, only a limited number of technical support equipment and facilities are essential if the hospice is not attached to a hospital. However, these free-standing hospices are still very expensive because they are usually small, yet need staff from many disciplines.

Home care hospice programs are often affiliated with a hospital-based or free-standing hospice facility. Patients often go back and forth between the hospice unit and their own home. They may go into the hospital or free-standing unit while drug dosage is being determined and then go back to their home; if a change in condition develops they go back to hospital; or they go there for family respite. In a recent study 60 percent of the home care hospice patients still had hospital care. Of course this care is often given in a regular acute-care unit because many home care hospices at present do not have an inpatient affiliation.

What the home care hospice program does is allow the person to go through the dying process in his own home surrounded by his family, while at the same time a professional support system is involved in treatment. It allows the person to continue to participate in family life. If, in the past, the terminally ill person stayed in his home, the family usually felt helpless because it was uncertain whether professional medical personnel would make house calls. In a home care hospice program the person and his family do not feel so alone, because a professional support team guarantees help; it closely monitors the patient's health by regular visits and even makes emergency night calls when necessary. This team works with the family to provide pain control and emotional support.

In the New Haven hospice program the home care division has a team administered by a full-time hospice physician; the team includes medical, nursing, physical therapy, social, and pastoral care workers as well as volunteers. When a new patient enters the program the team evaluates her needs and those of her family, schedules visits (from once a week to three times a day, depending on the situation), and holds up-to-date review sessions on the patient's condition. This team is available around the clock for emergencies. After the patient's death, the home care team continues to work with the family (Lack, 1977).

Hospice programs have developed in many parts of the United States over the last five years. Medicare moved in 1983 to reimburse costs for those patients deemed terminally ill. This should spark still greater growth of such services in the future. Whether the emphasis will be on the home care hospice or hospital-based hospice is yet to be seen. The National Hospice study described at the 1983 Gerontological Society meetings by Sherwood, Morris, and Wright showed hospital-based hospices were better in controlling pain and discomfort but the home-based hospice allowed a much higher level of social involvement and many more hours of caring (chatting, visiting, comforting). On a quality-of-life measurement scale, patients in this study seemed to be at about the same level whether in a home-based hospice or hospital-based program. Since the home-based program is considerably the cheaper, one might well expect government incentives to stimulate this type.

At this writing Medicare reimbursement is causing the hospice movement a number of problems. In late 1983 this grass roots movement, with its unique philosophy, gained acceptance for reimbursement by Medicare, only to find itself faced with many certification problems that could change its form. While Medicare reimbursement meant stable funding and, for the predominantly volunteer programs in some areas, the chance to add more professional staff, requirements meant standardization and add-ons (as do state licensing requirements). While hospice leaders have always been concerned about the quality of member groups (Osterweis and Champagne, 1981), rigid requirements mean the program is less flexible as to what is a hospice and what is not. They also amount to an imposition of standards by legislators outside the hospice movement. As of 1984 hospice leaders were working to rewrite a number of federal regulations for Medicare reimbursement to fit their programs better. And they were apprehensive as to what Medicare regulations might do; they asked themselves whether some of unique features of the hospice might be lost, and whether hospice leaders could maintain the hospice atmosphere within hospital facilities (*California Hospice Report*, 1984).

The many small, home care hospice programs are the ones having the hardest time meeting the Medicare requirements. These home care programs (as of 1984) are required to contract with a hospital or skilled nursing facility for inpatient care (some hospitals are turning areas at their disposal into skilled nursing facilities for hospice use). The small, home care hospices would rather have Medicare recognize instead several types of hospice, such as inpatient and home care. However, Medicare regulations requiring a program to have both types of care do follow the general hospice philosophy of working with the person both when he is at home and when he is in crisis and needs to move to the hospital or when respite for the family requires inpatient care (Medicare distinguishes between these types of inpatient care).

The problem is that many home care hospices have never provided or coordinated inpatient care, relying instead on traditional acute hospital care. Now they must contract for these and they worry about the problem of taking responsibility for care given by a contracting facility. In addition they worry about writing a formal contract and the possibilities of litigation (*California Hospice Report*, 1984). Calls by these hospices for inpatient hospital or skilled nursing home providers may go unanswered; nursing homes have few vacant beds, and while hospitals might benefit from filling some vacant beds, the Medicare reimbursement level is lower than what they receive when a regular oncology ward is used for such patients.

Other stumbling blocks to certification are staffing requirements. The regulation on medical supervision raises problems. The regulation that the hospice itself cover the core services such as nursing, medical social services, physical services, and counseling poses difficulties for small hospices that want to contract out for nursing care. It especially affects home care hospices that are of the "coalition" type, i.e., which coordinate access for their terminally ill patients to services provided by other agencies.

A more general issue is the questionable ability of the small hospice to provide the interdisciplinary staff required by Medicare: this is simply too expensive for many of them. The reimbursement paid for routine care under Medicare is low—and was recently reduced. Even the payment for a patient's temporary hospital treatment for acute symptoms or pain is low. Concerning costs, hospices also worry about the total Medicare maximum payment or "cap," now set at $6,600; they feel they will be responsible for some patients who need long periods of care or be responsible for expensive treatment if they take on patients and as required meet their full care. Some hospices are also reluctant to be certified for Medicare payment because many of their patients are under age 65. (If they are already certified as a home health care agency, as a number are, this makes matters easier).

Thus even the government's acceptance of the hospice approach has not been an unmixed blessing. It would be sad if many hospices decided not to become certified, because this would deprive many of an excellent source of help, help they truly need. I believe that in fact both the in-hospital and the home care hospice are necessary and that they should be made to function as a single unit. The effort must be made to make the inpatient hospice a place with a truly hospice-like atmosphere.

Conclusion

Discussion of the hospice movement leads us to consider new ways of delivering long-term care. Ideally, long-term care for any chronically ill person should be through services integrated to provide for the total needs of the elderly, preferably through a single comprehensive agency with multidisciplinary staff or by a coordinated effort among agencies. There should be a single point of entry and a single source for assessment of overall needs. The individual should be able to reenter the system at different points according to her situation at the time. For such a system, case management will be very important (Koff, 1982).

CHAPTER **12**

Income Maintenance Programs for the Elderly

The elderly in the United States, as a group, are not well-off. About a fifth of them live below the poverty level or in near-poverty. Minority elderly and single elderly, especially those over 75, are in an even worse financial position. The main monthly source of income for many elderly is their Social Security check, part of a federal income maintenance program. For the elderly poor, there can be a supplement to this: SSI assistance (Supplemental Security Income).

Social Security: Old Age Survivors and Disabled Insurance (OASDI)

Most elderly, when they retire, receive a monthly check from a program they or their spouse (or ex-spouse) have paid into during their working years. This government pension program—Old Age Survivors and Disabled Insurance (OASDI)—is the cornerstone of our social service system and surely the most sacred of all our social welfare legislation. While other programs have come and gone, this one has remained for five decades. It is in a period of financial crisis now, but it is extremely unlikely to disappear. To most American aged, it is the economic sine qua non for their retirement plans, guaranteeing them some comfort and economic security after they have left the workplace. There has been considerable social evolution as to the source of income for elderly in retirement. While many still receive the traditional

237

pension from their former employers in the private sector, older Americans today receive much of their retirement income from government sources: now some not only get Social Security money but, in a number of cases, state or local government pensions or special federal benefits. Attitudes have also changed, so that it is now widely assumed that all older Americans have a "right" to retirement benefits (Anderson, 1983).

The American elderly today are psychologically dependent on Social Security to carry them along in old age. Viscusi and Zeckhauser (1977) claim that the elderly value Social Security not only for its substantial financial benefits per se, but also for the *security* it provides. Unlike other investments, such as bond or corporate stock investments, Social Security functions like an annuity that insures against the uncertain duration of one's life span. OASDI is a universal program for all older Americans, rich and poor. Almost all retired Americans over 65—with the exception, until 1984, of federal government employees and a few other public service and nonprofit workers—now receive checks. The members of the latter groups are now also being brought into the system.

In 1982 almost 36 million Americans received periodic Social Security checks; this included the nonelderly disabled. The total estimated cost of payments to the elderly was $121 billion (in addition some $47 billion went to the Medicare program for FY 1983) (U.S. Office of Management and Budget, 1982).

History of Government Pension Plans

Government pension plans took much longer to develop in the United States than in Europe. In 1889 workers in Bismarck's Germany started to receive pensions, financed equally by employers, workers, and the state. This was a kind of risk sharing among individuals, similar to private insurance funds except for the government part of the funding. Contributory and compulsory, this program marked a break with the past, when local authorities, charity groups, and the church had given aid to the aged poor. In Britain pensions emerged in the early twentieth century. A general pension scheme was introduced in 1908, a simple transfer payment from general revenues to those of low income.

By 1929 government-subsidized pension schemes existed in 35 industrialized countries; some were noncontributory and some were noncompulsory. After World War II, such programs were the mainstay of the welfare state. In countries such as France, Denmark, Sweden, Holland, and West Germany, these pensions represent a very high proportion of total government spending. In general, they have been very generous, provided a high percentage of former wage income, and have increased regularly with inflation. For example, in Sweden in 1981 the minimum was $805 and the maximum $1,419 for a couple aged 65. Some of these European countries are now slowing down their inflation-related increases; for instance, in West Germany automatic pension adjustments were even suspended for six months, and the elderly were required to contribute to health insurance starting in 1983.

In the United States we have been slow to move toward a universal pension program for all elderly. The federal government up to the Depression period was reluctant to provide any type of welfare payments, although it early got into veterans' payments, assistance to native American Indians, and eventually some mental health provisions. Many states brought in means-tested old age pensions in the 1920s. Presidential candidate Teddy Roosevelt proposed a national social insurance program in 1912—but it was never enacted. Another Roosevelt, 23 years later, made history by introducing a broad social security program. In that year, 1935, the country was suffering a severe economic depression that had devastating effects on the elderly as well as on those in the work force. The individual states were too short on funds to cope with the rising need themselves. The economic climate stimulated citizen support for a national program of social security. As Roosevelt promised, this pension program helped protect people against the vicissitudes of life, and at least partially protected the average citizen and his family from poverty-ridden old age.

In pioneering this insurance scheme, Roosevelt and his advisors did not want the plan to look like charity or a dole. By making it contributory, they hoped that older Americans would consider receipt of payments later as a "right," a benefit due to them because they had contributed to the fund in their working years. Social Security continues to be one of the most popular of all government programs because, although it is a transfer from young to old, each person contributes and thus, in a sense, "buys" the right to benefits.

By keeping Social Security contributions in a fund separate from general revenues and from other forms of taxation, the Roosevelt Administration established a program it intended to be separated from politics. With this Social Security trust fund, they assured the American people benefits would be paid at the statutory rates without new congressional authorization—even if payroll tax receipts for a brief period did not cover current benefits and reserves had to be used. People paid a special Social Security tax and were paid from a special Social Security fund.

In 1935 Congress passed the Social Security Act, with this pension plan for the elderly (OASDI) as a major component. (Other parts included the unemployment insurance program, Aid to Dependent Families [now AFDC], and the welfare program for elderly poor [OAS, now called SSI].) At the outset this pension plan was quite modest. It covered only workers in industry and commerce, and benefits averaged only $22 a month in 1937. Payments started at age 65. Since life expectancy for both men and women was much lower than today, most received benefits for only a few years, if at all.

By 1939 the scope of the program began to change. In that year, coverage was extended so that when a pensioner died his widow and children would continue to receive benefits. The occupational categories of workers covered also expanded: eventually they included the self-employed, farm workers, domestic workers, state government and nonprofit organization employees (optional membership), religious personnel, and the military. Coverage was extended in the 1970s to divorcees who had been married to a beneficiary at least 10 years. It also included survivors after their 18th birthday if attending school (a provision now rescinded except for youth who are still in high school, who are covered until age 19).

Essential Features of the Social Security Plan

Over the years, two essential features of the government pension plan in the United States have emerged. First, although the plan is contributory, it also has a redistributive nature. Second, it is compulsory, not voluntary. With a few exceptions, which until recently included government workers, wage earners in the United States are required to contribute to Social Security. These two features are essential characteristics of the Social Security plan, but they are also controversial. As a later section details, Social Security experts and politicians have questioned these twin features in recent years as part of their attempt to reform the system to make it economically more viable.

CONTRIBUTORY VERSUS REDISTRIBUTIVE NATURE OF SOCIAL SECURITY

This, then, is a *contributory* insurance scheme: during his working life, each person and his employer contribute to the special Social Security fund, each paying half of the OASDI tax. A person qualifies to receive a pension by working so many quarters, by being the survivor of an eligible person, or by being disabled. The size of the payment to the beneficiary is determined by the salary or wages of the contributor; survivors receive a percentage of the same payment. At present there is a minimum pension payment, so that even those in low income categories, such as nuns, will receive something; this provision however, is being changed. There is also a maximum. For a single person the minimum in 1983 was $122 and the maximum was $729. However, the *average* payment in 1982 was $406 for a single person and $695 for a couple. Pension amounts are determined by the beneficiary's average monthly indexed earnings (excluding a few low years in the average);

the scale of benefits favors low-income earners. Benefits are indexed to increase with inflation.

While the program is contributory, one can quickly calculate that some beneficiaries, especially those who live 30 years after retirement, have not paid nearly enough into the system to justify, in purely financial terms, such a large payout of benefits. Thus, in reality, the payments from retirees come both from their contributions in the past and from the contributions of current contributors—today's working population. Social Security can be called an intergenerational transfer system which taxes those working and transfers the proceeds to the retired group; it is a pay-as-you-go system, paid for by payroll taxes, although up to the mid-1970s there was considerable surplus in the trust fund from past contributions.

Income does *not* accumulate in each worker's individual account as it would in a private savings-retirement pension plan. Instead, virtually all income collected through taxes on existing workers and employers is paid out to those retiring in the near future.

The current Social Security system is, in fact, an odd mixture of old-age insurance and welfare provisions (Parsons and Munro, 1977). As an insurance program, benefits are at least loosely tied to contributions and are not affected by the recipient's wealth and assets. From the welfare program perspective, however, the relationship between benefits and contributions is relatively tenuous. Benefits depend on circumstances beyond control of the individual—particularly the presence or absence of a spouse—and benefits are only proportional to earnings in a limited way.

The redistributive nature of the benefit payout can be seen by comparing the ratio of benefits to taxable wages for a worker with over 30 years of Social Security credit. Using 1976 calculations, Parsons and Munro (1977) provide an illustration of a worker who earned an average $100 per month (subject to Social Security taxes) over his working life—but receives almost $200 in monthly benefits when he retires. The transfer or welfare role of Social Security has evolved over time. The program was originally designed to support an impoverished group and to put purchasing power back into the economy. By removing the elderly from the labor force in the Depression, the program made room for younger workers. In contrast, today's program transfers resources from relatively affluent working population to relatively poor elderly beneficiaries. The program still could be—and indeed has been—justified as a means of letting all individuals in society benefit from growing productivity (Viscusi and Zeckhauser, 1977).

COMPULSORY VERSUS VOLUNTARY PARTICIPATION IN SOCIAL SECURITY

The Social Security system is a type of forced savings. Participation is mandatory; the exception until the 1983 amendment was mainly federal government and nonprofit organization employees and state or local government workers, who could vote themselves out. Now new federal employees and all nonprofit organization employees must join, and state and local government employees cannot terminate their participation. This mandatory feature is often defended on the grounds that many people would not save for their retirement if this was not mandatory; they might then become an economic liability to society in their old age, particularly if people begin to believe that society will always provide funds for their future. Others argue that the existence of the program decreases saving (Feldstein, 1974).

Americans have never been great savers. Their house is usually their main asset, and that is not a liquid asset. Only about a third of all Social Security beneficiaries have private pensions—and most of these are small, averaging under $100 a month in 1981. Thus, it is not surprising that a quarter of the elderly depend almost entirely on their Social Security checks for their monthly subsistence. These checks keep a large number of the elderly slightly above or at the poverty level.

These two factors—the low savings rate and the paucity of private pension plans—make Social Security an especially important, *guaranteed* form of insurance. Private pension plans in America have a very poor record (Myles, 1983). Most are seriously underfunded to employees. Most elderly, for a variety of reasons, do not receive private pensions in any case. Some never become eligible because they did not stay with one particular company for long enough to qualify. Most of the American public is very mobile. In 1981, for example, men changed jobs every 4.5 years and women every 2.6 years. It is not unusual for eligibility of employees (vesting) to be unequal or fraudulently handled (President's Commission on Pension Policy, 1980). Employees are often laid off shortly before they reach retirement age so they cannot qualify for the pension; or companies go bankrupt, which means that their employees never get the pensions they would otherwise have received. Finally, many nonunion benefit plans are coordinated with Social Security payments. The company makes up the difference between Social Security and a replacement earnings goal, that is, a percentage of preretirement income.

Private pensions have improved in recent years, but still suffer from these problems (President's Commission on Pension Policy, 1980). After long hearings, an Employee Retirement Income Security Act (ERISA) was passed in 1974 to regulate private pension plans, look into funding and vesting of employees, and set minimum standards of participation. Under ERISA's rules, the worker is vested in the plan after a certain number of years of work, usually 10; then he is entitled to at least some of its benefits even if he leaves before the official retirement age. ERISA also established the Pension Benefit Guaranty Corporation, a federal insurance company financed by premiums from the various plans covered to protect retirees from loss of benefits if their pension plans should be terminated—by a corporate bankruptcy, for example.

Establishing the Pension Benefit Guaranty Corporation provided workers with some protection, since it requires company actuaries to "certify" their assumptions and methods and explain themselves if they changed them. It did not, however, address other issues of vital importance to retirement security. Change of job is the greatest threat to retirement security. Pension plans, unlike Social Security, cannot be moved from company to company. In 1980, only about 31 percent of employees working for companies with pension plans were actually enrolled in plans, and only 28 percent of those who retired were eligible for benefits. Women workers were especially unlikely to get pensions (Moss, 1983). Thus, experts predict that many elderly will never have a private pension plan; in the future at most only about 50 percent of all those working at retirement age will actually get pensions. Some experts place this figure even lower, at 35 to 40 percent (Rich, 1978). Reforms in private pension plans have not therefore lessened the need for a government-backed pension available to all.

Problems of the Social Security System

While private pension plans have serious problems, the Social Security system, from the mid-1970s onward, has also run into a number of difficulties. Stated most succinctly, payout to recipients exceeds revenue coming into the trust fund. Demographic, economic, and political factors have contributed to this imbalance between costs and revenues. First, the number of beneficiaries has increased, while the ratio of workers to beneficiaries has decreased. From time to time, Congress has extended coverage to additional groups, thereby increasing the number of beneficiaries. Fluctuating birth rates have contributed to a large cohort of retiring elderly and smaller cohorts of persons in the labor force, thus reducing the ratio of contributors to beneficiaries. Second, longer life expectancy and earlier retirement add up to longer periods of coverage for beneficiaries. Third, high unemployment and high inflation in the past decade have further reduced revenues and increased costs. Fourth—and finally—in 1972 Congress added an amendment which inflated benefits through double indexing (Derthick, 1979).

NUMBER AND RATIO OF BENEFICIARIES

Over the years, the number of beneficiaries has increased as additional groups have been included. These groups, mainly noncontributors to the system, included dependent children; widows (whose benefits were moved up to 100 percent of their deceased spouses' in 1972); divorcees, if married a certain number of years to a beneficiary; and survivors over 18 still in school. (The latter group has been eliminated except for those in high school up to age 19). From 1956 on, the disabled were brought into a separate trust. In total, these additions meant there were almost 36 million beneficiaries in

1982, including the disabled. About one American out of six now receives a Social Security check each month.

The ratio of active workers to retirees has also decreased. Some cohorts of worker payee groups today were born in the 1930s and 1940s when the birth rate was low; this group, now in its 40s and 50s, is small in size compared to earlier worker groups. Those early cohorts of older workers have now reached retirement age. Because of this increased number of retirees and the later low birth rate, the ratio has moved down to three workers per beneficiary.

This demographic situation will be even worse by the year 2015, when persons born in the "Baby Boom" after World War II begin to retire. The small size of cohorts that follow them (1963 onward) will again mean there are even fewer workers to keep the fund solvent, while still more retirees draw money from it. Lower birth rates will shrink the number of workers in the labor force, forcing them to pay astronomically high taxes if the system is to remain self-financed. The ratio of those paying into the system versus beneficiaries would be very low, perhaps 2 to 1 or lower.

On the other hand, if there is heavy immigration in the next twenty years, the number paying may increase. Or the birth rate may move up due to recent major immigrations of Vietnamese and other Asians, as well as Mexican–Americans, Cubans, and other Hispanics—all groups with traditionally high birth rates. This would mean that by 2030 these young people should begin to swell the number paying into the fund. Another factor to keep in mind when predicting the future ratio of active workers to retirees is the length of time that young people stay in the educational system. Today young people enter the work force later than their parents because more youth now go on to higher education. This means they start paying substantial Social Security taxes at a later age. The contributor/beneficiary ratio is thus by no means a simple matter to calculate. Silver linings may appear, but we would not be anticipating them so keenly if we were not so apprehensive about the clouds we know will darken the picture.

LIFE EXPECTANCY AND EARLY RETIREMENT

In addition to this increase in the number of retirees and reciprocal decrease in the number of workers, Social Security has to cope with longer life expectancy and earlier retirement—both of which add up to longer periods of coverage for beneficiaries. When the architects of Social Security devised the system, they anticipated that most beneficiaries would live only a few years beyond retirement. In 1937 the average life expectancy for men was around 50; by 1982, life expectancy had increased to 70 for men and 76 for women. Thus, instead of drawing on Social Security for only a few years, retirees were, on the average, receiving benefits for at least five to ten years (Schulz, 1980).

Sixty-five is the age at which one can get full benefits from the system if one's earned income in that year is under a specified amount: the benefits are reduced if more is earned. Many are now retiring earlier, albeit at slightly reduced benefit rates. Since 1956 women have been able to start receiving benefits at age 62; from 1961 on, men have been able to do likewise. By 1982, two-thirds of the work force was retiring before age 65— even though that meant lower benefits.

Many experts have debated the relationship between Social Security and early retirement (Munnell, 1977). In years past, poor health and involuntary unemployment were generally the causes of early retirement, but it has been persuasively argued that increases in Social Security now encourage early retirement. Some contend that the increase in Social Security benefits is directly correlated with the increase in early retirement. Other experts take a more middle-of-the-road position: they see the growth of private pensions, in *combination* with increased Social Security benefits, as leading to early retirement. They also point out that later cohorts have accumulated more assets, principally in the form of housing, and that these assets have risen in value. In addition, diminished job opportunities in the 1970s may have played a role in many decisions to opt for reduced benefits at an early age (Schulz, 1980).

HIGH UNEMPLOYMENT AND HIGH INFLATION

Even with an increased number of retirees receiving benefits for longer periods of time, the Social Security trust fund maintained a substantial surplus up to 1970. The combination of high unemployment and high inflation has decimated the fund in the past decade. In the 1973–74 recession, lower income from taxed workers as well as high payouts began to decrease the surplus. Unemployment seldom ran any higher than 4 to 6 percent in the early postwar years, but in 1978 it moved up to 8 percent. In 1981 and 1982, this unemployment situation was even worse—10 to 11 percent were unemployed—so that there was a shortage of funds coming into the system and an increase in the number of those retiring largely due to growing layoffs of older workers.

Some argue that if unemployment is high, it is better to have older rather than younger workers out of the work force (Munnell, 1977). Presumably the founders of Social Security themselves, under the influence of the Great Depression, believed that if someone had to be idle it might as well be the elderly. It may be that younger workers now pay a tax whose yield entices older workers to leave the labor market (the proverbial carrot), while the earnings test,* together with company retirement rules (the stick), force them out.

*Social Security regulations restrict the amount one may earn while continuing to receive full potential benefits.

During the past decade this country has suffered from high inflation as well as high unemployment. Ex-Commissioner of the Social Security Administration Ball points out that the combination of recession with a high rate of inflation damaged the Social Security system from 1974 onward. High inflation has led to increases in the size of payments. Between 1950 and 1972, benefits were increased eleven different times. These increases not only raised general benefit levels but also formed a higher base upon which future increases would build (Ball, 1978).

Congressional Amendments of 1972

Prior to 1972 Congress alone determined when benefits should be adjusted to keep up with inflation. In 1972, however, it enacted legislation to systemize these increases rather than have them depend on political timing and congressional generosity. Under Wilbur Mills, head of the House Ways and Means Committee, Congress—motivated partly by the large surplus in the Social Security fund at the time—enacted a bill to raise benefits about 20 percent. The 1972 amendment brought in an automatic "Cost of Living Adjustment" (COLA), which made it mandatory from 1975 on that, when the consumer price index was 3 percent higher than during the previous 12 months, benefits would be raised the same percentage by the following July. Many applauded this move, since it meant that the increases needed to compensate for inflation would be granted automatically without the political uncertainty which had formerly prevailed. The elderly no longer had to fear that benefit increases might not occur as needed—and that consequently, inflation would eat away at their income.

While COLA was hailed at the time as an improvement in Social Security's ability to provide inflation-proof benefits, increased outlays during the 1974–77 period of high inflation began to deplete funds in a serious way. Critics have pointed out two serious flaws in this amendment: use of the consumer price index (CPI) as a guide for increases and double indexing.

Tying benefits to the CPI has been the most important factor in creating a crisis in the system, some say. The CPI is based partly on increases which the elderly are not likely to suffer from: increases in home mortgage or automobile payments, for example. Many elderly have full equity in their homes and are not purchasing new homes or cars. (High increases in such items during the 1970s inflated the CPI.) Rather than use the consumer price index, which may not be a reliable guide to increases for the elderly, some critics suggest using a more limited consumer index covering basic items.

The second problem, double indexing, was created by a defect in the benefit formula of the 1972 amendment. Munnell (1977) describes over-indexing as "an irrational and correctable feature of the benefit formula that tend[ed] to overcompensate workers for inflation. . . . With this error rectified, the projected deficit shrinks to a more manageable magnitude." This calculation method gave future retirees a double increase in benefits every time there was an increase in the cost of living, first from adjustment of the benefit formula and second, from the higher taxable wage base owing to higher earnings. In 1977 Congress tried to correct these defects by phasing in some benefit reductions over the next few years. However, the damage had already been done. Double indexing and high cost-of-living increases meant larger payouts from an ever-dwindling fund. Weaver (1982) claims these 1972 amendments destroyed the integrity of the whole system:

> Few citizens or politicians knew the damage that had been done to Social Security in 1972. In one fell swoop the new indexing provisions converted a system characterized by ad hoc growth to one of automatic and uncontrolled growth; converted the system from one in which economic growth and reserve accumulation preceded legislated expansion into one in which expansion, if properly financed, would necessitate economic growth; and converted a system that was—for a pay-as-you-go system—financed in a relatively conservative way into one that would be chronically under-financed.

The 1977 amendments did, of course, correct the double-indexing problems described by Weaver (1982), who is probably more critical about the 1972 amendments than most analysts. Many liberals, and groups lobbying for the elderly, view them more positively. After all, they *did* bring in an automatic cost-of-living increase. Other provisions were the increase in widows' benefits from 82.5 percent to 100 percent of deceased workers' monthly benefits, and special minimum benefits for low-income workers.

Early Solutions to Short- and Long-Term Crises in the System

Loss of Confidence in the System

The various problems of the Social Security system have caused some to lose confidence in it as a viable pension fund. Since it has been on the brink of insolvency, its critics have been able to scare the public into thinking that it will go bankrupt. Members of Congress report that inquiries flood their offices whenever Social Security financing issues and related uncertainties are in the news (Cowan, 1981).

The elderly fear the system will become insolvent and that their monthly checks will no longer arrive. The elderly and near-elderly, whose lifetime saving decisions have already been shaped on the assumption of a viable Social Security pension system, become concerned about the solvency of the program and the security of their future incomes. Even the 1983 National Commission on Social Security Reform had to consider measures specifically aimed at restoring confidence. Public confidence in the system has been dangerously undermined, even though experts contradict forecasts of doom for the Social Security system (Weaver, 1981; Estes, 1983a). Moreover, various polls reveal this lack of confidence. A 1981 New York Times/CBS poll indicated that 70 percent of the 18–29 age group doubted that they would be paid their full benefits. These young people questioned how much of a return they will get out of the system. However, the majority of Americans—according to a November 17, 1982 poll—wanted the system to continue. Moreover, these people were willing to pay higher Social Security taxes, even though they admitted they may not get full benefits themselves ("How to Save Social Security," 1982).

Early Solutions to the Crisis

INCREASED TAXES, 1977

In 1977 Congress increased the Social Security tax to help keep the system solvent (Robertson, 1978). At the time many members of Congress believed these increases would keep the system running for decades. The congressional act increased the amount of the individual's income subject to tax. In 1982, up to $32,400 of one's earnings could be taxed at 6.7 percent. The maximum Social Security tax (1982) was $2,170; as recently as 1970, the maximum had been only $374.

Increases in the tax, because it hits the lower-income harder than the middle-income worker, have caused an outcry: some pay more to Social Security than to income tax. Social Security, it is argued, is a regressive tax, unfairly imposed with regard to the poor. On the other hand, many young people think the current system is unfair: they pay large amounts into a fund that may go bankrupt before they can collect what is their due.

Unfortunately the increases imposed in the 1977 amendments did not bring in enough money to forestall a serious fiscal crisis in 1982–83. The continuing recession and resulting unemployment decreased payments into the fund at the same time the automatic COLA increased benefits to more beneficiaries than ever before—a group which had also grown due to early retirement during this recession.

By October 1982 the Old Age Survivors Insurance (OASI) fund had run out of money. The 1983 National Commission on Social Security Reform estimated a $150–200 billion shortfall in revenues over the next seven years. A short-term solution (borrowing from other trust funds) was authorized in late 1982. Within the Social Security system there are three trusts: the Old Age Survivors Insurance Trust, the Disability Insurance Fund, and the Medicare Fund. The latter two had considerable surpluses in 1982 (although by 1984 Medicare's surplus was almost gone; see Chapter 2). Congress approved a temporary transfer of funds from the Medicare and Disability Insurance trust funds.

Short-Term and Long-Term Crises

Some experts saw this financial problem as a short-term crisis—the increased payments would create a "breathing period" of solvency from the late 1980s or 1990 to either 2015 or 2030. Alicia Munnell (1977), a Federal Reserve Bank official and Social Security expert, believes the Social Security fund will be in great shape in the 1990s. Viscusi and Zeckhauser (1977) point out that around the turn of the next century, the percentage of elderly in our society will decline because the low-birth, Depression-era generation will then enter old age. Low birth rates during the Depression and Second World War years mean that there will be only a small addition of new recipients between 1990 and 2025: they may well be covered by more payees in the system from the "Baby Boom" group, who will then be in their prime years. Others fear that deficit financing will continue right through the 1990–2015 period unless serious measures are taken to halt the deficit's exponential growth. All agree that the retirement of the very large "Baby Boom" group and the low birth rate for worker cohorts contributing to the fund will create a long-run problem from 2015 or 2030 onward.

SHORT-TERM CRISIS, 1980–2015

Experts do not agree on the severity of the short-term crisis. Some have thought minor reforms could alleviate the crisis, but others have been less optimistic. Pechman, in 1977, thought that finances could improve with some minor moving-around of funds. The National Commission on Social Security Reform (1983), set up to deal with the problem, was less optimistic about matters, although it perceived the crisis as extending primarily through the 1980s, and not into the 1990s.

LONG-TERM CRISIS AFTER 2015

Virtually all authorities agree that there will be a serious financial crisis in the Social Security program from 2015 or 2030 on. As Ball (1978) explains:

> The short answer is the baby boom, followed by the "baby bust." The baby boom lasted from shortly after World War II until the early 1960's. The resulting huge, wave-like bulge in the population has been causing social dislocations of various kinds, as the peak population born in that period moves through the years. First, obstretrical wards in hospitals were overcrowded; now they are half-empty. Then the public schools had to use trailers for classrooms and schools went on double-shifts; now we have more teachers than we

need. At this time the job market is having great difficulty in absorbing the large number of young people looking for their first jobs. During the first decade of the next century, the baby boom generation will begin to enter retirement, and the number of persons over 65 will shoot up dramatically.

Entry of the Baby Boomers into the retirement population would not be so serious if the following generations were also large. However, since 1962 the U.S. birth rate has moved down: it has been exceptionally low after 1971 (although it moved up slightly in 1982 and 1983). It *could* climb way back up, but experts are pessimistic about a dramatic change. Most experts base their low estimates on the same assumptions as Ball (1978): "the fertility rate will not quickly climb back to a 2.5 rate or greater . . . and will continue to be lower than the 1967–70 period due to birth control methods and other factors."

But Ball himself warns against predicting many years ahead, due to uncertainties about the size of the work force and the future of other factors. For example, immigrants, both legal and illegal, may push the birth rate back up—as previously mentioned. On the other hand, earlier retirement and longer life expectancy than calculated can up the number of beneficiaries.

This intergenerational nature of the program or "pay-as-you-go" approach, whereby generations of retirees are promised benefits on the basis of future contributions of others, makes it more imperative than ever to find far-ranging solutions to this long-term crisis.

Current Solutions for the Financial Crisis

After OASI became insolvent in late 1982, it became obvious that the short-run solution of borrowing from other federal trust funds would not suffice. In 1982 and 1983, the National Commission on Social Security Reform debated a number of alternative solutions. Their principal aim was, as ex-Commissioner Robert Ball puts it, to restore full financing of the program with as few changes as possible. Each proposal for change, of course, had its own drawbacks. Since the elderly constitute a major voting block in the United States, politicians are reluctant to deprive them of their present benefits (Myles, 1983).

Yet something clearly had to be done in 1983 to make the system solvent. An interruption in benefit payments was politically unthinkable (Anderson, 1983)—as the conservative economist Milton Friedman (1977) concluded:

> Social Security cannot be abolished outright on both moral and political grounds, for the American government has made a moral commitment to the contributors. . . . We should discharge these commitments, so far as we can do so without imposing still greater inequalities on others.

Liberals wanted to make minor changes, while some conservatives wanted to reconstruct the program in major ways. The solutions agreed upon represent short-run measures to keep the system solvent for the next few decades (Harrington, 1983). In 1983 the solutions proposed fell into two groups of recommendations.

One focused on *increasing revenues:* including government employees in the program, increasing the ceiling on taxable income, or adding to the employers' part of the tax. Liberals, labor unionists, and lobbyists for the elderly groups favored such solutions. The second group of recommendations came from Republican leaders and conservative academics; they supported measures to *reduce cost,* i.e., reduce the benefits or categories covered or increase requirements. A more doctrinaire group wanted a variety of more drastic solutions—such as making Social Security a voluntary program (Weaver, 1982) or restructuring it as strictly an annuity program (Boskin, 1977). Individuals supporting these two major types of solution were about equally represented on the National Commission on Social Security Reform; their recommendations were regarded as a compromise between the two positions. Congress enacted into law many of these recommendations as the Social Security amendments of 1983.

REFORM MEASURES TO INCREASE REVENUES

Several 1983 reform measures focused on increasing the revenues available to the Social Security system. These included increasing the Social Security tax and combining OASDI with public employee funds.

Increasing the Social Security Tax. Liberal experts approved of the 1977 decision to increase the Social Security tax, and advocated this as a method to solve long-term problems. They proposed moving the tax increases scheduled for 1985 and 1990 to 1984 and 1988, and this was done in the 1983 act. They argued that bringing in tax increases early would substantially increase revenues. The National Commission on Social Security Reform staff estimated that many additional billions could be brought in from 1984 to 1989 by moving these increases forward far enough to close a large part of the projected Social Security budget gap. In the 1983 amendments these increases were moved forward—even though the Reagan administration was initially against any tax increases, fearing that the public would be hostile to such increases and that any large increase in Social Security taxes would retard economic recovery. In the end many experts rejected Rosen's (1977) finding that raising taxes did not seem either economically or politically viable. Some experts thought that young people—already pessimistic about the system—might revolt at a tax increase (Weaver, 1982). Yet protest has been minor, even though some young people ask why they must be in the Social Security system, when they can earn more on their own private savings.

Combining OASDI and Public Employee Funds.   The National Commission on Social Security Reform also recommended that government employees gradually be brought into the Social Security system. The 1983 amendments made it mandatory for *new* federal workers—and even for nonprofit workers—to join the OASDI system instead of participating in separate pension systems. This stopped the practice (by some state and local governments) of terminating their coverage. In the 1970s a number of state and local government employees, using the option to exempt themselves from the program, did so—although in many places such groups have done just the opposite, voting to be part of the system. Rita Campbell (1977) reports that the trend to withdraw from the Social Security system has accelerated in recent years. One survey reports that in 1981 an estimated one-third of state and local employees were not in the Social Security system.

The aim of the 1983 amendments is to make the Social Security system universal, i.e., mandatory for all workers, including the groups that previously had been able to opt out—such as state and local government workers. Federal employees long have had a separate retirement system which made higher payments under more liberal regulations. There are more than 38 major plans for federal employees, whose programs are more generous than the average private plan. These federal employee plans allow "double-dipping," whereby employees have access both to a government pension and to Social Security. Because federal employees can retire at age 55, some receive government pensions at a relatively early age and subsequently work the minimum number of quarters outside government in order to be eligible for Social Security pensions as well: "double-dipping," is the term which accurately describes this practice. Since the average earnings on which their Social Security benefits are based are low, former government employees get an extra advantage from the weighted-benefit formula intended for low-wage earners. Munnell (1977) estimates that about 40 percent of those receiving civil service retirement benefits received Social Security benefits as well. Under the 1983 amendments a "windfall" clause reduces benefits for workers entitled to a pension based on work not covered by Social Security *but* who have also been long enough in a job covered by Social Security to merit benefits: this applies to 1985 retirees and their successors.

In addition, persons who receive their spouse's Social Security benefits and pensions from their own employment with federal, state, or local governments—not covered by Social Security—will get a reduction in Social Security benefits. This, too, will decrease double-dipping.

While there was a strong government workers' lobby against joining Social Security, there was also incentive for federal, state, and local employees to move over to the Social Security system because the pension funds of these groups were in relatively poor condition. In 1981 the Civil Service Retirement Fund, the largest of the federal plans, had an unfunded liability of billions; the Railroad Retirement system was not much better off.

The picture was even bleaker for state and local government employees. Over the past few years the growth of state and local work forces has slowed, while many former workers have retired. The result strains public funds, because there are now fewer workers paying in—and more retirees to pay out to (Cavanaugh and Murphy, 1981).

Unfunded pension liabilities are staggering. Because of the inability of some cities to meet pension obligations, Carmen Elio, head of the Massachusetts Retirement Law Commission, has remarked that "something has got to give. . . . The decision may have to be made—do you abrogate your pension obligation or do you sacrifice your police or fire protection?" (Sheils, 1981).

Use of General Revenues

Some experts (e.g., ex-Commissioner Robert Ball) have asked why Social Security payments should not be underwritten by the overall federal budget—i.e., paid for by general revenues. The 1983 amendments retained the special fund concept, but debate on the issue continues. In most European countries social security does come from general revenue. One alternative to permanent use of general revenue would be temporary use of general revenue funds to alleviate short-term deficits in Social Security; ex-Commissioner Ball has recommended this ("How to Save Social Security," 1982).

Munnell (1977) discusses the pros and cons of general revenues for Social Security payments, stating that with redistribution as the major goal there are strong arguments for financing benefits through the most progressive sources of revenue, general revenues. She says there are several precedents for the use of general revenues within the Social Security system, and gives as an example the use of general revenue financing of some hospital payments. She adds that, at a late 1970s conference on social security, general revenue financing was considered appropriate on the ground that the existing program is in any case a compromise between a wage-related benefit program without redistribution of benefits to those of low income and a tax transfer scheme similar to many other major government programs.

Milton Friedman (1977) also favors use of general revenues to make up the difference between tax and payout if the payroll tax is inadequate to finance current benefits. His major concern is that employment taxes not be increased to cover the deficit, a concern shared by Pechman (1977), who thought the tax was regressive and hit hardest at low-income workers.

Cowan (1981) predicts that in the long run it is easy to imagine that Social Security will lose its separate identity if a situation develops in which general revenue covers a large share of benefit payments: The result might well be integration of the payroll and personal income taxes.

Many experts do not feel comfortable about the prospect of using general revenues for Social Security funding because this would mean a break with precedent—and a break in the perceived link between individual contributions and benefits. Anderson (1983) finds that this alternative is unappealing because Social Security is supposed to be self-supporting: dipping into general revenues would only mean the U.S. Treasury would have to borrow more. The problem with use of general revenues may be, above all, that there is just not enough money in the budget to pay the bills; cuts are already being made in a variety of programs.

Reform Measures to Reduce Costs

Several other reform measures focus on reducing costs, rather than on increasing revenues to Social Security. The 1983 amendments include reducing cost-of-living-adjustments, taxing Social Security benefits, and increasing the age of retirement. Another, even more conservative proposal is a voluntary, not mandatory plan (Cowan, 1981).

COST-OF-LIVING ADJUSTMENTS

Many think that automatic increases in benefits, tied to the COLA, are too high, and recommend changes in this formula. These experts say the present cost-of-living adjustments are inflationary and unrealistic because they are based on the CPI. As previously mentioned, this index overemphasizes housing and mortgage costs. Many experts prefer indexing pension increases to wage increases, which have been lower than COLAs in recent years.

One suggested solution has been to put a "cap" on the COLA at a level below annual price rises. Many National Commission staff members favored tying future COLAs to economywide wage gains (if high inflation continues). This would save money in the long run. Such a change would help to pacify the workers paying into the system, who have seen their wages (before taxes) increase by 30 percent between 1979 and 1982, while Social Security payments increased by 40 percent in this period. In the 1983 amendments a complicated formula, taking wage increases into account, has been enacted. The act states:

> Starting with 1984 if the balance in the combined Social Security (OASDI) trust funds is less than 15 percent of the expected year's benefit payments, the cost of living benefit increase will be based on the lesser of the increase in the consumer price index or the increase in average wages.

In 1983 one solution related to the COLAs was to delay, by a number of months, the mandatory automatic cost-of-living increases. Even this one-shot use saved many billion dollars. In 1984 there is discussion of doing this again. The elderly lobbies have raised strong opposition, and Congressman Claude Pepper has fought hard to stop any reductions in COLAs. The National Council of Senior Citizens has spoken out against changing the COLAs. As their director, Jacob Clayman, says: "No matter what you do with the COLA, whether you take only $10 a month away, you're hurting the elderly" (Anderson, 1983).

TAX ON SOCIAL SECURITY BENEFITS

Another solution enacted through the 1983 amendments that cuts benefits is to tax Social Security benefits—or at least half of them or half of income over a certain amount. It is estimated that this will not hurt the elderly poor, most of whom pay no tax. Three-fifths of all Social Security elderly beneficiaries pay no tax at all, because their incomes are too low and their exemptions too high for them to be hit by such a tax. Taxes paid by the other two-fifths may be recycled back into Social Security, and thus help to build reserves. Only those elderly with incomes over $25,000 for singles and $32,000 for couples filing jointly are taxed. While this income provision seems to make the measure noncontroversial, such is not entirely the case. Social Security is so sacred by now that many elderly perceive *any* tax placed on them as dishonest and a double tax on earnings, since they feel that they—in their working years—contributed to the system. The government, however, has enacted this tax.

INCREASING THE AGE OF RETIREMENT

Another way to save money is to increase the age of mandatory retirement—and this was done also in the 1983 amendments. This was done more to solve the long-term crisis, because this change in age cannot be done abruptly for it is a controversial political issue (Brodsky, 1982). For example, when the Carter administration's Secretary of the Treasury, Juanita Kreps, suggested an increase in eligible retirement age to 70, there was a major outcry by groups lobbying for the aged. And when the Reagan administration (in 1981) proposed discouraging retirement at age 62 by decreasing benefits for early retirement from 80 percent to 55 percent of full benefits, the Senate voted 96 to 0 against the measure. The Senate at that time was against it because such a move would be an inconceivable blow to people who had already made plans to retire within the next year. The relevant 1983 amendment included measures to discourage early retirement mainly by decreasing allowable earnings by beneficiaries; it also changed the age of retirement to 67, but this provision does not go into effect until 2000. Even then, it starts out gradually: the age of retirement will be 65 years and 2 months in 2000, then 65 and 4 months the next year, and so forth.

Munnell (1977) gives one of the major arguments for increasing the age mandated for retirement:

> Considering the improved health and life expectancy of today's elderly it is more logical to prolong their working life than shorten it, and to encourage them to active and productive employment beyond the customary retirement age of sixty-five. Increased labor-force participation by the elderly who are physically able and who want to continue working would be beneficial to them, to the social security system, and to society as a whole. Many of the problems affecting the elderly are directly related to the economic hardship caused by retirement, and naturally these would be relieved by earnings from continued employment. Working might also alleviate their isolation in a society that seems to have no place for them, and restore their dignity and self-reliance.

Munnell thinks that workers below 65 who are unemployed due to physical disabilities could be taken care of more appropriately by an extended disability program rather than a retirement program that pays benefits to everyone. She does admit that for older workers who are unemployed because they have been displaced by automation, early retirement may be a logical course, since retraining the elderly may be impractical. (Lobbyists for elderly groups agree that many of their constituents are pushed out of the labor force at age 60 or 62.)

One reason some sources have argued for allowing early retirement at age 62 is because some of those in their 60s lack the vigor necessary to keep them working after that age (Ball, 1978). While raising the retirement age for the nonmanual worker may be appropriate, manual laborers are usually too worn out to stay on the job that long. Many elderly would complain that they have put in enough years—usually 40 or more—on the job by age 62; they feel entitled to slow down and benefit from the many years of contributions put into the Social Security system.

Another way to increase revenues is to give people increased incentives to stay in the work force until they are 65 or older. Proponents of this solution suggest decreasing benefits for people retiring between 62 and 64, and rewarding those who work after 65 or 67. Even in 1982, some of those who held off retirement beyond 65 were given a bonus as an incentive: for each year that the person stays at work after 65 he or she gets a 3 percent increase in eventual retirement benefits. Between 1990 and 2008, this will be increased gradually to 8 percent, according to the 1983 amendments.

The earnings limitation for Social Security beneficiaries has always constituted a disincentive to work; those receiving benefits should be truly those in need of retirement income. Introducing changes in earning limitations to keep people on the job has been hotly debated, with some conservatives crying out that there should be no earnings limitations at all. The 1983 amendments provided incentives for people to keep working, especially those under 65. In 1984 those under 65 can earn only $5,160 and still collect benefits, while those of age 65 to 70 can earn up to almost $6,960 with full benefits; for every $2.00 earned over this "cap" the person's benefits are reduced by $1.00. Starting in 1990 this will be liberalized: only $1.00 in benefits will be withheld for every $3.00 earned. As is true now, after age 70 full benefits are granted, regardless of what one earns.

VOLUNTARY VERSUS MANDATORY PENSION PLAN

While the 1983 amendments increased the number of workers under a *mandatory* Social Security plan for all Americans, some conservative experts are recommending just the opposite, a purely voluntary plan. Writers favoring such a measure discuss development of a system of choice and competition—a system made attractive by returns on contributions and by "fairness." They want a system, as Weaver (1982) explains, in which tax payments truly constitute "contributions." Such a reformed system would not need to coerce others to remain in it simply to protect their own expected income. Free choice for participants would eliminate the potential for discriminatory and involuntary income redistribution. In an institutional environment, permitting free choice among competing private—and possible public—suppliers of retirement benefits would assure everyone of "income security" (Weaver, 1982).

Of course a voluntary system, if it is to be competitive in attracting middle-class participants, could not shape its rules to give the low-income contributor a minimum benefit: in general, it could not be a redistributive system. Payments would be based on previous contributions to the system. In other words, the much-touted "reform" would amount to an annuity system (Boskin, 1977). Such a system would be unacceptable to those who benefit as low-income contributors. Furthermore, it is also unacceptable to most social policy experts who believe that universal participation is necessary for a genuine social security system to work. Finally, a voluntary system is not desirable because if people are not forced to save for their retirement, some will later need to turn to the state for support in any case. Strongly advocating a compulsory system, Rosen (1977) makes this point:

> There are good social reasons for mandatory participation in a pension scheme, of course, that are not necessarily anti-libertarian nor necessarily based on paternalistic views that a government knows more about what is best for its citizens than they do themselves. These concern the fact that unlucky or unwise individuals can and do throw themselves on the mercy of the state; fellow citizens do not knowingly allow people to starve in their old age. If this kind of implicit social "insurance," random though it may be, is available through private or public philanthropic organizations, incentives are provided for many people not to look into the future, to be less careful about their investment and to be less prudent in their savings behavior—that is, it tends to promote those very instances where the mercy of the state must be invoked. Mandatory self-provision of a basic level of support is prudent social policy action under these circumstances.

Summary

Social Security is a contributory program in which workers pay into the system during their wage-earning years. At the same time it has some characteristics of an income transfer program, since it is in some measure redistributive, providing those of low income with much more in retirement payments than they in fact paid into the system. This program involves intergenerational transfer payments, for it is a pay-as-you-go system, depending on present workers to pay amounts into the fund for present retirees. Social Security is mandatory for all workers except for the various government employees who opted out in the past.

The system has changed considerably since its conception during the Great Depression. Many groups of workers have been added, and benefits are now provided not only to widows and survivors but to divorced women married to a qualified beneficiary for a certain number of years, regardless of whether he is retired or not. A separate fund covers the disabled. The number of beneficiaries has greatly expanded over the years due to these additions, to longer life expectancy for the elderly, and the trend to earlier retirement.

The problems the Social Security system encounters are due to the expansion of beneficiaries, high unemployment, high inflation, the COLA, and a low birth rate in certain age cohorts. Most experts anticipated a short-term crisis reaching out until 1990; that crisis may have been averted by the 1983 amendments and by an improvement in the financial situation—partly due to the "Baby Boom" cohort groups paying into the system. All experts see a long-term crisis when this "Baby Boom" group starts retiring (from 2015 onward) because the wage-earning group at that time is likely to be small because of the low birth rate of those born after 1962. The worker–retiree ratio will be very low.

A number of solutions have been suggested to improve the financial situation of the system. When the fund went broke in late 1982, money was borrowed from the other two Social Security funds (disability and Medicare). Earlier on, Congress set up a schedule of gradual increases in the Social Security tax rate and in the maximum income that can be taxed. The increase scheduled for 1985 and 1990 has been moved up to take care of the present financial crisis. Other solutions include taxing up to half of Social Security payments to high-income retirees. Some measures to decrease the costs of Social Security introduced in the 1983 amendments include gradually changing the age of retirement, providing incentives to postpone retirement, and tightening up regulations on survivor benefits.

Despite all the problems and recommendations for change in the system, Social Security remains, after half a century, the most important source of support for America's elderly.

Supplemental Security Income (SSI)

Supplemental Security Income is a program for those elderly of 65 and over whose income, even with a Social Security payment, is so low that they remain below the poverty level. Then the federal government, in conjunction with the separate states, provides a supplement; this source of assistance is also available for the small group of elderly not eligible for Social Security. The amount of the supplement is calculated in terms of other sources of income, including Social Security. It is a means-tested program: the applicant must provide evidence of assets and income. However, the regulations are liberal, disregarding as assets the elderly person's car, a limited amount of savings, and a house (thus allowing the applicant to retain his home and still apply). SSI also allows one to disregard a small amount of earned income (Rigby and Ponce, 1980).

This SSI program, which also serves the disabled and blind, was put into operation in 1974 to replace a more stringent and stigmatizing program run by the welfare departments along with AFDC.

Because the present program is run by the Social Security Administration, it has had an improved image. Various other efforts have been made to make it less stigmatizing than its predecessor, such as easier application forms, liberation of allowable assets, and publicity inviting use.

Because SSI is a federal program financed from general revenues, government officials set eligibility requirements and a minimum level of payment—a sort of guaranteed annual income. The federal portion of the cost for payment to the elderly (not disabled and blind) came to $3.1 billion in FY 1983. States are allowed to supplement federal payments, and many do so. The amount of the supplement varies from state to state and can change in relation to a state's willingness to provide cost-of-living adjustments. The federal government can also change its provision of cost-of-living adjustments, as it did with the 1983 amendments, which postponed COLAs for six months.

Because the number of people covered by Social Security has increased, and because Social Security payments have been more substantial in the last few years, the number of elderly applying for SSI (only a few million) has decreased. However, the number of those who apply is considered far below that of those who are eligible. Perhaps this is a reflection of the attitudes of the elderly poor who are still reluctant to apply for a means-tested program which they see as "charity." Brown and O'Day (1981) report that when the program was initiated in 1974, an estimated 3.8 million non-institutionalized elderly were eligible—but as of 1975 only 2.5 million eligible aged were recipients.

Besides underutilization, SSI suffers from its low level of payments, which make it hard for the elderly to subsist with them. The monthly payment in 1982 averaged $264.70 for an individual living alone (if living in another person's household, usually a relative's and receiving support in kind, SSI was reduced by a third). For two eligible individuals—husband and wife—the monthly average payment in 1982 was $397 (Gelfand, 1984).

Conclusion

These income maintenance programs are essential to the elderly if they are to keep their independence. While this book has mainly focused on services, the top priority for the elderly is enough money to live on. The erosion of savings and decreased worth of their dollars due to inflation are a continual source of worry.

Because many services, such as medical care, require a client contribution, adequate monetary resources are necessary for their use. The Social Security program provides this basic monetary underpinning as a "right," given without a means test; SSI supplements it when necessary, although a means test is required. These programs help the elderly to live in their own homes and to continue their own style of life, rather than resort to dramatic reductions in living arrangements and/or heavy financial dependence on their children. Social Security has in fact revolutionized the conditions under which our aged population lives. There would be a considerable upheaval in the economy if these many seniors, one out of nine Americans, did not have the wherewithal to buy what they need in their own communities.

Social Security money is needed today at least as much as when the system was founded in 1935, because of the very long—and lengthening—life expectancy of older people. This means that their savings from years of work are unlikely to meet their monetary needs in their many years of retirement. We need some type of mandatory annuity: Social Security, while not a true annuity, does that job better than any other current program. It gives the elderly assurance there will be some (minimal) sum coming in every month for the rest of their lives. In addition, the elderly person has the assurance that Medicare will pay some part of medical bills.

Most young Americans understand and accept this system, whereby they make Social Security payments during their working years in the knowledge that they can live on decent retirement income during their long nonworking retirement years. They also understand that the system makes monetary contributions to their parents which they would have to bear if it did not exist. Most of these young people have faith that the government will not let them down and will continue to fund a system they feel benefits them both now and later.

While conservatives may cry out that cutbacks and revisions of Social Security are necessary, most Americans do not want the system to lower payments or drop COLAs. Many do not support cutoff of groups such as divorcees, even though they may complain that the burden of payroll tax deductions is high.

It is unlikely that the American public will let any administration roll back the clock to the days when the elderly depended upon their children for income or moved to the poorhouse or county old-age home. The lobby group of the elderly is strong enough to prevent such a throwback—and it is joined by the adult children of the elderly.

Some services also provide a substitute for monetary outlay, such as housing. Public and nonprofit services are needed because they provide assistance not easily available with the same reliability and quality in the marketplace. Thus these services are needed by the middle-income elderly as well as those with low income. Both income assistance *and* services, not just one or the other, should be provided to the elderly who need them.

Bibliography

ABT ASSOCIATES. *Property Tax Relief Programs for the Elderly: A Compendium.* Cambridge, Mass.: Abt Associates, 1975.

ACHENBAUM, W. ANDREW. *Shades of Gray: Old Age, American Values, and Federal Policies Since 1920.* Boston: Little, Brown, 1983.

ADULT SENIOR CENTER *Report,* 1978.

AMSDEN, D., AND M. SIMOWSKI. "Cost-Effectiveness Measurement Criteria for Title III-B Services: An Area Agency Strategem." *Gerontologist* 22 (1982):87 (Abstract).

ANDERSON, HARRY. "The Social Security Crisis." *Newsweek,* January 24, 1983, 30–35.

ANDERSON, W. A., AND N. D. ANDERSON. "The Politics of Age Exclusion: The Adults Only Movement in Arizona." In R. B. Hudson (ed.), *The Aging in Politics.* Springfield, Ill.: Charles C. Thomas, 1981, 86–97.

Annual Housing Survey of 1974, 1975, 1977. See U.S. Bureau of the Census.

"ARCHITECTURAL DESIGN: HOUSING FOR THE ELDERLY." *Progressive Architecture* 62 (1981):59–75.

ATCHLEY, ROBERT. *The Social Forces in Later Life.* 2d ed. Belmont, Calif.: Wadsworth, 1977.

————. *Aging: Continuity and Change.* Belmont, Calif.: Wadsworth, 1983.

AUDAIN, M., AND E. HUTTMAN. *Beyond Shelter.* Ottawa: Canadian Council for Social Development, 1973.

BALL, ROBERT. *Social Security: Today and Tomorrow*. New York: Columbia University Press, 1978.

BARROWS, GEORGIA, AND PATRICIA A. SMITH. *Aging, Ageism and Society*. St. Paul, Minn.: West Publishing, 1979.

BATTLE, M., AND ASSOCIATES. "Relationship Between Self-Esteem and Depression." In *Psychological Evaluation of Information and Referral Services for the Elderly*. Washington, D.C.: GPO, 1977.

BENGSTON, VERN L. *The Social Psychology of Aging*. Indianapolis: Bobbs-Merrill, 1973.

BENNETT, RUTH, BARRY GURLAND, AND DAVID WILDER (eds.). *Coordinated Service Delivery Systems for the Elderly: New Approaches for Care and Referral in New York State*. New York: Hawthorn Books, 1983.

BERNARD, JESSE. *The Female World*. New York: Free Press, 1981.

BINSTOCK, ROBERT, J. GRIGSBY, AND T. LEAVITT. "The Complexities of Targeting: A Multi-Dimensional Overview of Strategy Options." Paper presented at the Gerontological Society meetings, San Francisco, November 1983.

BIRREN, J. E., AND K. W. SCHAIE (eds.). *Handbook of Psychology of Aging*. New York: Van Nostrand Reinhold, 1977.

BLAU, ZENA SMITH. *Aging in a Changing Society*. 2d ed. New York: New Viewpoints/Franklin Watts, 1981.

BLENKNER, MARGARET. *Final Report: Protective Services for Older People.* Cleveland: Benjamin Rose Institute, 1974.

BORUP, J. H., D. T. GALLEGO, AND P. G. HEFFERNAN. "Relocation and Its Effect on Morality." *Gerontologist* 19 (1979):135–149.

BOSKIN, MICHAEL (ed.). *The Crisis in Social Security: Problems and Prospects*. San Francisco: Institute of Contemporary Studies, 1977.

BOVBERG, R. R., AND J. HOLAHAN. *Medicaid in the Reagan Era: Federal Policies and State Choices*. Washington, D.C.: Urban Institute, 1982.

BRANCH, LAURENCE G., AND PAUL R. BRANCH. "Service and Non-Service Expenditures in a State Aging Program." *Gerontologist* 23 (1983):479–485.

BRICKNER, P. W. "Health Care Services for the Homebound Aged Maintain Independence, Limit Costs." *Hospital Progress* 61 (1980):56–59.

BRODSKY, D. M. "Raising the Social Security Retirement Age: A Political Economy Perspective," *Gerontologist* 22 (1982):211 (Abstract).

BRODY, ELAINE M. "Community Housing for the Elderly: The Program, the People, the Decision-Making Process, and the Research." *Gerontologist* 18 (1978):121–128.

———. "Aged Parents and Aging Children." In P. K. Ragan (ed.), *Aging Parents*. Los Angeles, Calif.: University of Southern California Press, 1979, 267–287.

———. "Women in the Middle and Family Help to Older People." *Gerontologist* 21 (1981):471–480.

——— (ed.). *A Social Work Guide for Long-Term Care Facilities*. Washington, D.C.: National Institute of Mental Health, 1977.

BRODY, ELAINE, P. JOHNSON, M. FULCOMER, AND A. LANG. *The Dependent Elderly and Women's Changing Roles.* Final report on AOA grant 90 A1277. Washington, D.C.: Administration on Aging, 1982.

BRODY, STANLEY J. "Comprehensive Health Care for the Elderly, An Analysis: The Continuum of Medical, Health and Social Services for the Aged." *Gerontologist* 13 (1973):412–418.

BROTMAN, H. B. *Every Ninth American.* An Analysis for the Chairman of the Select Committee on Aging, House of Representatives. Washington, D.C.: GPO, 1982.

BROWN, CHARLANE, AND MARY O'DAY. "Services to the Elderly." In Neil Gilbert and Harry Specht (eds.), *Handbook of the Social Services.* Englewood Cliffs, N.J.: Prentice-Hall, 1981, 102–150.

BRYANT, NANCY H., LOUISE CANDLAND, AND REGINA LOWENSTEIN. "Comparison of Care and Cost Outcomes for Stroke Patients With or Without Home Care." *Stroke* 5 (1974).

BULTENA, GORDON, AND VIVIAN WOOD. "The American Retirement Community: Bane or Blessing?" *Journal of Gerontology* 24 (1969):209–217.

BURGESS, ERNEST. *Aging in Western Societies.* Chicago: University of Chicago Press, 1960.

BURKHARDT, JON E. "Evaluating Information and Referral Services." *Gerontologist* 19 (1979):28–33.

BUTLER, ROBERT. "The Life Review: An Interpretation of Reminisence in the Aged." In Bernice L. Neugarten (ed.), *Middle Age and Aging: A Reader in Social Psychology.* Chicago: University of Chicago Press, 1968, 486–496.

————. *Why Survive? Being Old in America.* New York: Harper & Row, 1975.

————. "Public Interest Report no. 26: Compassion and Relief from Pain." *International Journal of Aging and Human Development* 9 (1978–79):193–195.

————. "Improving Health Care by Using Functional Diagnoses." Paper presented at Gerontological Society meetings, Boston, November 1982.

BYERTS, T. O. "Comparison of Mover and Non-Mover Applicants to a New Congregate Public Housing Setting: Year 1." *Gerontologist* (1982):82 (Abstract).

CAIN, L. "Evaluative Research and Nutrition Programs for the Elderly." In *Evaluative Research on Social Programs for the Elderly.* Washington, D.C.: GPO, 1977.

CALIFORNIA DEPARTMENT OF AGING. *California Long-Range Plan.* Sacramento, Calif.: Department of Aging, 1978.

CALIFORNIA DEPARTMENT OF HEALTH. *Adult Day Health Service: Its Impact on the Frail Elderly and the Quality and Cost of Long Term Care.* Sacramento, Calif.: State Department of Health, 1977.

————. *Commission on Nursing Home Reform. Report.* (Little Hoover Commission.) Sacramento, Calif.: State Department of Health, 1983.

CALIFORNIA DEPARTMENT OF HOUSING AND COMMUNITY DEVELOPMENT. *A Consumer's Guide to Mobile Homes.* Sacramento: Calif. State Department of Housing and Community Development, 1980.

California Hospice Report. 1, Sept. 1983; 1, Dec. 1983; and 2, March 1984. San Francisco: Northern California Hospice Association.

CAMPBELL, RITA. *Social Security: Promise and Reality.* Stanford, Calif.: Hoover Institute Press, 1977.

CANTOR, MARJORIE H. "The Informal Support System: Its Relevance in the Lives of the Elderly." In Neil McClusky and E. F. Borgatta (eds.), *Aging and Society: Current Research and Policy Perspectives.* Beverly Hills, Calif.: Sage Publications, 1980.

CARAGONNE K., AND DAVID AUSTIN. *Final Report: A Comparative Study of the Functions of the Case Management in Multi-Purpose, Comprehensive and in Categorical Programs.* Austin: University of Texas School of Social Work, 1984.

CARP, FRANCES. *Future for the Aged.* Austin: University of Texas Press, 1966.

————. "Congregate Housing: Concept and Role." Paper presented at National Conference on Congregate Housing for Older People, Washington, D.C., November 1975.

————. "Housing and Living Environments of Older People." In Robert Binstock and Ethel Shanas (eds.), *Handbook of Aging and the Social Sciences.* New York: Van Nostrand Reinhold, 1977a, 256–259.

————. "Impact of Improved Living Environment on Health and Life Expectancy." *Gerontologist* 17 (1977b):242–250.

CAVANAUGH, THOMAS, AND RICHARD MURPHY. "Urban Institute's Report on State and Local Pensions." *Pension World* 17 (1981):39–42.

CHELLIS, ROBERT, JAMES SEAGLE, JR., AND BARBARA SEAGLE (eds.). *Congregate Housing for Older People: A Solution for the 1980s.* Lexington, Mass.: D. C. Heath, 1982.

CICIRELLI, V. G. "Sibling Influences Throughout the Lifespan." In M. E. Lamb and B. Sutton-Smith (eds.), *Sibling Relationships: Their Nature and Significance Across the Lifespan.* Hillsdale, N.J.: Erlbaum, 1982, 267–284.

CLAYMAN, JACOB, NATIONAL COUNCIL OF SENIOR CITIZENS. Quoted in Merrill Sheils, "The Turmoil in Pension Plans," *Newsweek*, June 1, 1981, 28 31.

CLAYTON, L. "Family as Care Providers." *Gerontologist* 22 (1982):79 (Abstract).

COHEN, CARL, AND ARLENE ADLER. "Network Interventions. Do They Work?" *Gerontologist* 24 (1984):16–22.

COLLIN, LOU. *Elders in Rebellion: A Guide to Senior Activism.* New York: Anchor Press, 1979.

COONS, DOROTHY. *Alzheimer's Disease: Subjective Experiences of Families: Final Report.* Los Angeles: AARP-Andrus Foundation, 1983.

CORMICAN, ELIN J. "Task-Centered Model for Work with the Aged." *Social Casework* 58 (1977):490–494.

————. "Social Work and Aging: A Review of the Literature and How It Is Changing." *International Journal of Aging and Human Development* 2 (1980):251–257.

CORR, CHARLES, AND DONNA CORR. *Hospice Care.* New York: Springer, 1983.

COTTRELL, F. "Transportation of the Rural Aged." In Robert Atchley (ed.), *Environments and the Rural Aged*. Washington, D.C.: Gerontological Society, 1975.

COWAN, EDWARD. "Drive on Social Security Deficits Being Mounted by Congressmen." *The New York Times*, January 2, 1981.

COYLE, JEAN. "Attitudes Toward Provision of Services to the Elderly in Rural Communities: Two Case Studies." *Gerontologist* 22 (1982):135 (Abstract).

CRYSTAL, STEPHEN. *America's Old Age Crisis: Public Policy and the Two Worlds of Aging*. New York: Basic Books, 1982.

CUMMING, ELAINE, AND WILLIAM HENRY. *Growing Old—The Process of Disengagement*. New York: Basic Books, 1961.

CURTIN, SHARON. *Nobody Ever Died of Old Age*. Boston: Little, Brown, 1972.

CUTLER, N. E. "A Computer Simulation of Title III Intrastate Funding Formulas in Alternative State Environments." Paper presented at the Gerontological Society meetings, San Francisco, November, 1983.

DAATLAND, SVEIN OLAV. "Care Systems." *Ageing and Society* 3, 1983.

DAVIS, KAREN. Statement at Hearings, U.S. Senate, Special Committee on Aging, *The Future of Medicare*, 98th Cong., 1st sess. Washington, D.C.: GPO, 1983.

DENNETT, S., AND L. C. MULLINS. "The Professional Attitudes and Training of Nursing Home Nurses and Nurses' Aides." Paper presented at Gerontological Society meetings, Boston, November 1982.

DERTHICK, MARTHA. *Policymaking for Social Security*. Washington, D.C.: Brookings Institution, 1979.

DIBNER, A. S. "Utilization of Lifeline Emergency Response Service." *Gerontologist* 22 (1982):152 (Abstract).

DILLMAN, DON A., AND DARYL J. HOBBS. *Rural Society in the U.S.: Issues for the 1980s*. Boulder, Colo.: Westview Press, 1982.

DONAHUE, WILMA B., MARIE MCGUIRE THOMPSON, AND D. J. CURREN (eds.). *Congregate Housing for Older People*. (U.S. Senate Hearings on Congregate Housing.) Washington, D.C.: GPO, 1977.

DOUGLAS, R., A. HICKEY, AND E. NOEL. *A Study of Maltreatment of the Elderly and Other Vulnerable Adults*. (Final Report of the U.S. Administration on Aging and the Michigan Department of Social Services.) Ann Arbor: Michigan Department of Social Services, 1978.

DOUGLAS, RICHARD. *Heating or Eating? The Crisis of Home Heating, Energy Cost and Well-Being of the Elderly in Michigan*. Ann Arbor: University of Michigan Institute of Gerontology, 1982.

DUNKLE, RUTH, S. WALTER POULSHOCK, BARBARA SILVERSTONE, AND GARY DEIMLING. "Protective Services Reanalyzed: Does Casework Help or Harm?" *Social Casework* 64 (1983):195–199.

DUNLOP, B. D. "Expanded Home-Based Care for the Impaired Elderly: Solution or Pipe Dream." *American Journal of Public Health* 70 (1980):514–519.

ELLOR, J. W., S. M. ANDERSON-RAY, AND S. S. TOBIN. "The Role of the Church in Services to the Elderly." In H. P. von Hahn (ed.), *Service Provision and Support Systems*. Vol. 17, *Interdisciplinary Topics in Gerontology*, 119–131. Basel, Switzerland: Karger, 1983.

EMLING, DIANE CARPENTER. *Adult Chore Services*. Lansing: Michigan Department of Social Services, 1976.

ERIKSON, R., AND K. ECKERT. "The Elderly Poor in Downtown San Diego Hotels." *Gerontologist* (1977):440–446.

ESTES, CARROLL. *The Aging Enterprise: A Critical Examination of Social Policies and Services for the Aged*. San Francisco: Jossey-Bass, 1979.

————. "Social Security: The Social Construction of a Crisis." *Millbank Memorial Quarterly/Health and Society* 61 (1983a):445–462.

————. "Fiscal Austerity and Aging." In Carroll Estes, Robert J. Newcomer, et al. (eds.), *Fiscal Austerity and Aging*. Beverly Hills, Calif.: Sage Publications, 1983b, 17–40.

ESTES, CARROLL, AND P. R. LEE. "Policy Shifts and Their Impact on Health Care for Elderly Persons." *Western Journal of Medicine* 135 (1981):511–517.

ESTES, CARROLL, AND ROBERT J. NEWCOMER. "The Future for Aging and Public Policy: Two Perspectives." In Carroll Estes, Robert J. Newcomer, et al. (eds.), *Fiscal Austerity and Aging*. Beverly Hills, Calif.: Sage Publications, 1983b, 249–269.

ESTES, CARROLL, ROBERT NEWCOMER, ET AL. (eds.). *Fiscal Austerity and Aging: Shifting Government Responsibility for the Elderly*. Beverly Hills, Calif.: Sage Publications, 1983a.

FALLCREEK, STEPHANIE, AND NEIL GILBERT. "The Aging Network in Transition." *Social Work* 26: May 1981.

FEDER, J. M., AND W. SCANLON. "Regulating the Bed Supply in Nursing Homes." *Milbank Memorial Fund Quarterly/Health and Society* 58 (1980): 54–87.

FEDERAL COUNCIL ON THE AGING. *Annual Report to the President—1978*. Washington, D.C.: Federal Council on the Aging, 1979.

FELDSTEIN, MARTIN. "Social Security, Induced Retirement, and Aggregate Capital Accumulation." *Journal of Political Economy* 82 (1974):905–926.

FINCH, CALEB E., AND LEONARD HAYFLICK (eds.). *Handbook of the Biology of Aging*. New York: Van Nostrand Reinhold, 1977.

FLEISHER, D., AND B. H. KAPLAN. "Effectiveness of a Neighborhood-Based Informal Support System." *Gerontologist* 22 (1982):226 (Abstract).

FOLLETT, S. "Protective Services for Adults." In *Encyclopedia of Social Work* 17th ed., Vol. 2, 1107–1114. Washington, D.C.: National Assn. of Social Workers, 1977.

FOX, PETER, AND STEVEN CLAUSER. "Trends in Nursing Home Expenditures: Implications for Aging Policy." *Health Care Financing Review*, Fall 1980, 65–70.

FRANKFATHER, DWIGHT, MICHAEL J. SMITH, AND FRANCIS CARO. *Family Care of the Elderly*. Lexington, Mass.: D. C. Heath, 1981.

FRENZEL, C., AND A. SCHARLACH. "Respite Care: Alternative to Institutionalization?" *Gerontologist* 23 (1983):110 (Abstract).

FRIEDMAN, MILTON. "Payroll Taxes, No; General Revenues, Yes." In Michael Boskin (ed.), *The Crisis in Social Security: Problems and Prospects*. San Francisco: Institute of Contemporary Studies, 1977, 27–29.

FRITZ, DAN. "The Administration on Aging as an Advocate: Progress, Problems and Perspectives." *Gerontologist* 19 (1979):141–150.

GAITZ, CHARLES, coordinator. Symposium, "Addressing Mental Health Needs of Impaired Elders: Perspectives from Community Long-Term Care." Gerontological Society meetings, San Francisco, November 1983.

GANS, HERBERT J. *The Urban Villagers.* New York: Free Press, 1965.

GELFAND, DONALD. *The Aging Network.* New York: Springer, 1984.

GLASS, BETTY. "The Biology of Aging." In Antoinette Bosco and J. Porcino, *What Do We Really Know About Aging?* Stony Brook, N.Y.: State University of New York, 1977.

GLENN, JOHN. Statement, Hearings of U.S. Senate Special Committee on Aging, *The Future of Medicare*, 98th Cong., 1st Sess. Washington, D.C.: GPO, 1983.

GLICK, P. G. "The Future Marital Status and the Living Arrangements of the Elderly." *Gerontologist* 19 (1979):301–309.

GOLANT, STEPHEN. "Intraurban Transportation Needs and Problems of the Elderly." In M. Powell Lawton, Robert Newcomer, and Thomas Byerts (eds.), *Community Planning for an Aging Society.* Stroudsburg, Pa.: Dowden, Hutchinson and Ross, 1976, 282–308.

GOODMAN, CATHERINE. "Natural Helping Among Older Adults." *Gerontologist* 24 (1984):138–143.

GOTTESMAN, L., AND N. BOURESTOM. "Why Nursing Homes Do What They Do." *Gerontologist* 14 (1974):501–506.

GOTTESMAN, LEONARD, BARBARA ISHIZAKI, AND STACEY MACBRIDE. "Service Management—Plan and Concept in Pennsylvania." *Gerontologist* 19 (1979):379–385.

GRAY, V. KATERINE. "Providing Support for Home Care Givers." In M. A. Smyer and M. Gatz (eds.), *Mental Health and Aging: Programs and Evaluations.* Beverly Hills, Calif.: Sage Publications, 1983, 197–213.

GROSS, RONALD, BEATRICE GROSS, AND SYLVIA SEIDMAN (eds.). *The New Old; Struggling for Decent Aging.* Garden City, N.Y.: Doubleday, 1978.

GROTH-JUNKER, A., AND J. ZIMMER. "Home Health Care to Homebound Chronically and Terminally Ill Elderly." Paper presented at Gerontological Society meetings, Boston, November 1982.

GUTHRIE, M. B., AND B. BRODBAR. "Coping with Attrition: The Channeling Experience." *Gerontologist* 23 (1983):111 (Abstract).

GUTOWSKI, MICHAEL. "Integrating Housing and Social Services Activities for the Elderly." In E. Boynton (ed.), *The Housing of Independent Elderly.* Occasional Papers in Housing and Community Affairs, vol. 1. Washington, D.C.: GPO, 1978.

HALL, JOYCE, AND ANNA TUCKER. *Rhode Island Department of Elderly Affairs Elderly Abuse Program: January 1981 to December 1983.* Providence: Rhode Island Department of Elderly Affairs, January 1984.

HANDSCHU, SUSAN. "Profile of the Nurse's Aide—Expanding Her Role as Psycho-Social Companion to the Nursing Home Resident." *Gerontologist* 13 (1973):315–317.

HANSSEN, A., ET AL. "Correlates of Senior Center Participation." *Gerontologist* 18 (1978):193–199.

HARBERT, ANITA, AND LEON GINSBERG (eds.). *Human Services for Older Adults: Concepts and Skills*. Belmont, Calif.: Wadsworth, 1979.

HAREL, ZEV, AND BERNICE HAREL. "On-Site Coordinated Services in Age-Segregated and Age-Integrated Public Housing." *Gerontologist* 18 (1978):153–158.

HARRINGTON, CHARLENE. "Social Security and Medicare: Policy Shifts in the 1980s." In Carroll Estes, Robert Newcomer, et al. (eds.), *Fiscal Austerity and Aging*. Beverly Hills, Calif.: Sage Publications, 1983, 83–112.

HARRIS, DIANA K., AND WILLIAM COLE. *Sociology of Aging*. Boston: Houghton Mifflin, 1980.

HARRIS, LOUIS. See Louis Harris and Associates.

HEINTZ, K. *Retirement Communities for Adults Only*. New Brunswick, N.J.: Rutgers University, Center for Urban Policy Research, 1976.

HENDRICKS, JON, AND C. DAVIS HENDRICKS. *Aging in Mass Society: Myths and Realities*. Cambridge, Mass.: Winthrop Publishers, 1977.

HESS, BETH. "Old Women: Problems, Potential, and Public Policy Implications." In Elizabeth Markson and Gretchen Batra (eds.), *Public Policies for Aging Population*. Lexington, Mass.: D. C. Heath, 1980.

_____. "Aging Policies and Older Women: The Hidden Agenda." Paper presented at the American Sociological Association meetings, Detroit, September 1983.

HEYMAN, DOROTHY, AND GRACE POLANSKY. "Social Services in the Community." In Richard A. Kalish (ed.), *The Later Years*. Monterey, Calif.: Brooks/Cole, 1977.

HICKEY, TOM, AND RICHARD DOUGLAS. "Neglect and Abuse of Older Family Members: Professionals' Perspectives and Case Experiences." *Gerontologist* 21 (1981):171–173.

HILL, REUBEN. "Hill's Response to By-the-Way (Three-Generation Family Study)." *Journal of Marriage and the Family* 39 (May 1977):251–252.

HOCHSCHILD, ARLIE RUSSELL. *The Unexpected Community*. Englewood Cliffs, N.J.: Prentice-Hall, 1973.

_____. "Disengagement Theory: A Critique and Proposal." *American Sociological Review* 40 (1975):553–569.

HODGSON, JOSEPH, AND JOAN QUINN. "The Impact of the Triage Health Care Delivery System on Client Morale, Independent Living, and the Cost of Care." *Gerontologist* 20 (1980):356–363.

HOLMES, D., AND E. HUDSON. *Evaluation Report of the Mosholu-Montefiore Day Care Center for the Elderly in the Northwest Bronx*. New York: Community Research Applications, 1975.

HOLMES, MONICA, AND DOUGLAS HOLMES. *Handbook of Human Services for Older Persons*. New York: Human Sciences Press, 1979.

HORSTMAN, PETER. "Protective Services for the Elderly: The Limits of Parens Patriae." In Jonathan Weiss, *Law of the Elderly*. New York: Practicing Law Institute, 1977.

"How to Save Social Security." *Business Week*, November 29, 1982, 81–85.

HUTTMAN, ELIZABETH. *Housing and Social Services for the Elderly.* New York: Praeger, 1977.

———. "The Different Roles Played by Adult Day Care Centers in the Care of the Physically and Mentally Impaired Elderly." Paper presented at the Western Gerontological Society meetings, San Francisco, March 1979.

———. "Social Work Services in the Housing Field." In Neil Gilbert and Harry Specht (eds.), *Handbook of the Social Services.* Englewood Cliffs, N.J.: Prentice-Hall, 1981, 281–310.

———. "Multi-Level Housing Facilities for the Elderly in Denmark and Holland." *Housing and Society* 9 (1982):20–30.

HUYCK, MARGARET H. *Growing Older.* Englewood Cliffs, N.J.: Prentice-Hall, 1974.

IRWIN, THEODORE. "After 65: Resources for Self-Reliance." In Ronald Gross, Beatrice Gross, and Sylvia Seidman (eds.), *The New Old: Struggling for Decent Aging.* Garden City, N.Y.: Doubleday, 1978.

JACKSON, JACQUELYNE. "Children and Parents in the Black Community." Paper presented at Gerontological Society meetings, Boston, November 1982.

JACKSON, JACQUELYNE, AND BERTRAM E. WALLS. "Myths and Realities about Aged Blacks." In Mollie Brown (ed.), *Readings in Gerontology.* St. Louis: C. V. Mosby, 1978, 95–113.

JACKSON, RAYMOND. "Transportation for the Elderly: Sec. 16(b)(2) in Massachusetts." *Gerontologist* 23 (1983):155–165.

JACOBS, B. *Senior Centers and the At-Risk Older Person.* Washington, D.C.: National Institute of Senior Centers, 1980.

JACOBS, BELLA, AND ALLENE MAGANN (eds.). *Involving Men: A Challenge for Senior Centers.* Washington, D.C.: National Council on Aging, 1974.

JACOBS, JERRY. *Fun City.* New York: Holt, Rinehart and Winston, 1974.

JENKINS, LOWELL, AND ALICIA S. COOK. "The Rural Hospice: Integrating Formal and Informal Helping Systems." *Social Work* 26 (1981):414–416.

JOHNSON, COLLEEN, AND DONALD CATALANO. "A Longitudinal Study of Family Supports to Impaired Elderly." *Gerontologist* 22 (1982):78–79 (Abstract).

JOHNSON, ELIZABETH, AND BARBARA BURSK. "Relationships Between the Elderly and Their Adult Children." *Gerontologist* 17 (1977):90–96.

JOHNSON, PETER, AND ALLEN RUBIN. "Case Management in Mental Health: A Social Work Domain." *Social Work* 28 (1983):49–53.

JOHNSON, SHEILA K. *Idle Haven.* Berkeley: University of California Press, 1971.

KALISH, RICHARD, ELINORE LURIE, RICHARD WEXLER, AND RICK ZAWADSKI. *On Lok Senior Health Services: Evaluation of a Success.* San Francisco: On Lok Senior Health Services, 1975.

KALISH, RICHARD A. (ed.). *The Later Years.* Monterey, Calif.: Brooks/Cole, 1977.

KAPLAN, J. "Goals of Day Care." In E. Pfeiffer (ed.), *Day Care for Older Adults.* Durham, N.C.: Duke University Press, 1976.

KART, CARY, AND BARBARA MANARD (eds.). *Aging in America: Readings in Social Gerontology.* 2d ed. Sherman Oaks, Calif.: Alfred Publishing Co., 1981.

KART, CARY S., EILEEN S. METRESS, AND JAMES F. METRESS. *Aging and Health: Biological and Social Perspectives.* Menlo Park, Calif.: Addison-Wesley, 1978.

KAYE, IRA. "Transportation." In Don A. Dillman and Daryl Hobbs (eds.), *Rural Society in the U.S.: Issues in the 1980s.* Boulder, Colo.: Westview, 1982.

KELL, DIANE, AND CARL PATTON. "Reaction to Induced Early Retirement." *Gerontologist* 18 (1978):173–178.

KNOWLTON, JACKSON, STEVEN CLAUSER, AND JAMES FATULA. "Nursing Home Pre-Admission Screening: A Review of State Programs." *Health Care Financing Review* 3 (1982):75–87.

KOFF, THEODORE. *Hospice Caring Community.* Cambridge, Mass.: Winthrop, 1980.

———. *Long-Term Care: An Approach to Serving the Frail Elderly.* Boston: Little, Brown, 1982.

KRETZ, LINDA. Director of Hayward Social Day Care Center. Interview with author, Hayward, Calif., November 16, 1983.

KROUT, JOHN. "Correlates of Senior Center Utilization." *Research on Aging* 5 (1983):339–352.

LACK, SYLVIA. "Referral: Hospice." In Robert A. Kalish (ed.), *The Later Years.* Monterey, Calif.: Brooks/Cole, 1977, 351–358.

LA JOLLA MANAGEMENT CORPORATION. *Medicaid Program Characteristics.* Washington, D.C.: Health Care Financing Administration, 1982.

LAMB, H. RICHARD. "Therapist-Case Managers: More than Brokers of Services." *Hospital and Community Psychiatry* 31 (1980):762–764.

LAMB, M. E., AND B. SUTTON-SMITH (eds.). *Sibling Relationships: Their Nature and Significance Across the Life Span.* Hillsdale, N.J.: Erlbaum, 1982.

LANG, A., AND ELAINE BRODY. "Characteristics of Middle-Aged Daughters and Help to Their Elderly Mothers." *Journal of Marriage and the Family* 45 (1983): 193–202.

LAWTON, M. POWELL. "Assessing the Competence of Older People," in D. R. Kent, R. Kastenbaum, and S. Sherwood (eds.), *Long Term Care.* New York: Behavioral Publications, 1972, 122–143.

———. *Planning and Managing Housing for the Elderly.* New York: Wiley, 1975.

———. "The Housing Problems of Community-Resident Elderly." In E. Boynton (ed.), *The Housing of Independent Elderly.* Occasional Papers in Housing and Community Affairs, vol. 1. Washington, D.C.: GPO, 1978.

———. *Environment and Aging.* Monterey, Calif.: Brooks/Cole, 1980.

——— (ed.). *Community Housing—Choices for Older Americans.* New York: Garland Press, 1982.

LAWTON, M. POWELL, AND THOMAS BYERTS. "Planning Physical Space." In Robert A. Kalish (ed.), *The Later Years.* Monterey, Calif.: Brooks/Cole, 1977, 261–265.

LAWTON, M. P., M. GREENBAUM, AND B. LIEBOWITZ. "The Lifespan of Housing Environments for the Aging." *Gerontologist* 20 (1980):54–56.

LEANSE, JOYCE, AND SARA WAGNER. *Senior Centers: Report of Senior Group Programs in America.* Washington, D.C.: National Council on Aging, 1975.

LEBEL, J. O. "A Case for Lifelong Learning as a Planning and Service Network Priority." *Gerontologist* 22 (1982):86 (Abstract).

LEE, GARY, AND MARIE LASSEY. "The Elderly." In Don A. Dillman and Daryl J. Hobbs (eds.), *Rural Society in the U.S.: Issues for the 1980s*. Boulder, Colo.: Westview Press, 1982, 85–93.

LEHMANN, VIRGINIA. "Guardianship and Protective Services for Older Persons." *Social Casework* 62 (1961): 252–257.

LEMON, B. W., V. L. BENGSTON, AND J. PETERSON. "An Exploration of the Activity Theory of Aging: Activity Types and Life Satisfaction Among In-movers to a Retirement Commonity." *Journal of Gerontology* 27 (1972):511–523.

LESNOFF-CARAVAGLIA, GARI. "The Five-Percent Fallacy." *International Journal of Aging and Human Development* 9 (1978–79):187–192.

LIEBOWITZ, BERNARD. "Implications of Community Housing for Planning and Policy." *Gerontologist* 18 (1978):138–141.

LIND, RONALD. "The Importance of Volunteers." *Senior Center Report* 4 (1981):2–3.

LINNANE, PATRICK D. *Ombudsman for Nursing Homes—Structure and Process*. Washington, D.C.: Department of Health, Education and Welfare, 1977.

LITWAK, EUGENE. "Helping Networks Among the Aged: Alternative Substructures and Tools." Roundtable presentation at American Sociological Association meeting, Detroit, September 1, 1983.

LOETHER, HERMAN J. *Problems of Aging: Sociological and Social-Psychological Perspectives*. 2d ed. Encino, Calif.: Dickenson Publishing Co., 1975.

LONGINO, CHARLES, JR. "Retirement Communities." In F. J. Berghorn and D. E. Schafer (eds.), *The Dynamics of Aging*. Boulder, Colo.: Westview Press, 1981.

LOPATA, HELENE. *Women as Widows: Support Systems*. New York: Elsevier, 1979.

LOUIS HARRIS AND ASSOCIATES. *The Myth and Reality of Aging in America*. Washington, D.C.: National Council on Aging, 1975.

LOWY, LOUIS. "Social Welfare and the Aging." In M. Spencer and J. Dorr, *Understanding Aging*. Englewood Cliffs, N.J.: Prentice-Hall, 1975.

———. "Adult Children and Their Parents: Dependency or Dependability?" *Long Term Care and Health Services Administration Quarterly*, Fall 1977.

———. *Social Work with the Aging*. New York: Harper & Row, 1979.

———. *Social Policies and Programs on Aging*. Lexington, Mass.: D. C. Heath, 1980.

LOZIER, JOHN, AND RONALD ALTHOUSE. "Retirement to the Porch in Rural Appalachia." *International Journal of Aging and Human Development* 6 (1975):7–15.

LUND, M. "Adult Day Care: An Alternative with a Future." Discussion at Gerontological Society meetings, Boston, November 1982.

LURIE, E., R. KALISH, R. WEXLER, AND M. L. ANSAK. "On Lok Senior Day Health Center." *Gerontologist* 16 (1976):39–46.

LURIE, ELINORE. "Acute Hospital Referrals to Community-Based Care." Paper presented at Gerontological Society meetings, Boston, November 1982.

MACE, NANCY, AND PETER RABINS, discussants. Day Care for Alzheimer's Disease Workshop, Gerontological Society meetings, San Francisco, November 1983.

MACE, NANCY L., AND P. V. RABINS. "Areas of Stress in Families of Dementia Patients: A Two-Year Follow-up." *Gerontologist* 22 (1982):128 (Abstract).

MADDOX, GEORGE. "Activity and Morale: A Longitudinal Study of Selected Elderly Subjects." *Social Forces* 42 (1963):195–204.

MAHONEY, K. *Outside the Day Care Center: Additional Support for the Frail Elderly.* Hartford: Connecticut Department of Aging, 1978.

MARIN COUNTY, CALIFORNIA. Marin Area Agency on Aging. "Analysis of Needs of Older Adults, Resources or Gaps in the Service System." *Area Plan on Aging: Three-Year Plan FY1983–86.* San Rafael, Calif.: Marin Area Agency on Aging, 1982.

MEHTA, N., AND C. MACH. "Day Care Services: An Alternative to Institutional Care." *Journal of the American Geriatrics Society* 23 (1976): 498–504.

MELLOR, J. "Education of Caretakers Toward Self-Help." Paper presented at Gerontological Society meetings, Boston, November, 1982.

MENDELSON, M. A., AND D. HAPGOOD. "The Political Economy of Nursing Homes." *Annals of American Academy of Political Science* 415 (1974):95–105.

METRESS, SEAMUS. "Nutrition in Old Age." In Cary Kart and Barbara Manard (eds.), *Aging in America: Readings in Social Gerontology.* 2d ed., 189–207. Sherman Oaks, Calif.: Alfred Publishing Company, 1981.

MICHIGAN, UNIVERSITY OF. *Housing Adjustment of Older People.* (Sandra Newman, chief investigator.) Ann Arbor, Mich.: Institute of Social Research, 1978.

————. "Incontinence Comes Out of the Water Closet." *The Research News,* October–November 1983.

MINDEL, CHARLES, AND ROOSEVELT WRIGHT, JR. "Assessing the Role of Support Systems among Black and White Elderly." *Gerontologist* 22 (1982):205 (Abstract).

MITCHELL, J. B. "Why Won't Physicians Visit Nursing Homes?" *Gerontologist* 22 (1982):131 (Abstract).

MOBERG, D. O. "Religion and the Institutional Church." In Richard A. Kalish (ed.), *The Later Years.* Monterey, Calif.: Brooks/Cole, 1977.

MONK, ABRAHAM. "The Emergence of Day Care Centers for the Aged." Paper presented at National Conference on Social Welfare, San Francisco, May 20, 1974.

———— (ed.). *The Age of Aging: A Reader in Social Gerontology.* Buffalo, N.Y.: Prometheus Books, 1979.

————. "Social Work with the Aged: Principles of Practice." *Social Work* 26 (1981):61–63.

MONTGOMERY, JAMES. "The Housing Patterns of Older People." In Richard A. Kalish (ed.), *The Later Years.* Monterey, Calif.: Brooks/Cole, 1977, 253–259.

MOOS, R. H. "Specialized Living Environments for Older People: A Conceptual Framework for Evaluation." *Journal of Social Issues* 36 (1980):75–94.

MORAN, G. "Case Management as a Targeting Strategy." Paper presented at Gerontological Society meetings, Boston, November 1982.

MORRIS, ROBERT. "Alternative to Nursing Home Care: A Proposal." Hearings, U.S. Senate, Special Committee on Aging, 92d Cong., 1st Sess., October 1971.

————. *Allocating Health Resources for the Aged and Disabled: Technology Versus Politics.* Lexington, Mass.: D. C. Heath, 1981.

Moss, Anne. "Social Insecurity: Pension Plans Shortchange Women." *Women's Political Times*, February 1983.

Moss, Frank E., and Val J. Halmandaris. *Too Old, Too Sick, Too Bad: Nursing Homes in America*. Germantown, Md.: Aspen Systems, 1977.

Motenko, Aluma. "Coordinating Support Systems by Area Agencies on Aging in Facilitating Family Helping Network." Paper presented at Gerontological Society meetings, Boston, November 1982.

Mukherjee, M. R. "House Sharing by Non-Relatives in the Private Housing Market." Paper presented at Gerontological Society meetings, Boston, November 1982.

Munnell, Alicia H. *The Future of Social Security*. Washington, D.C.: Brookings Institution, 1977.

Munnichs, J. M. "Linkages of Old People with Their Families and Bureaucracy in a Welfare State, the Netherlands." In Ethel Shanas and Marvin Sussman (eds.), *Family Bureaucracy and the Elderly*. Durham, N.C.: Duke University Press, 1977.

Myles, John. *Political Economy of Pensions*. Boston: Little, Brown, 1983.

Nahemow, N. "Nutrition Patterns and Health Status among Low-Income Black Elderly." *Gerontologist* 22 (1982):206 (Abstract).

National Center for Health Statistics. *Selected Operating and Financial Characteristics of Nursing Homes*. Washington, D.C.: GPO, 1977.

National Commission on Social Security Reform. *Final Report*. 1983.

National Council on the Aging. *Aging in the Eighties: America in Transition*. Washington, D.C.: NCOA, 1981a.

——. *NCOA Public Policy Agenda, 1980–81*. Washington, D.C.: NCOA, 1981b.

National Council for Homemaker–Home Health Aide Services. *Interpretation for Standards for Homemaker–Home Health Aide Services*. New York: National Council for Homemaker–Home Health Aide Services, 1976.

National Institute of Adult Day Care Centers. Brochure. 1979.

National Institute of Senior Centers. *Senior Centers Report of Senior Group Programs in America*. Washington, D.C.: National Council on Aging, 1975.

——. "Adult Day Care: An Overview." *Senior Center Report* 1 (1978):3–8.

——. "Dedication Held for New Jacksonville Center." *Senior Center Report* 4 (1981):1.

Neuhaus, Ruby H., and Robert H. Neuhaus. *Successful Aging*. New York: Wiley, 1982.

Newcomer, Robert, and L. Frise. "Housing in the Continuum of Care." *Generations* 3 (1979):13–14.

Newcomer, Robert J., A. E. Benjamin, and Carroll Estes. "The Older Americans Act." In Carroll Estes, Robert Newcomer, et al. (eds.), *Fiscal Austerity and Aging*. Beverly Hills, Calif.: Sage Publications, 1983.

Newcomer, Robert J., and Charlene Harrington. "State Medicaid Expenditures: Trends and Program Policy Changes." In Carroll Estes, Robert Newcomer, et al. (eds.), *Fiscal Austerity and Aging*. Beverly Hills, Calif.: Sage Publications, 1983, 187–206.

NEWMAN, SANDRA, AND RAYMOND STRUYK. "An Alternative Targeting Strategy for Housing Assistance." *Gerontologist* 24 (1984).

OKTAY, J., AND H. PALLEY. "A National Family Policy for the Chronically Ill Elderly." *Social Welfare Forum, 1980.* New York: Columbia University Press, 1981.

Older Americans Reports. See "Vehicle."

O'MALLEY, HELEN, ET AL. *Elder Abuse in Massachusetts: A Survey of Professionals and Paraprofessionals.* Boston: Legal Research and Services for the Elderly, 1979.

OMB. See U.S. Office of Management and Budget.

ORR, MARTIN. *Development of Numerical Standards for Patient Placement in New York State Long-Term Care Facilities.* Albany: New York State Office of Health Systems Management, 1978.

OSTERWEIS, MARIAN, AND DAPHNE S. CHAMPAGNE. "The U.S. Hospice Movement: Issues in Development." In Cary S. Kart and Barbara Manard (eds.), *Aging in America: Readings in Social Gerontology.* 2d ed., 531–545. Sherman Oaks, Calif.: Alfred Publishing Co., 1981.

OZARIN, LUCY. "The Pros and Cons of Case Management." In John Talbot (ed.), *The Chronic Mental Patient.* Washington, D.C.: American Psychiatric Association, 1978, 167–172.

PALMORE, ERDMAN. "Total Change of Institutionalization among the Aged." *Gerontologist* 16 (1976):504–507.

PARSONS, DONALD, AND DOUGLAS MUNRO. "Intergenerational Transfers in Social Security." In Michael Boskin (ed.), *The Crisis in Social Security: Problems and Prospects.* San Francisco: Institute of Contemporary Studies, 1977.

PASTALAN, LEON (ed.). *Retirement Communities: An American Original.* New York: Hawthorn Books, 1983.

PEAR, ROBERT. "Fund Cuts Reduce Nursing Home Checkups." *New York Times,* March 5, 1982.

———. "Medicare Proposals Said to Burden Those Most Ill." *New York Times,* April 10, 1983.

PEARSON, CHRISTINE. "Housing Alternatives for the Elderly." Speech to class, California State University, Hayward, November 11, 1982.

PECHMAN, JOSEPH. "The Social Security System: An Overview." In Michael Boskin (ed.), *The Crisis in Social Security: Problems and Prospects.* San Francisco: Institute of Contemporary Studies, 1977.

PELCOVITS, JEANETTE, AND DOUGLAS HOLMES. "Nutrition for Older Americans." Paper for Administration On Aging, Washington, D.C., 1969.

PIERCE, N. "Elderly Freedom Is Riding on OATS." *Washington Post,* January 5, 1979.

PRESIDENT'S COMMISSION ON PENSION POLICY. *Interim Report.* Washington, D.C.: GPO, 1980.

PRITCHARD, DAVID. "The Art of Matchmaking: A Case Study in Shared Housing." *Gerontologist* 23 (1983):174–179.

PYNOOS, JON. "Setting the Elderly Housing Agenda." *Policy Studies Journal,* Fall 1984.

QUINN, J., H. RAISZ, AND J. SEGAL. "The Impact of Project Triage on Service Utilization over Time." *Gerontologist* 23 (1983):272 (Abstract).

RATHBONE-MCCUAN, ELOISE. "Geriatric Day Care: A Family Perspective," *Gerontologist* 16 (1975):517–521.

———. *Isolated Elders: Health and Social Intervention.* Rockville, Mo.: Aspen Systems, 1982.

RATHBONE-MCCUAN, ELOISE, AND M. ELLIOTT. "Geriatric Day Care in Theory and Practice." *Social Work Health Care* 2 (1976–77):153–170.

RATHBONE-MCCUAN, ELOISE, AND J. LEVENSON. "Impact of Socialization Therapy in Geriatric Day Care." *Gerontologist* 15 (1975):338–342.

RAWSON, I., J. WEINBERG, AND J. HOLTZ. "Nutrition of Rural Elderly in Southwestern Pennsylvania." *Gerontologist* 18 (1978):24–29.

REGAN, J., AND G. SPRINGER. *Protective Services for the Elderly.* Washington, D.C.: U.S. Senate Special Committee on Aging, 1977.

REGNIER, VICTOR, AND T. BYERTS. "Applying Research to the Plan and Design of Housing for the Elderly." In F. Spink (ed.), *Housing for a Maturing Population.* Washington, D.C.: Urban Institute, 1983.

REICHARD, SUZANNE, ET AL. *Aging and Personality.* New York: Arno, 1980.

RICH, SPENCER. "Private Pension Plans—Bad News for Workers." *San Francisco Chronicle,* November 15, 1978.

RICHMAN, J. "Family Therapy with the Elderly Suicidal Patient." *Gerontologist* 22 (1982):242 (Abstract).

RIGBY, D., AND E. PONCE. *The Supplemental Security Income Program for the Aged, Blind and Disabled: Select Characteristics of State Supplementation Programs.* Washington, D.C.: GPO, 1980.

RILEY, MATHILDA, AND A. FONER. *Aging and Society,* Vol. 1. New York: Russell Sage Foundation, 1968.

———. *Aging and Society: A Sociology of Age Stratification,* Vol. 3. New York: Russell Sage Foundation, 1972.

RIVLIN, ALICE. Statement at Hearings of U.S. Senate, Special Committee on Aging, *The Future of Medicare,* 98th Cong., 1st Sess. Washington, D.C.: GPO, 1983.

ROBERTSON, A. HAEWORTH. "Financial Status of Social Security Programs after the Social Security Amendments of 1977." *Social Security Bulletin* 41 (1978):21–30.

ROBINS, EDITH. "Models of Day Care." In E. Pfeiffer (ed.), *Day Care for Older Adults.* Durham, N.C.: Duke University Center for the Study of Aging, 1976.

———. *Directory of Adult Day Care Centers.* Rockville, Md.: Health Care Financing Administration, 1978.

———. "Adult Day Care: The Medicaid Perspective." Paper presented at Gerontological Society meeting, Seattle, April 13, 1981.

ROBINSON, BETSY, AND MAJDA THURNHER. "Taking Care of Aged Parents: A Family Cycle Transition." *Gerontologist* 19 (1979):586–593.

ROCKSTEIN, MORRIS, AND MARVIN SUSSMAN. *Biology of Aging.* Belmont, Calif.: Wadsworth, 1979.

ROGERS, C. J., S. MIZE-WRIGHTAM, AND S. SAELENS. "Comparison of Adult Day Care and Chore/Homemaker Clients," *Gerontologist* 22 (1982):236 (Abstract).

ROMBERG, DALE. "A Study of Rossmoor Leisure World." *Master's thesis.* Hayward: California State University of Sociology Department, 1983.

ROSE, A. M. "The Subculture of Aging: A Framework for Research in Social Gerontology." In A. M. Rose and W. A. Peterson (eds.), *Older People and Their Social World.* Philadelphia: F. A. Davis, 1965, 3–16.

ROSEN, SHERWIN. "Social Security and the Economy." In Michael Boskin (ed.), *The Crisis in Social Security: Problems and Prospects.* San Francisco: Institute of Contemporary Studies, 1977.

ROSENMAYR, L. "The Family—a Source of Hope for the Elderly." In Ethel Shanas and Marvin Sussman (eds.), *Family Bureaucracy and the Elderly.* Durham, N.C.: Duke University Press, 1977.

ROSENMAYR, L., AND E. KOCKEIS. "Propositions for a Sociological Theory of Aging and the Family." *International Social Science Journal* 15 (1963):410–426.

ROSOW, IRVING. *Social Integration of the Aged.* New York: Free Press, 1967.

RURAL MINI–WHITE HOUSE CONFERENCE *Report.* Washington, D.C.: Green Thumb Inc., 1981.

RUSSELL, R. M., N. R. SAHYOUN, AND R. WHINSTON-PERRY. "The Elderly: Nutritional Assessment." In E. Calkins (ed.), *The Practice of Geriatric Medicine.* Philadelphia: W. B. Saunders, 1984.

RUTHER, MARTIN, AND ALLEN DOBSON. "Equal Treatment and Unequal Benefits. A Reexamination of the Use of Medicare Services by Race, 1967–1976." *Health Care Financing Review* 2 (1981):55–83.

SANDS, DAN, AND THELMA SUZUKI. "Adult Day Care for Alzheimer's Patients and Their Families." *Gerontologist* 23 (1983):21–23.

SAUNDERS, CICELY. "Dying They Live: St. Christopher's Hospice." In Herman Field (ed.), *New Meanings of Death.* New York: McGraw-Hill, 1977.

SCHMANDT, JURGEN, VICTOR BACH, AND BERYL RADIN. "Information and Referral Services for Elderly Welfare Recipients." *Gerontologist* 19 (1979):21–33.

SCHMIDT, MARY. "Failing Parents, Aging Children." *Journal of Gerontological Social Work* 2 (1980):259–268.

SCHMIDT, W., K. MILLER, W. BELL, AND B. NEW. *Public Guardianship and the Elderly.* Cambridge, Mass.: Ballinger, 1981.

SCHRAM, S. "Elderly Policy Particularism: The Case of Title XX." Paper presented at the Gerontological Society meetings, Boston, November 1982.

SCHULZ, JAMES. *The Economics of Aging.* 2d ed. Belmont, Calif.: Wadsworth, 1980.

Senior Center Report 4, February 1981.

SHANAS, ETHEL. "Social Myth as Hypothesis: The Case of the Family Relations of Old People." *Gerontologist* 19 (1979a):3–9.

———. "The Family as a Social Support System in Old Age." *Gerontologist* 19 (1979b):169–174.

———. "Older People and Their Families: The New Pioneers." *Journal of Marriage and the Family* 42 (1980):9–15.

SHEILS, MERRILL. "The Turmoil in Pension Plans." *Newsweek*, June 1, 1981, 28–34.

SHERWOOD, S., J. N. MORRIS, AND S. M. WRIGHT. "Impact of Hospice on Patient Quality of Life and the Bereavement Experience." Paper presented at the Gerontological Society meetings, San Francisco, November 1983.

SICKER, M. "The AOA Advocacy Assistance Program: Origins and Directions." In *Aging*. Washington, D.C.: HEW, 1979, 18–21.

SIMS, RICHARD, AND SHIRLEY PACKARD. "A New Approach to Case Management of the High-Risk Elderly in a Primary Care Setting." *Gerontologist* 23 (1983):272 (Abstract).

SOCIAL SECURITY ADMINISTRATION. *1980 Annual Report of the Board of Trustees of the Social Security Trust Funds*. Washington, D.C.: GPO, 1981.

SOLDO, B. J. "Effect of Number and Sex of Adult Children in LTC Service Use Patterns." *Gerontologist* 22 (1982):129 (Abstract).

SOLDO, BETH. "Integrating Housing and Social Service Activities for the Elderly Household: Comments." In E. Boynton (ed.), *The Housing of Independent Elderly*. Occasional Papers in Housing and Community Affairs, vol. 1. Washington, D.C.: GPO, 1978, 138.

SOLDO, BETH J. *America's Elderly in the 1980's*. Washington, D.C.: Population Reference Bureau, 1980.

SOLOMON, JERRY. "A Study of the Miami Jewish Hospital Day Care Centers." Presentation at the American Orthopsychiatric Association meetings, March 1976.

SOLOMON, K., AND R. VICKERS. "Attitudes of Health Workers Towards Old People." *Journal of the American Geriatrics Society* 27 (1979):186–191.

SPITZ, B. *Medicaid Nursing Home Reimbursement: New York, Illinois, California Case Studies*. Baltimore: Health Care Financing Administration, 1981.

STEINBERG, RAYMOND, AND GENEVIEVE CARTER. *Case Management and the Elderly*. Lexington, Mass.: D. C. Heath, 1982.

STEINFELD, EDWARD. "Residential Repair and Renovation Services." In Monica Holmes and Douglas Holmes (eds.), *Handbook of Human Service for Older People*. New York: Human Sciences Press, 1979.

STEINMETZ, SUZANNE. "Elder Abuse." *Aging Magazine*, January/February, 1981.

STODDARD, SANDOL, *The Hospice Movement*. New York: Vintage Books, 1978.

STREIB, GORDON. "Social Stratification and Aging." In Robert Binstock and Ethel Shanas (eds.), *Handbook of Aging and the Social Sciences*. New York: Van Nostrand Reinhold, 1976, 160–185.

STREIB, GORDON F., AND CLEMENT SCHNEIDER. *Retirement in American Society*. Ithaca, N.Y.: Cornell University Press, 1971.

STRUYK, RAYMOND. *The Housing Situation of Elderly Americans*. Washington, D.C.: The Urban Institute, 1976.

————. "Housing Policies for the Elderly." Paper presented at Gerontological Society meetings, San Francisco, November 1983.

STRUYK, RAYMOND J., AND DEBORAH DEVINE. "Determinants of Dwelling Maintenance Activity of Elderly Households." Unpublished paper prepared for U.S. Department of Housing and Urban Development. Washington, D.C.: HUD, 1977.

SUGARMAN, J. H. "RSVP in New York City—A Study of Volunteer Impact and Opportunity." *Gerontologist* 22 (1982):208 (Abstract).

SUHART, MARIETTA, BRADLEY COURTENAY, DOUGLAS MCCONATHA, AND BOB STEVENSON. "A Data-based Model for Senior Adult Education." *Gerontologist* 22 (1982):86 (Abstract).

SUSSMAN, MARVIN B. "The Family Life of Old People." In Robert Binstock and Ethel Shanas (eds.), *Handbook of Aging and the Social Sciences*. New York: Van Nostrand Reinhold, 1976.

———. *Social and Economic Supports and Family Environments for the Elderly. Final Report*. Washington, D.C.: Administration on Aging, 1979.

SUSSMAN, R. B., AND F. STEINBERG. "The Aged in Public Housing." Unpublished paper, 1970. (Quoted in John Williamson, Linda Evans, and Anne Manley, *Aging and Society*. New York: Holt, Rinehart and Winston, 1980.)

TAIETZ, PHILIP. "The Impact of AAAs on the Development of New Services for the Elderly." Paper presented at Gerontological Society meetings, Boston, November 1982.

TAIETZ, PHILIP, AND SANDE MILTON. "Rural–Urban Differences in the Structure of Services for the Elderly in Upstate New York Counties." *Journal of Gerontology* 34 (1979):429–437.

"Tenderloin Hotel Tenants Protest Eviction Notices." *San Francisco Chronicle*, October 21, 1982.

THOMPSON, MARIE MCGUIRE. *Assisted Residential Living for Older People: A Guide for Tenant Selection and Preoccupancy Planning*. Washington, D.C.: International Institote of Gerontology, 1978.

TISSUE, THOMAS. "Social Class and Senior Citizen Center." *Gerontologist* 11 (1971):196–200.

TITMUSS, RICHARD M. *Essays on the Welfare State*. London: Allen and Unwin, 1981.

TOLLIVER, LENNE-MARIE. "Administration on Aging: Current and Future Directions." Paper presented at Gerontological Society meetings, Boston, November 1982.

TRAGER, B. "Adult Day Health Care." Report of conference held at University of Arizona, Tucson, 1979.

TROLL, L., S. MILLER, AND R. ATCHLEY. *Families in Later Life*. Belmont, Calif.: Wadsworth, 1979.

TSEMBERIS, SAM, AND ANN D'ERCOLE. "Social Support and Well-Being Among Older Men and Women." *Gerontologist* 22 (1982):248 (Abstract).

U.K. DEPARTMENT OF THE ENVIRONMENT. *Housing the Elderly: How Successful Are Granny Annexes?* London: Department of Environment, January 1976.

U.S. BUREAU OF THE CENSUS. *Annual Housing Survey of 1974*. Part A. General Characteristics for the United States and Regions. Current Housing Reports. Washington, D.C.: GPO, 1974.

———. *Annual Housing Survey of 1975*. Part A. General Characteristics for the United States and Regions. Current Housing Reports. Washington, D.C.: GPO, 1975.

———. *Survey of Nursing Home Utilization*. Washington, D.C.: GPO, 1976.

————. *Annual Housing Survey of 1977*. Part A. General Characteristics for the United States and Regions. Current Housing Reports. Washington, D.C.: GPO, 1977.

————. *Statistical Abstract of the U.S.: 1982–83*. Washington, D.C.: GPO, 1983.

U.S. CONGRESS. HOUSE. SELECT COMMITTEE ON AGING. *Transportation: Improving Mobility for Older Americans*. Washington, D.C.: GPO, 1976.

————. Subcommittee on Human Services. *Report*. Washington, D.C.: GPO, 1982.

U.S. CONGRESS. SENATE. SPECIAL COMMITTEE ON AGING. *Developments in Aging: 1963 and 1964*. Washington, D.C.: GPO, 1965.

————. *Developments in Aging: 1971*. Washington, D.C.: GPO, 1972.

————. *Developments in Aging: 1975*. Washington, D.C.: GPO, 1976.

————. *Developments in Aging: 1977*. Washington, D.C.: GPO, 1978.

————. *Developments in Aging: 1981*. Washington, D.C.: GPO, 1982.

————. Hearings, *The Future of Medicare*, 98th Cong., 1st Sess. Washington, D.C.: GPO, 1983.

————. Subcommittee on Long-Term Care. *Nursing Home Care in the United States: Failure in Public Policy*. Washington, D.C.: GPO, 1975.

U.S. CONGRESSIONAL BUDGET OFFICE. *Medicaid: Choices for 1982 and Beyond*. Washington: D.C.: GPO, 1981.

U.S. DEPARTMENT OF HEALTH AND HUMAN SERVICES. *Facts About Older Americans*. Washington, D.C.: GPO, 1980.

U.S. DEPARTMENT OF HOUSING AND URBAN DEVELOPMENT. *Housing for the Elderly and Handicapped: The Experience of Section 202 Programs from 1959–1977*. Washington, D.C.: GPO, 1979.

U.S. DEPARTMENT OF TRANSPORTATION. *Transportation and the Elderly: A Literature Capsule*. Cambridge, Mass.: Transportation Systems Center, 1977.

————. *Elderly Market for Urban Mass Transit*. Washington, D.C.: GPO, 1980.

U.S. GENERAL ACCOUNTING OFFICE. *Entering a Nursing Home: Costly Implications for Medicaid and the Elderly*. Report No. PAD-80-12. November 26, 1979.

————. *More Specific Guidance and Closer Monitoring Needed to Get More from Funds Spent on Social Services for the Elderly: Report by the Comptroller General*. Washington, D.C.: GAO, 1981.

U.S. OFFICE OF MANAGEMENT AND BUDGET. Health and Income Maintenance Division. "Federal Outlays Benefit the Elderly." In U.S. White House Conference on Aging, *Final Report, 1981*, Vol. 1, 13. Washington, D.C.: White House Conference on Aging, 1982.

"Vehicle Insurance Rates Lowered for Elderly Programs." *Older Americans Reports* 4 (1980).

VISCUSI, W. KIP, AND RICHARD ZECKHAUSER. "The Role of Social Security in Income Maintenance." In Michael Boskin (ed.), *The Crisis in Social Security*. San Francisco: Institute of Contemporary Studies, 1977.

VLADECK, B. C. "The Design of Failure: Health Policy and the Structure of Federalism." *Journal of Health Politics, Policy and Law* 4 (1979):522–535.

———. *Unloving Care: The Nursing Home Tragedy*. New York: Basic Books, 1980.

———. "Equity, Access and the Costs of Health Services." *Medical Care* 19 (1981):69–80.

VOLK, L. J., J. B. HUTCHINS, AND J. S. DOREMUS. "A National Cost-Containment Strategy for Long-Term Care." *Public Administration Review* 40 (1980):747–779.

VON BEHREN, RUTH. *On Lok Senior Health Services Adult Day Health Care—From Pilot Study to Permanent Program*. Sacramento: California State Department of Health publications, 1979.

———. Panelist, Day Care Symposium, Western Gerontological Society meetings, Seattle, April 1981.

WALKER, J. C., AND D. E. POTTER. "Analysis of Elder Abuse in a State-wide Reporting System." *Gerontologist* 23 (1983):151 (Abstract).

WARD, RUSSELL A. "The Meaning of Voluntary Association Participation to Older People." *Journal of Gerontology* 34 (1979):438–445.

WARD, RUSSELL, ET AL. "Subjective Network Assessments and Subjective Well-Being." *Journal of Gerontology* 39 (1984):93–101.

WASSER, EDNA. "Protective Practice in Serving the Mentally Impaired Aged." *Social Casework* 94 (1971):510–522.

———. "Protective Services: Casework with Older People." *Social Casework* 97 (1974):103–114.

WEAVER, CAROLYN. *The Crisis in Social Security: Economic and Political Origins*. Durham, N.C.: Duke University Press, 1982.

WEAVER, WARREN. "Poll Shows Americans Losing Faith in Future of Social Security." *New York Times*, July 17, 1981.

WEBER, RUTH. "Definitions, Case Identification and Sample Characteristics of Older Persons in Need of Protective Services." In Ella Liney (ed.), *A Crucial Issue in Social Work Practice*. New York: National Council on Aging, 1966.

WEG, RUTH. *Nutrition and the Later Years*. Los Angeles: University of Southern California Press, 1978.

WEILER, P., P. KIM, AND L. PICKARD. "Health Care for Elderly Americans: Evaluation of an Adult Day Health Care Model." *Medical Care* 14 (1976):700–708.

WEILER, PHILIP G., ELOISE RATHBONE-McCUAN, ET AL. *Adult Day Care*. New York: Springer, 1978.

WEINROBE, MAURICE. "The Adjustable Reverse Mortgage." In C. Garbacz (ed.), *Economic Resources for the Elderly*. Boulder, Colo.: Westview Press, 1983.

WEIS, JONATHAN. *Law of the Elderly*. New York: Practicing Law Institute, 1977.

WEISSERT, W. *Adult Day Care in the U.S.: Final Report*. Washington, D.C.: Trans–Century Corporation, 1975.

WEISSERT, W., T. WAN, B. LIVIERATOS, AND S. KATH. "Effects and Costs of Day Care Services for the Chronically Ill." *Medical Care* 18 (1980):567–584.

WEITZMAN, PHILLIP. "Mobile Homes: High-Cost Housing in the Low-Income Market." *Journal of Economic Issues* 10 (1976):576–597.

WELFELD, I. H., AND RAYMOND J. STRUYK (eds.). *Housing Options for the Elderly: Occasional Papers in Housing and Community Affairs*, Vol. 3. Washington, D.C.: GPO, 1978.

WILENSKY, GAIL. Statement at Hearings of U.S. Senate Special Committee on Aging, *The Future of Medicare*, 98th Cong., 1st Sess. Washington, D.C.: GPO, 1983.

WILLIAMSON, JOHN, LINDA EVANS, AND ANNE MANLEY. *Aging and Society.* New York: Holt, Rinehart and Winston, 1980.

WILSON, S. H. "Nursing Home Patients' Rights, Are They Enforceable?" *Gerontologist* 18 (1978):255–261.

WINDLEY, P. G., AND R. J. SCHEIDT. "Community Services in Small Rural Towns: Patterns of Use by Older Residents." *Gerontologist* 22 (1982):88 (Abstract).

WINOGROND, I. R., AND A. FISK. "Research in an Alzheimer's Disease Day Care Program, Implications for Therapeutic Intervention." *Gerontologist* 22 (1982):145 (Abstract).

WINOGROND, IRIS, AND MARLENE MIRASSOU. "A Crisis Intervention Service: Comparison of Younger and Older Adult Clients." *Gerontologist* 23 (1983):370–376.

WISHARD, WILLIAM R., AND LAURIE WISHARD. *Sixty Plus in California.* San Francisco: Cragmont Publications, 1981.

WOLF, ROSALIE, KARL A. PILLEMER, AND MICHAEL A. GODKIN. *Elder Abuse: The Final Report from Three Model Projects.* Worchester, Mass.: University Center on Aging, University of Massachusetts Medical Center, 1984.

XIQUES, LINDA. "Gray Panthers' Housing Fight." *Pacific Sun*, July 26, 1982.

YOUMANS, E. GRANT. *Older Rural Americans: A Sociological Perspective.* Lexington: University of Kentucky, 1967.

―――. "The Rural Aged." *Annals of the American Academy of Political and Social Science* 429 (1977):81–90.

ZALBA, J., AND J. MCVEIGH. "The Marriage of Research and Service: The Foster Grandparent Program Evaluation in the State of Michigan." *Gerontologist* 22 (1982):87 (Abstract).

ZARIT, STEVEN. *Aging and Mental Disorder: Psychological Approaches to Assessment and Treatment.* New York: Free Press, 1980.

ZARIT, S. H., K. E. REEVER, AND J. BACH-PETERSON. "Relatives of the Impaired Aged: Correlates of Feeling of Burden." *Gerontologist* 20 (1980):649–655.

Index